The Competence Connection
A Blueprint for Excellence

The
Competence
Connection

A Blueprint

for Excellence

Jay Hall, Ph.D.

WOODSTEAD PRESS

1755 Woodstead Court
The Woodlands, Texas 77380

ISBN 0-945804-07-5

Library of Congress Cataloging-in-Publication Data

Hall, Jay, 1932—
    The competence connection.

    Includes index.
    1. Organizational effectiveness. 2. Job enrichment. 3. Performance.
I. Title.
HD58.9.H34   1988   658.3'14   88-5578
ISBN 0-945804-07-5

Grateful acknowledgment is made to the following for permission to reprint previously published material:

Harper & Row, Publishers, Inc.: for specified material from *Management by Participation* by Alfred J. Marrow, David G. Bowers and Stanley E. Seashore, copyright 1967 by Alfred Marrow.

Holt, Rinehart & Winston, Inc.: for specified material from *Man for Himself* by Eric Fromm, copyright 1947 by Henry Holt, & Company.

The New York Times Company: for specified material from *The New York Times* by John Holusha, copyright 1985 by The New York Times Company.

Pantheon Books, a division of Random House, Inc.: for specified material from *Working: People Talk About What They Do All Day and How They Feel About What They Do* by Studs Terkel, copyright 1972, 1974 by Studs Terkel.

AMACOM, a division of American Management Associations: for specified material from *The Failure of Success* edited by Alfred J. Marrow, copyright 1972 by AMACOM.

Harper & Row, Publishers, Inc.: for the Epilogue which was abridged from pp. 43-46 in "The Principles of Scientific Management" from *Scientific Management* by Frederick Winslow Taylor, copyright 1911 by Frederick Winslow Taylor, renewed 1939 by Louise M. S. Taylor.

9-899

To Schmidt . . .
and all his progeny

Contents

Part Two: Proving the Premise

Preface

If excellence is our goal, we already have what it takes to get there. We are a people with both the *desire* and the *ability* to do good work! We are competent.

The achievement of excellence requires both a widespread competence among people *and* an environment which encourages and enables the expression of that competence. We are blessed with the first, but we have defaulted on the last. We have created organizations which punish rather than encourage and suppress rather than enable a full expression of human competence. There is an irony in all this which every leader should ponder.

This country was founded by individuals whose competence had been suppressed. Many of them were considered undesirable by an autocratic society. So they left their homelands to find opportunities for collaboration, commitment, and creativity. Finding them, their competence levels rose to heroism in government, religion, and business.

If excellence is truly our goal, leaders must work for a state of unsuppressed competence. Only then can we truly take pride in all that we do. Only then will excellence once again be commonplace instead of something we lost along the way and now must "search for." Excellence resides within every individual in the guise of unexpressed competence. Unfortunately, when suppressed and unexpressed, it can easily be misinterpreted as *in*competence.

I think we are about to rediscover excellence. The works of Tom Peters and Robert Waterman have struck a responsive chord because they remind us of an abiding yet neglected desire: to do our best and to take pride in our accomplishments. Peters and Waterman have done us a favor by legitimizing the notion of excellent performance, after a period of disuse and abuse. Their message is timely because, as a nation, we are where we are by virtue of losing sight of both the aspirations and standards of excellence. Many of our problems of productivity and quality of work life might be remedied by a new commitment to excellence on the part of our leadership.

At the same time, we must avoid the pitfalls of hollow rhetoric. The pursuit of excellence requires substance if it is to be a fulfilling rather than disappointing undertaking. Exhortations to excellence, alone, create a vacuum. We have been inspired to do better, but no one has provided adequate guidelines to accomplish this. In many respects, without a clear operational blueprint for the achievement of excellence, we are set up for failure — and for the ultimate frustration which can take a lofty ideal down with it.

This book is about rediscovering the basics that our founding fathers proved necessary for excellence. It is not based on theoretical surmise, armchair fantasy, or "what we've always done before." Rather, it is based on extensive studies conducted by Teleometrics International in organizations of many types, with fast-food and grocery chains, manufacturing firms, financial institutions, government agencies, health care facilities, and research and development organizations. The Teleometrics-developed Competence Process has been validated as a management methodology that goes far toward the achievement of excellence in such companies as IBM, AT&T, and Ford Motor Company.

The Competence Connection is offered, then, as a carefully researched, validated, and demonstrated blueprint for the achievement of excellence in any organization. Predicated on the core ingredient which makes excellence possible in the first place—the human desire and capability for doing what needs to be done, *The Competence Connection* spells out in detail a process which leaders can use to create a new cultural environment, one which both supports and releases human competence for its fullest expression in the doing of organizational work.

In this respect, the process is a road map for outstanding performance and productivity. But it is also a vehicle for renewal and health in the workplace. The organizational environment it describes enables people to feel good about themselves as a result of their labors. Morale soars and stress plummets under such conditions. This is important, for true excellence — the kind that endures and becomes a sustained national theme—requires both productivity and health.

In addition, the process described for the achievement of excellence requires a champion. It doesn't happen by itself. It needs ongoing thoughtful and creative management. As the book's title implies, people in positions of authority must learn to assume responsibility for connecting the competence of those who work to the tasks that need to be done. *Leaders, individually and collectively, are the Competence Connection.* They must, therefore, function as such if true excellence is ever to become a reality.

It is my firm belief that once we make the Competence Connection, this great people and great nation will once again resume their leadership role in productivity, creativity, and the balance of trade. Then our people will be both able to afford and willing to buy what they have produced. There is an outlet for the competence of every citizen once we unleash the excellence it produces. It is with this hope that I offer *The Competence Connection: A Blueprint for Excellence.*

Jay Hall, President
Teleometrics International

Acknowledgments

This book is an expansion and updating of the earlier *Competence Process*. It seems particularly fitting to me that a book about competence should reflect the contributions of so many competent people. I am indebted to each of these for their help in moving the original competence process from the realm of ideas to its present recorded, validated, and tested status.

For me, now as then, the fact of empirical confirmation is the major strength of the competence process. I am indebted to those several people who made validation possible by supplying data from their organizations. For the sake of organizational anonymity, I must refrain from personal references; but they know who they are and I want each of them to know, as well, that this volume is much more practical and pertinent because of their faith, willingness, and effort to share the real world of organizational life with us.

Without the help, support, and industry of Susan Donnell, my research associate, this book—quite literally—could never have been accomplished in the time it has. Susan coordinated and supervised the validation research every step of the way. She made major contributions to the development of proper scaling techniques. She personally saw to the numerous analyses of data. And no spur-of-the-moment test of hunches or requests for reanalysis diminished her enthusiasm or willingness to press on. She has been a research partner in the fullest sense of the word and her contributions have, in particular, colored the last half of this volume.

I am grateful to Leanne Lacey for preparing the manuscript. Having overcome my penmanship and any number of capricious "final" changes, she remained loyal to the project until I could deliver my best initial thoughts into the hands of my editor, Dr. John A. Shtogren.

I was fortunate to have so conscientious and caring an editor. John was colleague, friend, and mentor; and I am indebted to him for bringing order out of chaos in the original version. This volume, too, is immeasurably better because of his efforts.

Finally, I am indebted to those managers, consultants and trainers—and their organizations—who embraced the original *Competence Process*. In the six years since its 1980 publication, over 50,000 people in North and South America and Europe have moved to set the Process in motion. I am gratified by their commitment and, especially, by the willingness of many of them to share their experiences with me so that they might be included in this book for others to consider.

To all these outstanding friends my sincere thanks for what, together, we have been able to do.

Introduction

The Competence Connection. It is for managers of companies large and small who have begun to doubt that people really want to work anymore. It is for teachers who have begun to wonder if it is possible to teach anyone when so few seem to value learning and for public officials who have begun to believe it politically naive to expect both fairness and effectiveness in government.

It is also a book for those who are managed and lament the loss of meaningful tasks and the sense of accomplishment that once characterized work. It is for those who are taught but cannot see relevance or a concern for excellence in their classrooms. And it is for those who are governed, affected in virtually every segment of their lives by legislation, regulation, and policy—yet somehow barred from access to or reciprocal influence over the invisible forces in government which seem to prevail.

At the same time, this book is for those who persevere, not yet persuaded that mediocrity and frustration are the best they can hope for, that what is now ever shall be. It is for managers who refuse to accommodate themselves to diminishing productivity and malaise in the workplace; it is for teachers who feel that, as the shapers of an unformed precious resource, they *do* make a difference. And it is for public officials who recognize that good words are no substitute for good deeds and the rules of logic and equity, though often perverted and tested, are still the handmaidens of lasting societies. This is a book for those who work for reasons beyond economic gratification. It is for those whose pursuit of learning will not be compromised by lowered standards or diverted by busywork and automatic progression. And it is for those who acknowledge that while the process of government may sputter and falter, it can yet be a magnificent force for the common good.

The Competence Connection is a book for diverse interests, for people of many persuasions and different concerns. But it applies equally since it is about the common element that binds us all together and, at the same time, fosters that very diversity which is the source of creativity and accomplishment at all levels of society.

This is a book about human competence—the widespread and uniquely human capacity to do what needs to be done—and what managers, business owners, teachers, leaders, and people in general can do to insure that it is properly nurtured and cherished as a defining characteristic of our shared experience. It is about a process which people can set in motion—be it in their factories, their offices, their stores, their classrooms, their communities, or their own families—and through which the expression of individual accomplishment will flourish. *Competence abounds. Properly managed, it can become the dominant feature of our social institutions, enhancing both productivity and health.* That is the essential message from several years of intensive research. This book is about what needs to be done. It is about the ingredients of the process which will make latent human competence manifest.

A Personal View of the Competence Process

Here, in the Introduction, is my opportunity to indulge myself. It is here that I may share my personal concerns and it is in this context that I, the author, am allowed to encourage you, the reader, to take seriously what follows. I sincerely hope you will, for, with declining quality and production at home and challenges from abroad, there is much to be done. We need competent performance *now!* And I am convinced that the competence process—verified as it is by hard data, scientific scrutiny, and application in some of our most important organizations—has important implications for productivity and health in both the public and private sectors of our communities.

The book is written primarily to those who manage. Let me explain: While I believe this book offers something to anyone in a position of influence—parent, teacher, community leader or friend—I feel it is particularly pertinent for those who manage our organizations, from first-line supervisor to chief executive. This is because our formal organizations—the values they are founded on and the priorities and practices which characterize them—have become a dominant force in determining the day-to-day quality of life for each of us.

Industry, as a case in point, is no longer just the economic organ of our society; it is a trend setter as well. It influences local and national priorities and the way we live in numerous ways. In our schools, curriculum is at least partially based on what business and industry is perceived to want in its hirees. Communities decide zoning and taxation issues with industry in mind. And, because we admire and respect those who are highly placed in powerful and complex organizations, many organizational leaders sit on the boards and steering committees of our nonindustrial institutions. As a result, educational, community service, and health care agencies are often managed according to a logic more appropriate to ensuring the profitability of a multinational conglomerate than to the provision of human services for the good of the community. For good or ill, business and industrial organizations affect major segments of our working lives.

The same may be said of nonindustrial organizations. Whether we speak of a military complex, a large university, seats of government, or bustling medical centers, the interplay between organizations and communities occurs. The dynamics of influence are the same . . . and they tend to be one-way transactions. Only rarely do we hear of organizations voluntarily basing their priorities or modifying their practices in response to community influence.

That is why this book is addressed to managers. They have the tough job. They guide the organizations. They are among the major shapers of opinion and practice—of values, if you will—not only in their organizations but within our communities. This is a role that is seldom articulated, but I think the effects of management extend well beyond the company parking lot. If the average middle manager directly affects the work life of ten people, the likelihood is that he or she indirectly affects the lives of dozens of others—the families of those who are managed and how they, in turn, interact with their neighbors. The way a given manager thinks about work or feels about control or human dignity affects the productive and social well-being of scores of individuals in a tangible way. Multiply this by the tens of thousands of managers in our various organizations and you sense the scope of influence which reposes in our formal organizations. It *matters* how they are managed and what life is like at work, for our homes and communities and government agencies are but mirror images.

I envision organizations and communities characterized by competence. I believe the capacity to do what needs to be done is a fundamental attribute of the human condition. But competence must be valued and properly managed to become truly manifest. Unfortunately, in too many organizations and communities competence has been neither valued nor properly managed. And this is the root cause of many of the problems of frustration and poor performance we face today.

Competence must be reaffirmed. Any success and prosperity we have enjoyed has been due to the fact that human competence is such a powerful force that it asserts itself regardless of mismanagement, neglect, and lack of encouragement. But how long can this continue?

I propose we recognize that fundamental and uniquely human capacity to do what needs to be done and make it the cornerstone of our plans for organizing and managing for the accomplishment of work. When we do this, we will find that our priorities will change; we will ask different questions of ourselves than we have asked in the past; and we will begin to challenge some of our favorite assumptions about people and the conditions under which they might be expected to produce.

The competence process involves the management of competence so that it might be released into the bloodstreams of our organizations and communities. In the following pages, we will trace the development of this process, verify its basic premise, and assess its potential for increasing both productivity and health in our workplaces. And, as we do this, we will lay out the social technology of a more competent management than we have ever known before.

Part One

A Premise of Competence

I

Prophecies of Competence

In a free society, competence is an elementary duty. John Gardner believes competence is the glue that holds a nation together. In his provocative little book, *Excellence,* he wrote, "Men and women doing competently whatever job is theirs to do tone up the whole society."[1]

When I've discussed Gardner's ideas about competence with leaders of formal organizations, most are in agreement. They think men and women competently doing whatever job is theirs to do has something to do with productivity and competitive position. They think leaders should be concerned about such things. And, invariably, having agreed they then put a question to me: "But how do you get people to do that, work competently?" And I, invariably, reply, "You begin by *acknowledging* the competence that is all around you."

From time to time, we need to remind ourselves and one another of a fundamental truth. We are good at what we do. Not just one or two of us, but all of us have the capacity and need for working well. There is tangible evidence of our talents all about us. If we consider all the buildings and

[1] Gardner, J. *Excellence.* New York: Harper & Row, 1961.

bridges we have built, the development of the microchip and space exploration, the eradicaton of smallpox and breaking the genetic code, our many artistic achievements and the range of services we render, our capacity to accomplish is really quite remarkable. As people at work, we have displayed ingenuity, diligence, and concern. We are demonstrably competent.

I find it strange that so little is made of our inherent competence in books on organizational theory or management science. People perform so many tasks, and perform them well, that it is really amazing that so few theories of organization and management—our recorded notions of how best to accomplish work through people—make note of the human capacity to *do*.

Our theories are peculiar, actually biased, views of work. We exalt technology and management expertise when things go well; but when things go wrong we blame the people who do the work. More often than not, we organize and manage as if workers were deficient, as if incompetence rather than competence were the defining feature of the human condition. In management theory, for example, the emphasis is on control, executive decision making, and methods of performance appraisal; in structuring organizations, the emphasis is on coordination, cost effectiveness, job description, and authority relationships. These are primarily mechanisms for containing incompetence, for making sure that people don't foul things up. I have often wondered what would happen if we organized ourselves and managed with the emphasis on the simple premise that people are competent, that they can do whatever needs to be done. This is not just an idle question. There is evidence from a number of settings which indicates that people perform as they are *expected* to perform.

The Power of Prophecies

There are numerous cases on record where leaders—people in positions of influence—were led to believe that those they supervised were uniquely competent and geared their practices to this belief. In an elementary school in a major U.S. city, students from a lower socio-economic neighborhood actually increased their I.Q.'s—not to mention their classroom performance—because their teachers *believed* them to be brighter than their fellow students and taught them accordingly. Unknown to their teachers, these children were average in every way. In a Texas Job Corps program, a randomly chosen group of disadvantaged, chronically unemployed men and women outperformed their fellow trainees of similar backgrounds on four different measures of welding skill simply because their supervisors *believed* that they possessed special potentials for superior performance and managed them accordingly. At the United States Air Force Academy Preparatory School, randomly chosen airmen, when compared with their fellow airmen, demonstrated enhanced abilities in mathematics simply because they were *assigned* to a "high ability" class for instruction and trained accordingly. And at the Tulane University Biomedical Computer Center, a professor taught the janitor of the computer center to be a competent computer operator because of his *conviction* that he could teach and the janitor could learn. Today that former janitor is in charge of the main computer room and is responsible for training new employees to program and operate the computer. The unifying factor in all these cases, from elementary school children and society's disadvantaged to people in pursuit of advanced knowledge, was an expectation of competence on the part of those in charge.

These and similar examples of the self-fulfilling prophecy have been related by Robert Rosenthal of Harvard University.[2] They reflect the scientific evidence for what Rosenthal has titled the *Pygmalion Effect:* the subtle yet powerful way in which what *we expect* of others so influences how *we behave* toward them that we literally coax out of them those reactions and achievements we anticipate, much as the sculptor Pygmalion coaxed life from his statue in classic mythology. Rosenthal has suggested that, once we form an expectancy of how others will perform or once we label their potential in some way, we will communicate this by the way we interact with them. We will create warmer, more friendly and supportive "climates" for those we value than for people deemed less worthy or skilled. We will provide more helpful and complete "feedback" on performance to "special" people than to others. We will give more usable and challenging information to those of whom we expect more, and we will afford greater opportunities for expression along with more encouragement to do so when we have high expectations than when we expect little of others. In short, depending on what we expect or believe of others, we alter our *own* practices to such an extent that we virtually insure that we will get what we expect.

Lest we doubt that the applicability or sensitivity of such a subtle interpersonal influence, the dynamics of the self-fulfilling prophecy have been found to be so potent that they even influence the outcome of experiments with white mice.[3] Mice from the same genetic strain learned more or less rapidly depending on whether the experimenter believed

---

[2] Rosenthal, R. *Experimenting in Behavioral Research.* New York: Irvington Publishers, Inc., 1976.

[3] Rosenthal, R. "On the Social Psychology of the Self-fulfilling Prophecy: Further Evidence for Pygmalion Effects and Their Mediating Mechanisms." New York: MSS Modular Publications, Inc., 1974, Module 53, pp. 1-28.

them to be from a bright or dull strain. What, you may ask, does this have to do with how we organize and manage? Well, to paraphrase Rosenthal, if rats can become brighter when expected to by their experimenters, we can hardly consider far fetched the idea that *people* might become more proficient and productive when *expected* to by their *managers*. The point is worth pondering.

Prophecies of Incompetence: The Managerial Paradox

The prospects of the self-fulfilling prophecy raise a paradoxical question: if such a powerful yet simple mechanism for upgrading performance is indeed a reality, why aren't we all better off? Why are our organizations and people restive and discontented? Why is there, as Bruce Stokes has pointedly observed, a global malaise and universal slowdown of production?[4] Why, with all the traditional stimulants—technological innovation, capital investment, and sophisticated organization of production—is productivity still down and slowing daily virtually around the world? The answer lies in the fact that the self-fulfilling prophecy works both ways: our prophecies for performance, our managerial expectations if you will, fulfill themselves for good or ill.

"Nature will never deceive us," wrote the French philosopher Rousseau, "it is always we who deceive ourselves." That's our real problem: we have deceived ourselves . . . contrary to the evidence Nature has provided.

---

[4] Stokes, B. "Worker Participation—Productivity and the Quality of Work Life." *Worldwatch Paper 25*. Washington: Worldwatch Institute, 1978.

Many of our prophecies are founded in self-deceptions where the competence of others is concerned.

In the light of worker alienation and diminished output, we need to reassess the nature of our managerial prophecies. We need to reflect on the nature of those organizational structures and managerial practices which manifest our current prophecies. When we do this, as Chris Argyris has done, we can begin to see how we have deceived ourselves. And problems of productivity and malaise in the workplace will take on new meanings. Argyris, a distinguished and insightful observer of life in organizations, states the case succinctly:

> . . . *we have designed organizations which have ignored individual potential for competence, responsibility, constructive intent, and productivity.* We have created structures and jobs that at the lower levels alienate and frustrate the workers; lead them to reject responsible behavior, not only with impunity, but with a sense of justice; and tempt them to fight the organization by lowering the quality of what they produce. Products and services thus become the tangible expressions of the low quality of life within organizations.[5] (Italics mine.)

The design of organizations and structuring of work reveal managerial values and assumptions about people and the conditions under which they can be expected to produce. Argyris goes on to say that assumptions and values ". . . about human beings and organizations, no matter what they

[5] Argyris, C. "A Few Words in Advance." In A.J. Marrow (Ed.), *The Failure of Success.* New York: AMACOM, 1972, p. 3.

are, become self-fulfilling prophecies in the minds and hands of managements." Therein lies the crux of our managerial paradox. We have *expected* the worst and organized and managed accordingly.

Prophecies of Competence: The Managerial Challenge

We know what happens when we expect the worst; the evidence is painfully abundant. But what if we expected the best? Once more: what would happen if we organized ourselves and managed on the basis of the simple premise that people are competent, that they have the ingenuity, diligence, and concern to do whatever needs to be done? If we *expected* competence, then organized accordingly— if we *managed* on the basis of prophecies of competence—we might very well find it necessary to change the way we approach our own managerial tasks. And we might discover a heretofore untapped reservoir of human talent, at the ready for the tasks of the organization.

Prophecies of competence, if they are to be fulfilled, require much of the manager. They must be genuine and, moreover, they must be put into action. As J. Sterling Livingston has so accurately stated the case, much more than wishful thinking or positive regard is implied:

> To become self-fulfilling prophecies, expectations must be made of sterner stuff than the power of positive thinking or generalized confidence in one's fellowmen—helpful as these concepts may be for some other purposes . . . managerial expec-

tations must pass the test of reality before they can be translated into performance.[6]

In many respects, that is what this volume is all about: translating managerial prophecies of competence into practical reality, *reality defined by nothing less than productivity*. As we move from theory to practice in following chapters, we will concern ourselves with the "sterner stuff" of competence, with a definite *competence process* which every manager can set in motion to make maximum use of the human talent which abounds. We will examine the managerial action requirements of the process. We will apply the tests of reality, and present in Parts II and III the confirming data for the competence process. And we will, in the process, develop and refine a new technology for accomplishing work—a *social* technology pertaining to people rather than their tools.

The Miracle at Marion[7]

The first small step toward the competence process was taken more than three decades ago in the small town of Marion, Virginia. It was prompted by a drastic reduction in production at the Harwood Manufacturing Corporation, a problem which refused to yield to traditional remedies. Management made a break with the past and embraced radical new practices which, in turn, required a new set of managerial expectations. To say that they proceeded from prophecies of competence seems, in retrospect, to capture

---

[6] Livingston, J.S. "Pygmalion in Management." *Harvard Business Review*. July-August, 1969.

[7] The following material draws heavily from Marrow, A.J., D.G. Bowers & S.E. Seashore. *Management by Participation*. New York: Harper & Row, 1967, and selected sections are reprinted by express permission of the publisher.

the essence of their efforts. And to say that they worked a managerial miracle is a matter of historical fact. The problems faced by Harwood's management are timeless— but the miracle they wrought needs retelling so that, in pondering the past, we might better prepare ourselves for the future.

The Basic Dilemma

Harwood's management was worried about its very existence in the garment industry. Costs were spiraling and no matter how hard management tried or what they did, their employees were dissatisfied. Maybe if they had known that soon they would be parties to a classic breakthrough in organizational theory and the practice of management, things would have seemed brighter. But for the time being, all that concerned them was lost efficiency and worker unrest. The outlook was somewhere between bleak and desolate.

The pajama manufacturing business had always been whimsical at best, subject to changes in the market place. In response to demands for new styles and an appealing product mix, it was frequently necessary to introduce new methods for doing the work and to reassign personnel to different tasks or different work groups. Despite the fact that workers appeared to understand both the need and reasons for such change—and regardless of the fact that special monetary measures were taken to protect workers' interest— every time management made a change, productivity plummeted. Not just a little, not the nominal amount which would suffice to signify that people preferred the more familiar routine. Productiviy would drop anywhere from *25% to 50% below standard per hour!*

In addition, the effect on morale was disastrous. Following any given change, 62% of the workers affected could be expected to become chronically substandard operators or to *quit*. Among those remaining, outward aggression and open hostility toward supervisors, the time-study engineer, and higher management were commonplace. Clearly management had cause for its concern.

Perhaps the problem was the kind of employees management had to work with every day. The main plant was located in the Appalachian foothills. Most of the employees were recruited from the rural, mountainous areas surrounding the town and, typically, were hired without any previous industrial experience. Most were women; females outnumbered males by a five-to-one margin. Few employees had completed high school; in fact, the *average* education was eight years of grammar school. And most were young; the average age was 23 years. Maybe young, relatively uneducated, women from a rural setting simply could not cope with the demands and stresses of working in a highly competitive industrial complex.

Or maybe management was overly sensitive to the issue of employee wellbeing. Perhaps, in the process of striving for fairness and good human relations, management had merely become benevolent to a point where it effectively undercut its own needs for efficiency and productive enterprise. Certainly the company had invested substantial amounts of both time and money to make things comfortable for workers. Health services, lunchroom, and recreational programs were company-sponsored. And there was even piped-in music. The economic package was more than fair. Because of an individual piece-rate incentive system, employees could literally determine how much they would earn each pay period. So far as management could tell, the company enjoyed both good labor relations and the good will of the local community. And yet, management was confronted with problems of low efficiency, high turnover, chronic grievances, and restricted output sufficient to scuttle a lesser firm.

Management had exhausted its traditional options. Monetary solutions had failed; attempts to enlist the cooperation and aid of the union had failed; even layoffs based on individual productivity had failed. How, then, was Harwood to stay competitive in a field marked by changing market demands and rising costs when even the most simple change would wreak such havoc with morale and productivity?

The Guiding Philosophy

Harwood is a family concern; and in the late 1930's, its founder turned over its management to his two sons—one a psychologist and the other an engineer. And, because of their respective professional trainings, it was they who established the company policy that management problems would be solved on the basis of scientific knowledge. Harwood literally became a center of behavioral research in 1939 when the eminent psychologist Kurt Lewin began to work with the plant management on problems of leadership, group decision making, and interpersonal relations. Through the years following, Lewin worked closely with the Harwood owners and, indeed, brought in his students and colleagues to carry out a number of pioneering action-research projects.

To capture the tenor of the times, one has only to look at how problems were approached and solved. In one instance, Dr. John R. P. French, Jr., a protege of Lewin's and director of personnel research for the company, dealt with management's opposition to hiring older workers by successfully applying the "problem solving through scientific knowledge" rule favored by Harwood's owners. Following Lewin's lead, he involved management in its own research project into the costs associated with employing older women. French created an opportunity for managers to examine their personal beliefs in the light of hard data. Managers designed the study and devised the means for data collection. And they analyzed their own data; the project was their own and so were the findings.

The results were in sharp contrast to management's expectations. But they believed them because, as Lewin observed,

> . . . the facts became really their facts (as against other people's facts). An individual will believe facts he himself has discovered in the same way he believes in himself.

Management concluded, on the basis of their own study, that the benefits of hiring older people far outweighed the costs. Given this background, it is only natural and to be expected that problems of substandard production and worker malaise would be subjected to a more scientific analysis and, more to the point, that the method of scientific inquiry would be brought to bear in solving the problem.

The Classic Experiment

What transpired at Harwood's Marion plant—what was

revealed and the farreaching implications of the events set in motion—concern all who manage and all who work. In response to a problem of productivity—not unlike those which plague every generation of manager and every type of formal organization—the owners of Harwood broke with tradition and addressed themselves, not to new technology, or new sources of capital, or a different economic model, but to why people work as they do. They focused on the social dynamics of the workplace and how people felt about their work, management, and one another. The result was a lasting solution to the problem and a classic study in the annals of organizational dynamics.

Scientific Problem Solving

French and his colleague, Lester Coch, set in motion an "experimental" approach to solving the problem of declining productivity and worker malaise. Much as in a laboratory setting, ideas and processes flowing from scientific knowledge were put to the test in the real world of work. Here in the words of the late Al Marrow, Chairman of the Board of Harwood at the time, is an account of what was done and what happened as a result:

> The workers were divided into three groups, all of them matched in skill, and were advised of the impending job changes in different ways. Group I was called into the conference room and told that changes were to be made and why they were necessary. The production manager explained the new mode of work, the new job assignments, and the new piecework rates. The operators were invited to ask questions and were given frank answers. By and large, this was normal procedure.

Group II workers were asked to choose representatives to meet with management to discuss and decide upon the new job methods. They were given a full explanation of why the change was mandatory—orders had fallen off for the style currently in production. Unless fresh business was attracted by new models and lower prices, there might be layoffs. The urgency of cutting costs by simplifying the product was dramatized as vividly as possible. The group was asked to discuss cost reduction as a joint problem of management and workers. The situation was defined this way: "We don't want to sacrifice quality, and we don't want you to lose any income. What ideas do you have about this?" The group's spokesmen brought the workers' views to management, joined in outlining new methods, and then went back to their workers to explain the new job methods and rates and to help in the retraining.

Group III did not delegate decision-making to representatives but participated as a whole. Management and all operators sat together from the start until the methods and rates were agreed upon. Though no formal vote was taken, the decisions were reached by consensus at the meetings.[8]

There were obvious inherent risks with the new approach. In a time when the labor supply was glutted, Harwood's management sought to include openly hostile employees in the decision-making process. Not all management would have been so charitable. Moreover, management publicly

---

[8] *Ibid.*, p. 28.

committed itself in advance to implementing the plan thus achieved. Not all management would have been so fearless. What might we learn from this exercise in both restraint and trust? Marrow continues:

> What resulted from this three-pronged experiment? Production by Group I—the nonparticipative group—dropped 35 percent after the changeover and did not improve for a month thereafter. Morale deteriorated; and there was marked hostility toward the company, restriction of output, subtle non-cooperation. It turned out later than an agreement to "get even" with management had been explicitly made. Within two weeks after the change, nine percent of the operators had quit. Others filed grievances about the pay rates, although the rates were, in fact, a little too high.
>
> Group II learned the new methods at a remarkably fast pace. Morale was good, and the standard rate of productivity was recovered within 14 days. By the end of the month, productivity had exceeded what it had been before the changeover. The same supervisor whom Group I was criticizing received friendly cooperation from Group II. No one from Group II quit.
>
> Group III, the fully participating group, took the lead from the start. By the second day, the operators were back to their former level of production and steadily raised it to a point about 14 percent higher than ever before. They cooperated with their supervisor, and no one quit. Their excellent morale reflected their feeling that they were a team.

Two and a half months later, it was possible to confirm the results dramatically. Group I, which had to be broken up after six weeks because its low rate of production persisted, was reassembled when another new job opened up in the plant. But this time the change was made with full participation of all the members. The results were successful and the opposite of the earlier experience. There was rapid recovery after changeover: a new and higher level of output, no hostility, no terminations, high cooperation and morale.

Involving operators in making their own work-related decisions was identified as the key element responsible for the results obtained. Coch and French, in their formal presentation of the study, reported that the rate of recovery to standard was *directly proportional to the amount of involvement;* the more people participated in shaping the decisions governing their work, the more rapidly they reached—indeed, in some cases surpassed—the production standard.[9] In a similar vein, rates of turnover and aggression were *inversely proportional to involvement;* the less people participated, the more likely they were to be openly hostile or quit. And finally, involvement seemed to be a positive factor in more uniform, less sporadic, individual productiveness.

The Emergence of New
Managerial Values

Marrow describes the practices and underlying value

[9] Coch, L. & J.R.P. French, "Overcoming Resistance to Change." *Human Relations,* Vol. 1, No. 4, 1948, p. 512.

system of what he called participative management thusly:

> Since its early involvement with participative management practices in cooperation with behavioral scientists, Harwood's management has been convinced that a job is done best when employees feel that their needs are considered in a way that sustains their self-respect and creates a sense of responsibility. As employees they 'participate.' They do not feel the humiliation implied in the term 'hired hands.' They do not feel they are mere robots.[10]

> . . . In illustrating the managerial approach that has evolved in the company's development, Harwood's experiments also epitomized the human side of the management picture everywhere. Wages and hours are only part of that picture; the work climate must satisfy a range of human needs. Clearly, the findings are relevant to industry at a time when manufacturing methods and technology are changing with dramatic speed. These changes influence the attitude and behavior of the workers as they respond to frequent and often upsetting changes.[11]

New managerial values—new assumptions and expectations—were the defining feature of the Harwood experience. It is from these that we can learn; it is on such a foundation that we can build and begin to prepare for the future.

[10] Marrow *et al. Op. cit.*, p. 26.

[11] *Ibid.*, p. 30.

The Miracle in Restrospect

Management development specialist and author John A. Shtogren has observed that, given the prevailing autocratic approach to management of the time—just after World War II—the use of participative practices to solve a problem of worker unrest and purposely restricted output was just short of miraculous. "Given the complexity of the problem and the industrial context within which it occurred," writes Shtogren, "the use of such a simple and uncontrolling method as participation seems, in retrospect, as somewhat of a managerial miracle."[12]

But participative practices per se were not the miracle at Marion: the miracle was what lay behind such practices. Participative practices were founded on a managerial expectation that the people at Harwood could, given a proper opportunity, do what needed to be done. *The miracle at Marion was the emergence of a managerial prophecy of competence,* a belief that people by and large would energetically and creatively solve their work-related problems if management allowed them to and backed them up in their efforts. That presumption of competence so many years ago in a small Appalachian town is the true miracle of Marion.

The experience at Marion was a pioneering effort. In many respects it was primitive. But Marrow was acutely aware of the widespread competence available at Harwood and, although he did not employ the terms of competence which we will be using, he certainly noted the defining features of competence. His appreciation of the ingenuity, diligence,

---

[12] Shtogren, J.A. Introduction to "Involvement: The Neglected Factor in Performance." In J.A. Shtogren (Ed.), *Models for Management: The Structure of Competence.* The Woodlands, Texas: Teleometrics, Int'l., 1980.

and concern of the people at Harwood is apparent when he writes of their contributions:

> The question is often asked: Have the workers' opinions been of much value? That depends on *how much the participator knows and how important the matter is to him.* On matters which the workers know best—their own jobs, conditions in the shop, operation of machines—they have far more informed opinions than top managers who lack first-hand experience. Harwood found that workers can make practical suggestions of considerable merit. *Many are ingenious and inventive, capable of seeing short cuts, and aware of their own and their fellow workers' capabilities.*
>
> As an illustration, consider an operator who sews pockets on men's shirts. Under current manufacturing processes, an experienced worker will sew well over 100,000 pockets every year. The group in which she is a member may jointly sew a million pockets a year. *Is it not reasonable to expect, at least within the limits of their own direct experience and observations, that they are more expert in the details of their particular job than any of the supervisory staff?*[13] (Italics mine.)

Marrow had not only an appreciation of the reality of competence, but he *expected* competence to become manifest and began to manage accordingly. In embarking on such a bold and uncharted course, Marrow and his colleagues provided the first tentative answer to our question: What would happen if we organized ourselves and

[13] Marrow *et al. Op. cit.*, p. 26.

managed on the basis of the simple premise that people are competent, that they can do whatever needs to be done? The answer: *We will prosper in ways not even imagined by more traditional managerial minds.*

All of us in positions of influence—managers, teachers, parents, and elected leaders—can, I think, learn from the answer to that question: if, in spite of misgivings and trepidation, we proceed from a prophecy of competence, we will discover new alternatives and become open to new assumptions and values. In turn, this will encourage us to try new strategies and experiment with new practices. We will profit in new and exciting ways. And that is the key to the future: understanding and valuing human competence such that we can provide for its proper management. It is time, therefore, before looking to specific management strategies, to address ourselves to that fundamental competence which underlies productivity so that we might better understand the rich resource which is in our keeping.

II

A Presumption of Competence

Unexpressed competence appears much the same as incompetence. This is a point worth remembering, for competence in our organizations has been a shadow truth. Traditionally, many of us have predicated our managerial practices on a presumption of incompetence. Most of our theories of organization and many of our managerial efforts have been geared primarily to defending against *in*competence. Argyris' words bear repeating: ". . . we have designed organizations which have ignored individual potential for competence, responsibility, constructive intent and productivity." In doing so, we have erected barriers to the expression of competence.

We have fulfilled our prophecies of incompetent performance. And we have missed the point that this book seeks to make. More inclined to guarding against malfeasance than to encouraging excellence, we have overlooked the obvious. We have taken a narrow view of people, as if current behavior tells all about potential, and we have failed to ask how mature adults—when apparently unproductive and uncaring—might come to act contrary to their nature and own best interests. If we are to achieve excellence in our organizations and communities, we must be willing to reorient ourselves. We must make a presump-

tion of competence in the workplace rather than incompetence, for high level performance rests on the simple, yet
not widely accepted, premise that people will behave
competently if we will but let them.

The competence process, which will be described in detail
in later chapters, flows from an abiding belief in human
competence, a fundamental conviction that the people who
comprise our organizations—our factories and schools,
hospitals and farms, towns and cities—are capable of
doing what needs to be done. It is based in a hardnosed
faith in the capacity of people to deal productively with both
one another and the various demands and problems which
characterize the human condition. In our organizations this
means that people have the capacity for solving the
problems associated with personal and collective productivity,
that they possess the ingenuity needed for fashioning the
tools of their work and the skills required for superior
performance. And, perhaps most important, it means that
they are driven by a need to do these things well. The
investment of energy, devotion to accomplishment, and
personal sacrifice for the greater good which have punctuated
social and technical progress all denote a human desire to
do what needs to be done. It is upon this capacity and drive
for excellence that the competence process is founded.

But the sad fact is that too few people—particularly those
in charge—really *believe* in such a capacity and drive. That
is why, as a prelude to the competence process, we must
concern ourselves with the basic propositions upon which
the process turns: the historical fact of individual human
competence, its basic components and evidence of a
competence motive, and the absolute necessity of an
organizational context—created by managers—which will
nurture and sustain this competence so that it may be

expressed in the doing of work. Upon such a foundation we can build a social technology for competence in our communities and organizations.

Personal Competence: The Shadow Truth

Each of us—manager and worker alike—has reached an impressive level of personal competence long before joining a formal organization. We have learned how to deal with and solve any number of problems, how to innovate, how to continue to learn, and how to profit from our experiences so that personal competence is continually enhanced. One of the first things we must do is understand and appreciate competence as a generalized human trait, as a widespread capacity to do what needs to be done. Convention would often have us equate competence with the possession of some special expertise, but such a posture promotes a narrow view of the human potential available in our organizations. Competence is more fundamental than the special skills belonging to those we call experts. Without competence—without some fundamental capacity to do what needs to be done and to learn from past experience—there would be no special skills, no expertise.

To judge competence in terms of speciality alone diverts us from its more generalized distribution among people and fosters a subtle form of elitism which serves to compound the presumption of incompetence. If we take a narrow view of competence we not only misstate its probability, but we are tempted to deny the mantle of personal worth to all but those whose skills are most generally admired. Some skills command greater respect than others—they are "weighted" in terms of social desirability—but this does not mean that the fundamental competence underlying less imposing talents is any less worthy. The concept of competence must apply to all, lest, seduced by expertise, we default on the very talents we most need. John Gardner has described the pitfalls of elitism clearly:

> An excellent plumber is infinitely more admirable than an incompetent philosopher. The society which scorns excellence in plumbing because plumbing is a humble activity and tolerates shoddiness in philosophy because it is an exalted activity will have neither good plumbing nor good philosophy. Neither its pipes nor its theories will hold water.[1]

Our interest is in *generalized* competence because that is the norm. The attainment of competence is a natural part of the life process.[2,3,4] It is important to stress the fundamental nature of competence, lest we imbue the concept with such an enriched meaning that it seems unattainable and improbable. Competence *is* a rich attribute, entirely on its own merits, but it is also commonplace. Being able to do what needs to be done, dealing productively with other people, being able to solve problems and respond appropriately to the circumstances one encounters are part and parcel of normal human development. And, should any of us become unduly impressed by our own competence,

---

[1] Gardner, J. *Excellence.* New York: Harper & Row, 1961, p. 102.

[2] Smith, M.B. *Social Psychology and Human Values.* Chicago: Aldine Publishing Company, 1969.

[3] White. R.W. "Competence and the Psychosexual Stages of Development." In M. Jones (Ed.), *Nebraska Symposium on Motivation,* 1960, Lincoln: University of Nebraska Press, pp. 97-141.

[4] deCharms, R. *Personal Causation.* New York: Academic Press, 1968.

we might remind ourselves that competence—widespread and plentiful—is simply part of Nature's plan for us. Competence insures the survival of our species. It is why we have endured and, properly nurtured, it holds the way to our future.

Robert W. White, the first to call attention to the self-evident but unheralded fact of human competence, has defined competence as the key to *adaptive fitness:* the more competent we are the more *fit* we are to interact effectively with our social and physical surroundings, to respond productively to the demands they make on us.[5] If we view competence as adaptive fitness, we can be more precise and definite about competence. Adaptive behavior is defined as any behavior which helps one meet environmental demands, as an ability to make appropriate responses to changing circumstances. Two frequently used criteria of adaptability are the capacity to profit from past experience and the capacity to initiate new and more complex experiences. So it is that we have not only been able to develop the wheel but to make it work for us in ways not even imagined at its inception. So it is that children, having learned to stack blocks, go on to build tree forts and, perhaps one day, skyscrapers. Implicit in such behaviors are a basic creative mechanism and sustained commitment to responding appropriately. These strike at the core issues of competence. Focusing on creativity and commitment allows us to break competent performance down into its most basic dynamics so that we can better grasp its essence and prepare for its management.

[5] White, R. W. *Motivation Reconsidered: The Concept of Competence. Psychological Review,* 66, 1959.

The Competent Response:
Creativity Fueled by Commitment

The competent response is one part creativity. We know that to satisfy the requirements of adaptability, we must be able to sense the meanings of events and literally *create* appropriate ways of responding. In our daily lives, we do this routinely; we are adaptive by nature. We are able to solve problems and invent constructive action. In our organizations being adaptive means that people must not only be able to identify accurately their various interpersonal and task demands before they can respond to them in a truly productive fashion, but they must be able to perceive alternative solutions and predict consequences. This is basic problem-solving behavior and it requires a flexibility of thought that is unconstrained by false parameters, one that is based in an openness to possibilities. These are all *creative* processes. They require a freedom of action.

To be truly adaptive, the decision processes employed and their implementation must allow for novel insights—seeing connections between seemingly unrelated events. They should provide for the development of emergent skills—a sharpening of heretofore unrecognized talents. And they should take into consideration spontaneous reliance upon and use of unlikely resources—using the tools and materials at hand to get the job done regardless of their original intent. Such unconstrained and imaginative problem-solving activities are, again, basic to the creative process. And people possess the capacity for such activities in abundance. But without opportunities for creativity there will be little competence. And without commitment there will be little creativity.

The competent response is yet another part commitment.

For people to do what is required of them in a creative fashion, they must not only have the opportunity to put their talents to work, they must be *committed* to their tasks as well. Typically, the creative response denotes *interest,* a sense of personal identification with the task at hand and its outcome. While we are all creative from time to time, sustained creativity of a level and type to characterize a whole organization, for example, requires an investment of personal attention and concern on the part of people. This is an unlikely occurrence if people do not have a deep and abiding identification with what they are doing or feel that it is important to do it well. People tend to think about, be more occupied with, and give greater effort to that work in which they have a personal stake or sense of vested interest. The issue is ownership, the personal relationship one is able to establish with his or her work. The cabinet maker who can feel the wood and smell the shavings as he fashions a gift for his children in his own workshop will often give more care to his project than when his every movement is at the pleasure of a factory foreman concerned only with quantity, not quality. The difference is commitment. We know that committed people will, given the opportunity, try to perform more creatively than uncommitted people. Commitment—concern, vested interest, caring—fuels creativity.

A more precise definition of personal competence may be found in the interplay of adaptive-creative-commitment processes: *competence, as a state of adaptive fitness and response readiness, is the sustained capacity of people to respond in a committed and creative fashion to the demands placed on them by their environments.* People not only survive but prosper because they are adaptively fit. They are prepared by virtue of their own personal histories to solve problems and accomplish tasks. This is not a sporadic or episodic capacity but, rather, a sustained and far-reaching ability to do what needs to be done—a fundamental potential for behaving competently. And, as we shall see, people *need* to behave competently.

The Competence Motive: A Personal Need to Perform Well

While the capacity for competence makes the competence process possible, it is the *desire* for competence among people that makes its effects probable. A drive to perform is what makes the capacity for competence become manifest. A sustained capacity for committed and creative adaptivity —that is, basic competence—is well within the reach of most organizations because *the vast majority of the people who comprise organizations would prefer to work that way.* This is an important point for it addresses the core mechanism which energizes competence and makes it such a readily available resource. *There is a competence motive, a need among people to demonstrate their competence.*

One of the most important contributions Robert White has made to our understanding of human competence is to provide evidence of a *competence motive.*[6] He has marshalled an impressive array of data in support of the fact that people *need* to behave in a competent manner, not just for the sake of survival but for purposes of continued growth and self-enhancement. Infants strive to master simple tasks in return for the simple pleasure of having an impact on their environment. Children spontaneously explore and reach out for more complex surroundings so as to bring these too under their control. This never ending search for

[6] *Ibid.*

challenge is one we have all known in one form or another. The feats of learning and the perseverance required to master various life tasks clearly denote a basic desire, a need to be competent. Particularly when we consider the embellishments people have added—the active search for and acquisition of nonessential skills—we can agree with White that the range of accomplishments is so broad that they must ". . . be conceived to be motivated in their own right."[7]

We *learn* to be competent as a necessary means to survival in its most literal sense, but we *value* being competent as a personal expression of biological and psychological growth. Competence is its own reward; it requires no external impetus. Competence is intrinsically satisfying. But the *achievement* of competence—the opportunity to demonstrate one's capabilities—often depends on others.

This is the definitive feature, the core premise for managers to keep in mind—since people *want* to be competent, since they have a *need* to perform in ways that are appropriate and productive, the task of management is less one of leading or prodding, as traditionally thought of, and more one of providing a context within which competence can be expressed. We can provide such management for others in a mutually beneficial way if we become sensitive to the workings of the competence motive.

The Need for Efficacy and Personal Worth: Self-respect

For competence to be motivated, for there to be sufficient reason for people to undertake both the feats of learning

[7] *Ibid.*

necessary to attain adaptive fitness and to persist in the expression of competent behaviors, there must be a mechanism which *reinforces* competence. There must be something which makes adaptive behavior rewarding and therefore likely to occur again and again. There is such a reinforcing mechanism and it operates in a deceptively simple and straightforward manner: when people are competent, when they demonstrate their adaptive fitness, they experience what White has called *feelings of efficacy and personal worth.*[8] *They feel good about themselves.* Brewster Smith, past President of the American Psychological Association, extended the notion.[9] While White was primarily concerned with competence relative to the physical environment, Smith observed that there is important feedback from the social environment, reactions of praise and affirmation, which enhances self-esteem such that the real payoff of competence is *self-respect,* that most powerful of human incentives. And Erik Erikson, pointing to the significance of successful problem solving and task accomplishment for the youngster's self-concept, has described the rewards of competence in terms of the developing self-image. Competent behavior, says Erikson, provides ". . . a self-verification of lasting importance."[10] The opportunity to behave competently reaffirms and strengthens each of us, throughout our lives, and helps us feel good about who and what we are.

Mike Lefevre, the steelworker in Studs Terkel's *Working* understood such feelings. Reflecting on his job, Lefevre gives life to the competence motive:

[8] *Ibid.*

[9] Smith, M. B. *Op. cit.*

[10] Evans, R. I. *Dialogue with Erik Erikson.* New York: E. P. Dutton & Co., Inc., 1969.

> It's not just the work. Somebody built the
> pyramids. Somebody's going to build something.
> Pyramids, Empire State Building—these things
> don't just happen. There's hard work behind it.
> I would like to see a building, say, the Empire
> State, I would like to see on one side of it a foot-
> wide strip from top to bottom with the name of
> every bricklayer, the name of every electrician, with
> all the names. So when a guy walked by, he could
> take his son and say, 'See, that's me over there on
> the forty-fifth floor. I put the steel beam in.'[11]

Mike Lefevre understands what the competence motive is
all about—he wants to be allowed to do good work and he
wants others to know it is his.

Most of us have known such feelings and can attest to their
potency; we can, if we but reflect on our own personal
experiences, verify the fact that most people will tend to
repeat those acts which result in such feelings. We tell and
re-tell the stories we relate well; we continue to prepare and
serve our personal "specialties;" we join clubs and volunteer
for projects which cater to our personal talents. Indeed, if
we are honest, most of us would admit that we actively seek
out and pursue opportunities to demonstrate our competence again and again so that we might enjoy more often
the heady experience of efficacy and personal worth. And,
regardless of how our interests and personal expressions may
differ, it is basically the same with us all. We all want to
do those things which make us feel good about ourselves.

How strange it is that any one of us might overlook or

[11] Terkel, S. *Working*. New York: Avon Books, 1985, p. 2.

minimize in importance such a potent force in the lives of others. But, as managers, we erect barriers to competence—to the means to personal worth—every day in our organizations. We take managerial acts which block or dilute the expression of competence and impair the adaptive fitness of those who do the organization's work. We write job descriptions that ignore the people who do the work; we give power to decide on the basis of rank rather than knowledge of the task; we too readily impute incompetence rather than competence to those about us who falter.

Whether we do this out of some well-intended but misguided desire to help or out of a more common lack of appreciation of the human desire and capacity for competence, the effect is the same: people lose access to the fundamental rewards of work, they are deprived of self-respect, they become less productive, and the organization as a whole loses its ability to respond to the demands of its environment. *For work is the context of individual competence and the organization is the context for work.*

People come to the organization, capable and desirous of working competently. Managers then supply them with the policies and ground rules, standards and objectives, which will characterize their work. People supply the capacity and managers supply the context. Often the two collide because the context for doing work reflects few of the reasons people work at all.

Competence and the Meaning of Work

To appreciate the true essence of the competence motive and its implications for the quality of life, we must first understand work—and the personal meaning it holds for individual human beings. We are told that people labor only to subsist, or that to toil is inherently good, or that we *must* work as a way of preserving the social fabric. Such views are rooted in economic theory, in theology and political philosophy; and they reflect the values of their respective fields. But those concerned with mental health and the social dynamics of human development have a different view. *People work in order to be healthy.*

Freud, when asked what a person should be able to do to be considered normal, replied, simply, that he should be able *to love and to work.* According to Freud, human existence may ultimately be defined in terms of these two basic realities which characterize and make it unique. All our strivings, Freud says, are understood in terms of our efforts to reconcile and integrate our needs to love and be loved and our needs to produce and accomplish—to feel good about ourselves. Work, then, is part of the condition of normalcy. It is, in a manner of speaking, one of the two avenues open to us for expressing our humanity. It is through our work that we maintain contact with reality, with other people and our physical environment. It is in work that we are best able to express many of those skills and attributes which make each of us unique. It is through work that we are most able to influence and have impact on the world in which we live. And it is through work that we achieve and sustain a feeling of movement, that stimulation and sense of growth that is basic to the life process. Is it any wonder that we derive feelings of efficacy and personal worth—self-respect—from working well? By doing so, we reaffirm our normalcy. And is it any wonder that we respond in counterproductive ways—with hostility and antagonism, with apathy and indifference—to those who would disrupt our work or make doing it well more difficult for us? They bar us from the rewards of competence and deny us the means to normalcy.

A study by the Institute for Social Research underscores the importance of work for that emotional well-being that we equate with competence and normalcy. From their study of men who were out of work, researchers concluded that:

> . . . for most men in our culture, work is apparently the sole organizing principle and the only means of self-expression. Without work, men exhibit a certain deterioration of personality, loss of emotional stability and breakdown of morale. This malignant boredom threatens the organism as a whole.[12]

The competence motive, then, is tied directly to the simple goals of normalcy. The desire to do one's best, the need to feel good about oneself, the rewards of pride in accomplishment—none of these is extraordinary. They are simply the basic requirements of normal living. They require no outside impetus, threats or inducements, only opportunities for expression. Those who would deny such opportunities out of some misguided notion about the onerous nature of work or because of some elitist view of human capacities do us all a disservice; they make us, individually and collectively, something less than we truly are.

When Competence is Frustrated

Why is it then that competence sometimes appears to just

[12] Slote, A. *Closing at Baker Plant.* Indianapolis: The Bobbs-Merrill Co., 1969.

go away, to drop from our repertoires, when we join an organization? Chris Argyris some years ago asked essentially the same question and concluded that organizations are put together in ways that do not take human capacities into account.[13] The result is to reverse the natural process of growth; to encourage dependency rather than independence; to expect immaturity rather than maturity as the norm; and to promote psychological failure rather than psychological success. People learn under such conditions to *behave* incompetently. They *learn* to become passive and submissive, to avoid responsibility and risk. They learn not to care.

It is safe to say that such organizational structures are certainly not founded on a recognition of individual competence. Failure to recognize competence and the failure to provide for its expression are the first critical steps in the organizational loss of competence. The capacity for competence is innate but its expression is directly influenced by agents and events external to the person. As managers, we must face up to the fact that the expression of competence, the competent response, is *learned* and, as such, is subject to all the laws of learning and motivation. Properly rewarded, the competent response will intensify and become more probable. Unrewarded or, indeed, punished competence will be *extinguished.* It will weaken as a response tendency and become less and less probable until it virtually disappears. But the *need* to be competent, the competence *motive,* will not diminish. Indeed, deprived of satisfaction, it will become greater—and so will the sense of frustration.

In our organizations today we are encountering unprecedented signs of frustrated competence. Many managers

---

[13] Argyris, C. *Personality and Organization.* New York: Harper & Row, 1957.

have begun to wonder if it is even possible to manage at all anymore. So many apparently irrelevant issues have surfaced in the workplace that is hard to focus on the work itself. However, the vast majority of such issues may be not only very relevant to work but may result from barriers to the expression of competence. What is the abiding issue in complaints of sexism? It is the frustration of competence needs among women and all that this entails psychologically and economically. What is the core issue in ethnic complaints? It is the arbitrary denial to some of opportunities to express their competence; it is the withholding of the means to normalcy and self-respect on the basis of race. What really prompts labor grievances? Is it the economic benefits and fringe package everyone talks about or is it really unappreciated and mismanaged competence? And when we complain about the quality of work life and organizational stress, as many have begun to do recently, are we not really talking about the feelings and tensions that are triggered when competence is frustrated? The point is that, unaccustomed as we are to thinking in terms of human competence and its management, we misinterpret the signs of frustrated competence. Mismanagement of competence—failure to create the proper context for its expression—may well be responsible for most of the major problems of production and morale confronting us today.

Despite all the evidence in support, the concept of widespread competence will not appear to all. There will always be those who see their workers as unmotivated and unproductive. They will single out a few poor performers and cite the exception in order to disprove the rule. But exceptions do not challenge the principle of competence. We all know that there are people who neither care nor produce just as we all know that there are unfortunate individuals who do not function within the boundaries of normalcy. So what? What else is new? But to subscribe to the notion that the vast majority of people are uncaring and unproductive is just as tenuous a line of reasoning as to conclude that the vast majority of people are abnormal. The whole history of human accomplishment is tangible evidence to the contrary. Perhaps, as managers, we ought to take a hard look at our exceptions; more often than not, we will find that they are of our own making, that we have gotten in the way of the competence motive.

We must ask ourselves if we have organized *defensively:* apprehensive about the unrealized competence of 10% of the workforce, have we created structures and developed policies which constrain and limit the activities of the remaining 90% who are demonstrably competent? It is entirely possible— indeed, likely—that through a presumption of incompetence we have driven competence underground. We can do better than that.

We must recognize that, in dealing with other people, all of us— managers, parents, teachers, leaders of every sort—are dealing with *potentiality,* with talents and traits that not only will exist in the future but whose future existence is prepared in the present. Erich Fromm, the eminent psychoanalyst and social philosopher, has spoken eloquently to this important reality. He resorts to metaphor to make his point:

> This relationship between the present and the future stage of development can be described by saying the future virtually exists in the present. Does this mean that the future stage will *necessarily* come into being if the present stage exists? Obviously not. If we say that the tree is potentially present in the seed it does not mean that a tree

must develop from every seed. The actualization of a potentiality depends on the presence of certain conditions which are, in the case of the seed, for instance, proper soil, water, and sunlight. In fact, the concept of potentiality has no meaning except in connection with the specific conditions required for its actualization. The statement that the tree is potentially present in the seed must be specified to mean that a tree will grow from the seed *provided* that the seed is placed in the specific conditions necessary for its growth. If these proper conditions are absent, if, for instance, the soil is too moist and thus incompatible with the seed's growth, the latter will not develop into a tree but rot.[14]

And so it is with people at work.

Just as the unnurtured seed may never come to look like a tree, competence in our organizations may never surface unless its potential is supported and encouraged . . . with the ultimate irony being that unexpressed competence appears for all the world as incompetence. What if, as managers, we addressed ourselves to the soil, to the kind of organizations we have created rather than to the kinds of people who populate them? The people are not the problem. They are individually competent—because they want to be. It is management's job to harness this personal competence so that it may become collective competence. It is management's job to provide a context within which competence may be expressed, where commitment and creativity are allowed to flourish. The key at this point to

---

[14] Fromm, E. *Man for Himself.* Greenwich, Connecticut: Fawcett Publications, Inc., 1947, p. 210.

increased productivity and enhanced morale in the workplace is to shift our attention from individual capacities and focus on the organizational context which controls the expression of competence. Perhaps we might all begin to address ourselves to the creation of organizations which are *contexts for competence.*

III

Creating a Context for Competence

People in charge hold the key. They may release commitment and creativity—unleash competence—in their organizations by applying the proper principles and practices. The competence process may be set in motion to harness the abundance of talent and energy available in our organizations. But first, before considering the process, we must refocus, gain a more *personal* perspective on life and work in organizations. We have said that people are capable of doing what needs to be done; we have made a presumption of competence. Yet all about us we see evidence to the contrary. Al Marrow has commented on our discontent:

> Every citizen is aware of the failure of public and private institutions alike to meet the needs of the public they deal with—employees, customers, clients, the public. The complaints voiced are constant, pervasive, and increasingly strident: Cars, tires, TV sets, and other products are shoddy and often defective when delivered; workmanship is sloppy; repairmen are rude; managers are arrogant; workers are apathetic; service is poor. Similar deterioration of quality is reported in medical care,

education, transportation, and public utilities.[1]

Something is clearly wrong. But the problem is not a lack of competence so much as it is one of *unexpressed* competence. Marrow brought the issue into focus when he wrote that the level of production, particularly among some forty million workers in the service industries ". . . is estimated by authorities as only *50 percent of the potential available from existing human skills, initiative, and energy."*[2] (Italics mine.)

The problem is that people are simply not doing what they are capable of doing. Why? Given personal competence coupled with a personal need to perform competently, why do we operate at 50 percent of capacity in our various organizations? The answer is *management.* Management has discouraged competence. By creating impersonal organizations which are insensitive to the human need for efficacy and worth, managers have afforded contexts which frustrate the expression of competence. And they have replaced an attitude of hope among workers with one of despair. Productivity is but a mirror of the attitudes and aspirations management has encouraged among those who do the organization's work.

Management and Productive Orientation: The Crisis of Attitude

When repairmen are rude and service is poor, when

---

[1] Marrow, A. "For the Puzzled Executive—A Briefing." In A. J. Marrow (Ed.), *The Failure of Success.* New York: AMACOM, a division of American Management Association, 1972, preface, p. *v.,* May, 1984.

[2] *Ibid.*

workers are apathetic and workmanship is sloppy, when managers are arrogant and products are shoddy, it is because work itself has become a disappointing experience. When people do not do what they are capable of doing, it is because they have become frustrated, angry, and disaffected. Blocked from expressing personal competence and robbed of the hope that things might change for the better, people eventually stop trying. They lose what psychologist Erik Fromm has called their *productive orientation*. As defined in the psychological literature, one's productive orientation is that healthy ". . . *outlook* that permits him to be creative in work and social relations and to use well whatever potentialities he has."[3] (Italics mine.) In addition to its obvious implications for the accomplishment of work, at the personal level a productive outlook is a necessary precondition for such work-related notions as satisfaction, responsibility, commitment, and pride.

Productive orientation is an attitude, a mind set, a personal anticipation that the *prospects are good that competent performance will yield the psychological rewards associated with competence: feelings of efficacy and self-worth.* One's productive orientation is *learned.* As such, it may well be both the most critical and most neglected factor in the manager's pursuit of productivity. For the nature of a person's productive orientation determines whether or not one's competence will be expressed in the doing of work, whether or not striving for competent performance seems worth the effort. Managerial practices and organizational priorities determine what the prevailing productive orientation will be in the workplace. Managers *teach* the productive outlook to those they manage.

[3] English, H. & A. English. *A Comprehensive Dictionary of Psychological and Psychoanalytical Terms.* New York: Longmans, Green and Co., 1958, p. 411.

When workers join an organization, they are immediately faced with choice situations in which they really have very little choice at all. Personal and organizational values collide, and organizational values prevail. When faced with a choice of doing one's best or keeping the work *cost effective,* cost effectiveness wins every time, or so it seems. When faced with the option of doing a task better or doing it according to some standardized procedure, procedure wins every time. When faced with a choice of working for quality or staying with the production schedule, the schedule wins every time. Now these are adaptive people we are talking about; they *learn* very quickly. They learn that neither their ability nor their personal needs to perform competently are really very important in the organizational scheme of things. They learn that management doesn't really expect or want them to do what needs to be done—not if it costs too much, breaks with precedent, or challenges the status quo. They learn that to perform too well is, more often than not, to invite trouble. Management makes it more and more difficult for people to feel good about either their work or themselves. So they stop trying.

The following excerpt from a report, written by an insider at the Department of Agriculture under the pseudonym of James North, captures dramatically how productive orientation can be destroyed by the messages implicit in managers' practices and the organizational conditions they create.

In pondering what was wrong with his co-workers and the organization, North wrote:

> What was it with those people? They were all intelligent, potentially competent, as honest as the next guy. They had all entered Government service with enthusiasm and dedication. But

somewhere along the line they had all settled for far less than expected—and some had virtually embraced incompetence. The odd thing was that most took no joy in their malfeasance. A few delighted in petty corruption, but most were frustrated and dissatisfied. They felt that theirs was the only rational course open, that *the system demanded incompetence.*[4] (Italics mine.)

Then, in trying to explain how intelligent, honest, and at one time dedicated people could literally choose to be incompetent, he reflected:

One answer is obvious: *the pressure toward mediocrity is simply too enormous to resist.* To stand out one need perform only slightly better than the prevailing level of incompetence. To do much more is to play the fool—doing others' work—and invites the hostility of co-workers. (Italics mine.)

Good people, North reports, were led by the norms and prevailing conditions of that system to abandon their aspirations and embrace incompetence. They were caught up in a crisis of attitude. They exchanged attitudes of enthusiasm and dedication for those of frustration and dissatisfaction; they stopped anticipating that competent performance was the means to efficacy and worth in their place of work. Managers cannot afford such a decay of the spirit.

---

[4] "The Making of a Bureaucrat." *Time,* March 5, 1979, p. 17.

The Role of Management

Managers typically do not use phrases like "productive orientation;" they are content to leave such jargon to the social scientists. But they *talk about* productive orientation a good bit of the time: "Nobody wants to work anymore!" "He's not motivated," or "She's got a poor attitude," or "It's impossible to get good help these days." Such common managerial complaints are description of productive orientation or, to be more precise, of its absence. The attitudes of people at work are much on the managerial mind. And well they should be, for all too often they are the products of management.

Chris Argyris relates the story of a top executive who told him "the trouble with the workers today is that 5 percent of them work, 10 percent of them think they work, and 85 percent of them would rather die than work." When he was finished, Argyris asked the executive to repeat his observations and add at the end ". . . in my plant."[5] That's the perspective called for in exploring the significance of productive orientation in the competence process. We are interested in the outlooks of people in *our* organizations. We are concerned with the contexts *we* create. For our purposes, managers seem to control both the cause and the cure.

As managers, on behalf of our organizations, we are directly responsible for the mind set, the personal anticipation, the expectation of competence which will prevail. Through our policies and practices, we as much as state the odds that people will be able to work in such a way that they can

[5] Argyris. C. *Personality and Organization.* New York: Harper & Row, Harper Torchbooks, 1957, 1970, p. 48.

harvest the rewards of competence. We literally condition the productive orientation of those in the workplace. And we unwittingly set the limits—low or high— on productivity.

Productive Orientation and Productivity

The point is that, depending on the productive orientation we have fostered in our organizations—healthy or unhealthy views of the possible—the abundance of competence available to us will or will not be expressed in the doing of the organization's work. The presumption of competence still holds. The capacity of people to do what needs to be done does not change; but the *opportunity* to do so changes according to managerial practices. So it is that performance varies from manager to manager and organization to organization. The prevailing productive orientation among people predisposes them to be more or less productive. Managers hold the key to both outlook and performance: If people have high expectations, they will be productive; if they expect little, they will forego competent performance in the same spirit as they learned to lay aside their aspirations for self-worth and health through work. To prevent such malaise and the diminished productivity which accompanies it, managers must find ways of revitalizing the workplace. They must begin to manage for the widespread expression of competence.

Managing for Collective Competence

While the issue of personal competence is just that—a personal issue—competence in organizational settings is essentially a managerial issue because managers create and monitor the contexts within which people work. Managers have the hard job of translating individual competence into collective competence. It takes more than one hard-working individual to do the work of an organization; all must perform competently. The success of organizational efforts requires widespread, collective competence. And, just as Robert White has equated personal competence with the adaptive fitness of the individual, collective competence will dictate the organization's fitness for future action. Managers must be concerned not only with the present but with the future, with the adaptive fitness of their organizations. For, as James Thompson has written, "For the organization as a totality, the important question is not what it has accomplished but its *fitness for future action.*"[6] (Italics mine.) Managers can determine today what the future holds for their organizations.

When cars and tires, TV sets and medical care, education and transportation are shoddy, we should look to management because these products and services are not *uniformly* shoddy, even within the same organization. If we were to look at the management—rather than at the people or the technology—in both our competent and apparently incompetent organizations, those that have succeeded versus those that have failed, we would find that managerial practices differ for the two. We would find that some managers have created a more proper *context* for the collective expression of individual competence while others have not.

Given the organization's need for creative enterprise accomplished by committed people, the individual's desire

---

[6] Thompson. J. *Organizations in Action: Social Science Bases of Administrative Theory.* New York: McGraw-Hill, 1967.

to behave competently creates the potential for a symbiotic relationship between organizations and those who populate them: individuals and organizations may function to the mutual benefit of one another. As individual needs for competence are acted upon and satisfied, the organization's capacity for adapting effectively to its environmental demands is enhanced. Whether the potential for competence will be nurtured and brought to fruition within organizations depends in large measure on whether managers recognize the symbiotic relationship between organizations and those who do their work, on one hand, and whether they *do* anything to capitalize on such a state of affairs, on the other. The issue is really simple and straightforward: Organizations need people and people need organizations. It is managers who either recognize or ignore the competence potential inherent in a symbiotic coexistence of people and formal organizations; and it is managers, above all others, who are in the position to do something constructive and generative about such a potential.

Competence among individuals is a basic assumption, but a corollary assumption holds that none of this personal competence will ever become apparent or brought to bear on the work of the organization unless it is nurtured by management. Quite simply, competence will not become *manifest* unless a context is provided for its expression. The frequent complaint that people are no longer productive or no longer take pride in their work says less about the fundamental competence of people than it does about the organizational contexts we have created for the doing of work.

Again: *unexpressed* competence looks much the same as *in*competence. This is why, when managing for the widespread expression of competence, major emphasis is placed on the philosophic and structural properties of the organization; in all practical respects these *define* the context within which collective competence may be either directly expressed in productive output or frustrated by outdated managerial policies and practices. When managing for collective competence, the focus is on the organization's internal environment, the context within which people perform, and how the forces at work are experienced relative to the individual's need for competence. The emphasis is on those facets of organizational life directly amenable to managerial influence—job structure, decision processes, and the like—rather than on external demands such as changes in the market place or federal regulations over which managers have little control. In managing for collective competence, we are interested in the things the individual manager can do something about. And that is what the competence process is all about. On this note, then, let's consider the competence process and the task of management.

Basic Properties of the Competence Process

Achieving widespread commitment and creativity is the major objective pursuant to collective competence. A good deal is known about commitment and creativity. Basic research in the behavioral sciences has revealed numerous cause-effect dynamics, philosophic considerations, and support requirements in the incidence of both commitment and creativity. The competence process simply puts these findings into a proper perspective so that their implications for organizational objectives may become more apparent and managers may have a clear understanding of the actions required and, equally important, *why* they are necessary.

Individual versus Collective Competence

While individual competence is natural and intrinsic, collective competence of the type needed by organizations must be created; it requires extrinsic supports. People behave in committed and creative ways in their personal tasks because it helps them feel good about themselves, as individuals. Under what circumstances might they be expected to join with others in a committed and creative fashion for doing the tasks of the organization? This is the problem managers must solve and it is the question the competence process first addresses.

A subtle psychological difference separates individual from collective competence. Individual competence proceeds from a personal competence motive—a felt need leading to sustained energy—and the rewards are essentially personal. What are the organizational equivalents of the competence motive and personal feelings of efficacy and worth? The key, I think, lies in the fact that organizations provide the major outlets—the tasks—through which individual competence may be expressed and according to which its rewards may be accrued. The core issue is whether or not work is structured in a way and decision processes are such that people—individually and collectively—can expect that their personal competence is valued by management and can, in fact, be expressed.

In seeking an organizational equivalent to the competence motive and its rewards, managers may need look no further than to providing those opportunities for the full expression of personal competence which, in turn, will enhance productive orientation in the workplace. Managers need not "motivate" in terms of pushing or prodding; instead they can create conditions and provide supports for the free operation of those intrinsic needs for competence which people bring with them to the organization. When people can view the work they do as a vehicle for expressing what they know, for demonstrating skills in which they take personal pride, as a challenge to their problem-solving abilities, they perform competently. The key to widespread collective competence, therefore, is creating the conditions and providing the opportunities necessary to imbue the work of the organization with such meanings. This is what the competence process succeeds in doing. It bridges the gap between individual and collective competence by providing a context within which the individual commitment and creativity of many people may be expressed in concert. And it begins with the lesson learned at Harwood.

Collaboration: Bridging the Gap

The competence process has as its objective the widespread release of human commitment and creativity into the organization's bloodstream. Individual creativity is an outgrowth of personal commitment and both, in turn, are by-products of a third antecedent factor: personal involvement . . . the opportunity to influence and shape the course of one's efforts. Involvement is, of course, stimulated and facilitated by active participation. We saw the power of participation and the practical utility of a company-wide system of participative management at Harwood.

Opportunities to participate, to become personally involved in planning and goal-setting where one's work is concerned, afford a powerful *triggering* device for personal commitment and creativity. But, even though such opportunities may be offered to work teams, departments, and the like— assemblies of several people—the initial focus and the primary rewards of participation seem to concern *individuals* and the release of *personal* commitment and creativity. There is a private, all too self-centered, aspect to participation that must be recognized and re-directed if collective competence is to be achieved.

Douglas McGregor, the eminent psychologist, had this to say about the power of participation:

> Participation . . . offers substantial opportunities for ego satisfaction for the subordinate and thus can affect motivation toward organizational objectives. It is an aid to achieving integration. In the first place, the subordinate can discover the satisfaction that comes from tackling problems and finding successful solutions for them. This is by no means a minor form of satisfaction. It is one of the reasons that the whole do-it-yourself movement has grown to such proportion in recent years. Beyond this there is a greater sense of independence and of achieving some control over one's destiny. Finally, there are the satisfactions that come by way of recognition from peers and superiors for having made a worthwhile contribution . . . participation in departmental problem solving may have considerable significance in demonstrating to people how they can satisfy their own needs best by working toward organizational objectives.[7]

Implicit in McGregor's words is a preoccupation with the *individual* rewards of participation. The emphasis is on *the*

[7] McGregor, D. *The Human Side of Enterprise.* New York: McGraw-Hill, 1960, p. 130.

subordinate's ego-satisfaction, motivation toward organizational objectives, and sense of independence and control.

Now, all of these by-products of participation are highly desirable and worthy objectives. But, for the release of competence throughout an organization, such effects must be both widespread and coordinated. One of the things the management of Harwood discovered was that some people become so enamored of participation that they work to increase their share of air time, effectively disenfranchising less assertive but equally astute individuals. As Harwood's management became more sophisticated in participative methods, they finally introduced group dynamics training to promote greater sensitivity and norms of sharing across the workforce. What they sought was more than participation—a state of collaboration. As powerful a tool as participation can be, it must be managed such that it becomes a shared commodity—equally available to all, management and workers alike.

Collaboration, a genuine working *together,* is the key. In *The Human Animal,* Phil Donahue made a telling observation: "Most of our uniquely human accomplishments have been a combination of cooperation and individual achievement."[8] It is individual achievement geared to cooperative effort that is called for in the competence process. Collaboration—between worker and worker, manager and manager, and manager and worker—can bridge the gap between individual and collective competence. Not only can a collaborative posture on the part of everyone activate the critical components of competence—uncover needed resources, set the stage for commitment and creativity—

[8] Donahue, P. *The Human Animal.* New York: Simond Schuster, Inc., 1985.

but it can imbue the organization's work with personal meaning and its accomplishment with a shared sense of accountability and obligation. When collaboration is encouraged it becomes the mechanism of ownership; people begin to feel "the organization's work is *our* work." But, equally important is its *symbolic* value; norms of collaboration send a message throughout the organization that we want the best people have to offer, that the prospects for competence are good in our workplaces.

It is because of these effects—the fostering of a widespread sense of mastery, the discovery of multiple resources, the promotion of feelings of ownership and partnership, protection of individual rights, spirit of shared inquiry, and coordination of effort—that collaboration is considered a mandatory precursor to commitment and creativity.

The Structure of the Competence Process

To understand the competence process, we must appreciate the causal connections among the three factors of collaboration, commitment and creativity. In the competence process, collaboration is viewed as the well-spring from which commitment and creativity flow. It serves to *trigger* the process. We might portray the skeletal structure of the competence process thusly:

Figure 1. The structure of the competence process.

In Figure 1, collaboration is portrayed as the prime mover in a causal sequence of events which culminates in a response state of collective competence. As depicted, both commitment and creativity flow out of collaborative opportunities and, when they are achieved, combine to yield an adaptive response capability. As we shall see in later chapters, an organization's level of competence may be measured in terms of such dynamics, and performance outcomes may be estimated with a high degree of confidence. In the interim, however, it is important to focus in more detail on the sequence of events leading up to the state of competence, for much more than collaboration is required if the potentials unleashed are to be realized.

Collaborative dynamics, once set in motion, must be managed for task accomplishment if they are to prove meaningful and rewarding. This is why, in the competence process, the collaboration dimension is viewed primarily as a triggering mechanism for setting the process in motion. It affords a springboard to commitment and makes creative functioning more probable. But it does not guarantee the occurrence of either.

Commitment and creativity are competence dimensions in their own right and they require the same attention, emphasis, and careful planning that have customarily been given only to collaborative dynamics in the past. They are the primary task dimensions of the competence process. The systematic incorporation of these task-centered considerations makes the process viable and, at the same time, helps put the use of collaborative practices into proper perspective.

Dimensions of Competence

The competence process is a three-dimensional approach, with each dimension serving a different function yet interdependent with the remaining dimensions. To better understand both the functions served and the nature of the interdependencies, we may now consider the factors of collaboration, commitment, and creativity in terms of their dimensional status. In the context of collective competence, each stands for a dimension of organizational life which is manifested in organizational policies, practices, and procedures. And each is equally important. The manner in which organizations are put together—the policy structure, incentive system, reporting relationships, supervisory practices, all these and more—may be looked upon in terms of how they serve collaboration, commitment, and creativity.

Every policy, written or unwritten, every practice, and every priority characterizing an organization may realistically be considered as a force in the lives of its members; they exert pressure, they lead and direct, they facilitate or make impossible, they prescribe and reward or punish. How they bear on people's needs to become involved through collaboration, feel committed, or be creative is the core issue in widespread competence. The people who comprise organizations take their cue from prevailing ground rules. They experience and interpret them, they feel pressured by them in identifiable ways.

For our purposes, the underlying principle is straightforward and simple: the people who manage the organization create conditions which give it its basic character and serve to transmit to its personnel the values embraced, priorities deemed important, the range and type of tolerable behaviors, what can be expected and what should not. The norms *define* the organization for people—their roles in it, prevailing standards and sense of purpose—and establish the context within which work is to be done. They literally *teach* people what is considered important, acceptable, and feasible. People hear the message; and, just as those described earlier by James North, they learn it, internalize it, and perform accordingly.

The point, of course, is that the message conveyed by an organization's leaders may be one that encourages and enables competence or something less. Through the management of organizational conditions, those who lead organizations can set in motion a competence process such that the organization is better equipped for meeting its adaptive demands or they can discourage competence and impair adaptive fitness. Some managers pursue competence intuitively; some do not, opting instead for conditions which either purposely frustrate or ignore the needs for collaboration, commitment, and creativity.

My assumption is that a managerial frustration of competence is due more to a lack of appreciation of the psychological significance of organizational policies and practices than to any malevolent intent. Many managers come to their positions because they have performed well in other professional spheres. The outstanding engineer is often "promoted" to management with little additional training; the excellent teacher is made a principal or dean; the creative accountant is made president. Principles of management are left to on-the-job learning.

Once in management they also must contend with archaic guidelines. We still organize ourselves according to the military phalanx principles enunciated by Julius Caesar and amended at the beginning of this century by the father of Scientific Management, Frederick Taylor. Our incentive systems and economic postures still bear the imprint of the 18th century economist Adam Smith. And every day a manager somewhere takes some protective action in memory of Samuel Gompers' success as a union organizer. We are too often mired in historical precedent. But nowhere will a backward glance at the historical roots of current practices fall on issues of competence. To pursue competence we must readjust our sights and determine how our ways of organizing and managing serve the need for collaboration, commitment, and creativity. These are the dimensions of competence, and they have been sorely neglected in past treatments of life in organizations.

Conditions for Competence

What, then, are the conditions which promote and sustain that widespread sense of collaboration, commitment and creativity which is revealed in collective competence? This is the question which must be answered in preparing for the future. In our research we have identified and confirmed several requisites which are critical to both initiating and capitalizing upon each competence dimension. Through these, collaboration, commitment, and creativity come alive.

The dimensions of competence are merely abstract rubrics, a form of verbal shorthand used to organize and ease discussion. But each competence dimension may be thought of as being served or supported by certain specific, real, conditions. Without its supporting conditions, a given dimension is weakened and may cease to operate as a force for collective competence. Implied is that collaboration, commitment, and creativity—and, by extension, competence—require more than a philosophical commitment from organizational leaders. A dedication to competence must be translated into positive action steps geared to the creation of specific organizational conditions. In the next three chapters we will examine in detail both the defining characteristics of and the managerial actions necessary for creating a context for competence. We will develop, step by step, a new social technology for enhanced health and productivity in our places of work, be they in the public or private sectors of our communities.

IV

Conditions for Collaboration

Collaboration, the first dimension in the competence process, is a shared decision-making and problem-solving work experience. It is job analysis; it is planning and forecasting and the allocation of resources accomplished by people working together. With all its emotional overtones, collaboration is uniquely task centered. And from the doing of collaborative tasks, people emerge with a feeling that they have helped shape future events. They have a clearer picture of what is to be done and how to do it. They have a better sense of their own responsibilities as a result. They often feel more comfortable with the substantive guidelines governing their work because, as a result of the give-and-take of open discussion and analysis, they have satisfied themselves that most important considerations have been touched upon. People experience fate control in the workplace. This does not mean that management abdicates its role or sidesteps its responsibilities. Managers collaborate, as well. Management may still control problem focus and task identification, but the people charged with doing the work now directly influence how best to accomplish it.

Not too long ago, collaboration in the workplace was thought to rest on something as simple as a managerial invitation to become involved. "What would you do?" or

"What do you think?" or "How do you feel?" These were the magic phrases managers could rely on to become participative in dealing with their subordinates. They are still potent entrees but, as we have come to understand better the dynamics of participation, the participative issue has become more complex. It is now apparent that much more is required for a truly collaborative system whose objective is the widespread expression of competence.

Managers have needed resources too. A collaborative system allows the incorporation of managerial as well as non-management resources. Some managers are initially suspicious of collaboration, sensing an erosion of managerial authority. But in genuine collaboration, neither their authority nor ideas and opinions get lost in the shuffle.

Collaboration is an invitation to share *power.* When managers create opportunities for those affected by decisions to share in making them, they are inviting influence. They are asking, for all intents and purposes, that people share in the manager's traditional power to decide. They are making them partners in the decision-making process. And they are sharing control and ownership of the work to be done. But power is a volatile issue in many organizations. Therefore, managers must be sensitive to an important contingency effect underlying collaboration. In the minds of most personnel, their collaboration *is contingent upon being invited and encouraged by management to do so.* More often than not, there will be no collaboration unless management recognizes this contingency and takes the initiative in opening up the process so that others have opportunities to influence planning and decision-making activities. To comment openly may seem presumptuous or foolhardy to some subordinates; they need the reassurance of management. Managers must overcome this reticence by insuring both the occasion and the support necessary for people to get involved. When managers take the responsibility for doing this, they will find an enhancement of the emotional tone of the workplace.

The decision by a manager to employ collaborative methods should be based on an awareness of the power dynamics which underlie collaboration and of the implications for future policies. Affording collaborative opportunities, encouraging people to shape and influence decisions affecting their work, is a *symbolic* gesture on the part of management; it signifies that managers are voluntarily divesting themselves of a portion of their formally endowed power and reinvesting it in others. Unless this is the true intent, backed by the manager's willingness to relinquish personal control, collaboration will not work. People can sense the difference between genuine and gimmicky uses of collaboration; one denotes a managerial conviction worthy of confidence while the other is but a managerial technique to be viewed with suspicion. As Douglas McGregor has observed, "Techniques which are used as 'gimmicks' can . . . readily destroy confidence."[1]

When collaboration is genuine it creates among people a sense of vitality and self-direction. Individuals begin to feel that they have choices, that they have some control over those events in the workplace which affect them personally. Their prospects for competent performance improve. No longer are they organizational pawns to be moved and positioned, or simple badge numbers to be requisitioned and assigned. They become functioning human entities whose most valued attributes are ideas, opinions, and knowledge about how best to do the organization's work.

[1] McGregor, D. *The Human Side of Enterprise.* New York: McGraw-Hill, 1960, p. 138.

And they begin to feel good about themselves and their jobs. This is a potent beginning for the competence process, for it affects productive orientation, the anticipation that work may be a source of important psychological rewards.

Collaboration and Productive Orientation

How much satisfaction one derives from work, the personal feeling of responsibility for doing it well, sense of ownership and freedom from frustration, combine with pride to define that basic outlook which we have characterized in Chapter III as one's productive orientation. Opportunities for genuine collaboration have rather dramatic implications for how people feel about themselves and the work they do. In our research, we studied 9,600 people from over 30 different organizations regarding the degree to which they had opportunities to collaborate in planning and designing their work and their consequent feelings of satisfaction, sense of responsibility, emerging commitment, lack of frustration, and personal pride in output. Figure 1 summarizes our research findings of the influence of collaborative opportunities on those feelings.

As our data show, both healthy and unhealthy orientations are traceable to the management of collaborative opportunities. It is by the creation of opportunities to become involved that management first serves notice to others that their contributions are valued; collaboration keynotes and sets the tone for the productive orientation which management hopes will prevail in the workplace.

The profiles in Figure 1 portray two groups which differ on the basis of their collaborative experiences: one group

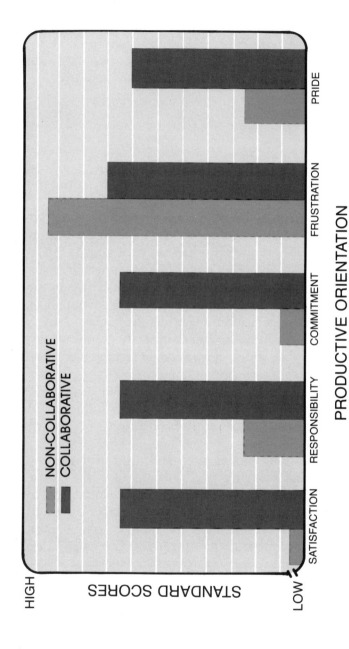

Figure 1. The effects of opportunities to collaborate on productive orientation.

of 1,539 individuals reported few opportunities to collaborate in work-related decisions and a second group composed of 8,061 people reported that they were routinely encouraged to join in making such decisions. As the data plots for the two groups indicate, collaborative opportunities are a potent influence on the productive feelings of people at work. The differences portrayed are so great as to be expected by chance alone fewer than one out of 10,000 times.[2]

These data pretty much speak for themselves. People who have enjoyed freedom to influence those decisions affecting their work—what is to be done, how it is to be accomplished, etc.—uniformly report higher potentials for job satisfaction, sense of responsibility, commitment, lower frustration with their work, and greater pride in accomplishment than do individuals characterized by few collaborative opportunities. They are inclined to a more positive outlook, a more healthy productive orientation. These feelings are of practical significance to organizations and their management because they have implications for whether or not people will be inclined to do what they are capable of doing. A safe inference is that people characterized by more positive feelings of commitment, responsibility, and the like are more likely to go that extra mile and do their best in implementing work-related decisions than are dissatisfied, uncommitted, frustrated individuals.

These findings have been replicated hundreds of times in numerous settings and are the basis for our thesis that collaboration, as the starting point in promoting a healthy productive orientation, is the wellspring—the prime prerequisite, the trigger—for the achievement of commitment

[2] See Table I of the Statistical Appendix for a summary of the data analysis for this study.

and creativity pursuant to competent performance. The actual achievement of competence, however, is not so simple as these data might imply.

A Collaborative Caveat

The effects of collaboration are not new to us. We have known about the substantial potentials of participative techniques for thirty years or more, ever since the classic work of Al Marrow and his colleagues at the Harwood Manufacturing Corporation as described in Chapter I.[3] We are familiar with the dramatic increases in productivity along with the virtual disappearance of several perennial problems of morale and employee turnover which resulted from introducing participative practices. These effects are more than a cultural artifact. Bruce Stokes—writing for the Worldwatch Institute—has recounted numerous benefits of participation in organizations throughout the world.[4] Nevertheless, the participative approach to management has received mixed reviews. This is because its expected effects are not always obtained.

I agree that participation does not always work as expected, but I attribute this to mismanagement of the process—to an incomplete appreciation of its complexities and support requirements—rather than to a weakness in involvement and power sharing per se. First of all, the private satisfactions of participation must be spread more widely through collaborative practices. But there is more than that

[3] Marrow, A. J., D. G. Bowers & S. E. Seashore. *Management by Participation.* New York: Harper & Row, 1967.

[4] Stokes, B. "Worker Participation—Productivity and the Quality of Work Life." *Worldwatch Paper 25,* Washington: Worldwatch Inst., 1978.

required. Collaborative practices were never intended as a panacea, but as the beginning of a process, never as an end in itself.

Collaboration implies future action. It is a preparation for *doing* something. And it must be followed by implementation if its potentials are to be realized. To collaborate for no reason, to invest time and thought to a project only to find that there are no plans for its implementation, to make suggestions which then lie fallow—all this renders the collaborative process a meaningless expenditure of energy. And people become frustrated, dissatisfied, and resentful as a result. Productive orientation suffers. Additional steps are required if the potentials unleashed by collaborative opportunities are to be realized.

For the full potential of collaborative practices to be realized—for people to avail themselves fully of the opportunities afforded—three support conditions are critical. There must exist a cultural backdrop where opportunities to collaborate are recognized as genuine and, moreover, where there is some personal incentive to take advantage of these opportunities. In addition, the way the organization is structured, physically and psychologically, must facilitate rather than hinder collaboration; information flow, geographic and logistical planning, interpersonal transactions, and organization of the work itself must be such that collaboration becomes a practical fact rather than a frustrated possibility. And finally, there must be evidence of managerial sincerity where collaborative opportunities are concerned; there is a "once burned, twice shy" quality to collaboration such that opportunities to verify management intent are important supports for a sustained sense of partnership and appreciation of collaboration.

The task of management, then, is to see that the proper support conditions for genuine collaboration exist and characterize the organizations. We have gathered these conditions and their related considerations under the collaborative rubric of *management values, support structure, and managerial credibility.* As depicted in Figure 2, the dimension of collaboration takes its strength from the combined effects of these conditions. And, in turn, these conditions begin to address the "sterner stuff" of our prophecies of competence and the hard questions of reality which managers must confront in their organizations. Each requires careful treatment so that both its meaning and role in the collaborative phase of competence can be appreciated.

Figure 2. Conditions for collaboration.

Management Values[5]

Every organization has a fundamental character or spirit—

[5] Recommended readings on both the promise and pitfalls associated with Management Values are:

Argyris, C. *Integrating the Individual with the Organization.* New York: Harper & Row, 1957.

Likert, R. "Human Resource Accounting: Building and Assessing Productive Organizations." *Personnel.* May/June 1973, pp. 8-24.

McGregor, D. *Op. cit.*

we might call it culture—which is revealed in a prevailing system of values, beliefs about the importance and basic nature of people, and norms of authority and influence. Typically, this organizational culture amounts to an amorphous mix of policy, day-to-day supervisory practices, employee expectations or apprehensions, and system of rewards and punishments. Its message is subliminal. People sense it rather than see it. However ill-defined the character of the organization may be, it is realistically a direct product of policy level decisions which, in turn, reflect the assumptions and basic outlook of organizational leaders. This is the ethos, the system of *management values,* which creates the cultural backdrop for collaboration. It is here that management *begins* the shaping of productive orientation.

Management values flow from the very core, from basic convictions about the *worth* of the people who do the work. Different convictions among managers yield different ways of organizing and relating to the people who do the work. Consider the likes of David Liederman and Debbie Fields, both owners and chief executives of successful cookie stores.[6] Reflecting on his approach to business, Liederman says, "You have to think at the lowest common denominator. One of the reasons we do so well in the cookie business is that a chimpanzee could take cookies out of that bag and more often than not put them on the tray properly . . . I'm terrified of sending anything out there where an employee has to do anything to the food." On the other hand, Fields has this to say, "Mrs. Field's Cookies is an extension of how I see the world. I believe people will do their best, I really do, provided that they are getting proper support . . . You say that people come to work for money, and I disagree with

---

[6] Richman, Tom, "A Tale of Two Companies," *Inc.* Boston: Inc. Publishing Co. July, 1984, pp. 38-43.

that. Money is part of a whole picture. People come to work because they need to be productive. They need to feel like they are successful in whatever they do . . . we want them to have fun." Liederman thinks Fields is an "air head."

Such managers send messages—different messages with different implications—and their meanings are clear to those on the receiving end. People are affected personally, in fundamental ways, and their capacity and will for competent performance are affected as well. Wittingly or not, management values impact on the self-images—the sense of personal worth—of those who work. Negative examples of the subtle effects of managerial policies and practices are more easily come by than positive ones, but we can learn from these as well. Consider Gus Maybry, a retired tool-and-die maker from Hughes Tool Company:

> My son asked me the other day what it used to be like at the plant, back when I was there. I said, 'Well, they sure knew how to keep us in our place. We had to punch in on a timeclock so they'd be sure we put in a full shift. They didn't want us to come early and wait around 'cause somebody might think we were loafing. Supervisors got their paycheck in a nice envelope with their names on it. We got ours' just handed to us so the whole world could see what we made. I used to walk two blocks in the rain *after* I found a parking place. Some 30-year old guy from the front office had a place right next to the entrance with his *name* on it. What really took the cake, though, was if you weren't in management, you couldn't take a cup of coffee to your work station. After 40 years I was pretty clear on how important I was to Hughes.' I said, 'I guess it's different now.' You know what he said? 'Not really.'

So it is that the values of management are transmitted through innocuous policies and practices. Impacting self-image and shaping productive orientation, the system of management values also affects the readiness of people to join in collaborative effort. If management truly wants a system of collaboration it must serve notice through the values it promotes.

Collaborative values are best set in motion by people with formal authority, those who speak for the organization. It helps when they come from the very top. A good example of the positive role top management can play in laying a foundation for collaboration comes from Ross Perot, founder and CEO of Electronic Data Systems, Inc. After EDS was purchased by General Motors for 2.5 billion dollars in 1984, Perot was asked if being under the GM umbrella would change things, whether EDS would come to resemble GM or vice versa. Perot replied:

> Everything (at EDS) is warm and very close. I spend lots of time with my employees and maintain an open-door policy. I deal with them as friends. There are no executive dining rooms at EDS . . . Look at the strength of EDS. The Japanese study us . . . Everybody here is an equal. We treat people fairly and respect them. We teach them how important they are and continue to stress being the best in the world. We deliver the best service at the best price. You listen to people who do a good job. You do these things and you will succeed.

Most people would agree that H. Ross Perot has done just that.

Perot's words exemplify the two most important messages conveyed via collaborative management values. First, management serves notice that it values the ideas and knowledge of its personnel and has faith in both their capacity and desire for productive enterprise. Secondly, through the values and practices it promotes, management reaffirms its concern for excellence. The first message essentially acknowledges humanity in the workplace; the second gives voice to the need for and commitment to the best possible work people can do. By disavowing policies and regulations which constrain people in their work, management serves notice that *results*—not slavish conformity to written procedure or cumbersome guidelines—have top priority. Excellence achieved in collaboration with competent people keynotes the theme advanced by management values of partnership and collaboration.

Douglas McGregor, in addressing the participative underpinning of collaboration, has captured the essence of the role played by management values in fashioning a collaborative system:

> The effective use of participation is a consequence of a managerial point of view which includes confidence in the potentialities of subordinates, awareness of management's dependency downward, and a desire to avoid some of the negative consequences of emphasis on personal authority.[7]

As a condition supporting collaboration in the pursuit of competence, *management values* recognize, philosophically and operationally, the human desire and capacity for

[7] McGregor, D. *Op. cit.*, p. 125.

competence and the mutual dependence of organizations and people:

- Policies reflect a sense of partnership and recognition of the essentiality of every member of the organization.

- People are managed as human beings who can gain personal satisfaction through doing the work necessary for the organization to meet its goals.

- Management sees that the organization and its people—while fundamentally different entities—are equally dependent upon one another.

- Policy encourages sharing of decision-making power, as well as rights, privileges, and economic returns, throughout the organization.

- A concern for excellence is demonstrated by management's willingness to provide or secure whatever training or support is required to enable people to do their best.

- The practices of management reflect the fundamental respect for others which a belief in their competence would denote.

We can ask the following kinds of questions to assess the effects of an organization's current management values on collaboration, how they are transmitted and define the roles of organizational members, set the limits for their expectations and aspirations, and condition their collective productive outlook. How a manager answers this type of question tells a great deal about the management values which prevail and whether or not the organization will be characterized by a collaborative system.

How are people valued in the organization? Are people at all levels accorded respect as human beings who are important because they perform the various tasks which the organization needs—or are they primarily valued according to the kind of work they do and particular positions they occupy?

How does management view the competence of its personnel? Does management expect the best and have confidence that people are both capable of and committed to doing the organization's work well—or does management doubt the abilities and intentions of its personnel?

What system of power and influence characterizes the organization? Is power shared with those who need it to get their work done—or do only those in positions of formal authority exercise power and make decisions?

The core issue in these questions is not so much monetary or privilege as it is *respect.* Respect, uniformly accorded throughout an organization, lays the groundwork for a collaborative system. People who have reason to believe they are not respected either fear or distrust opportunities to collaborate. Respect for the individual strikes at the core issue in both personal competence and a truly productive orientation. Depending on how such questions are answered, an organization may be said to operate from managerial values which promote or hinder collaboration. In general, the more positive and optimistic about employee potential and the fewer the vestiges of a powerbased class system, the more supportive of collaboration managerial values will be. And the more likely it is that the competence process, thus set in motion, may be sustained.

While the attainment of this supporting condition may require a basic reevaluation of management philosophy and a revision of existing policy, to settle for less is to opt for something other than widespread competence. Management values are self-fulfilling prophecies, be they for competence or less. Cultures based on a preoccupation with controls, authority-obedience norms of relating, subtle forms of elitism, manipulation, and the like undermine collaboration and make the achievement of widespread competence less probable.

Support Structure[8]

When management values are geared to sustained collaboration, their effects are most quickly discerned in the way management structures relationships within the organization; the structure of physical and psychological relationships is a second major requisite for collaboration.

Relationships exist between and among people and groups of people, between people and their work, people and their

---

[8] For additional insight into the manner in which the structure of relationships can affect collaboration and the emotional tone of the workplace, I recommend reading:

David, L. E. & A. B. Chernes. *Designing Organizations Around Human Values.* (2 Vols.). New York: Free Press (in press).

Hall, J. "Systems Maintenance: Gatekeeping and the Involvement Process." In J. A., Shtogren (Ed.), *Models for Management: The Structure of Competence.* The Woodlands, Texas: Teleometrics Int'l., 1980.

Likert, R. "An Integrating Principle and an Overview" and "The Interaction-Influence System." *New Patterns of Management.* New York: McGraw-Hill, 1961, pp. 97-118, 178-191.

Likert, R. "The Interdependent, Interacting Character of Effective Organizations." *The Human Organization.* New York: McGraw-Hill, 1967, pp. 47-77.

tools, between the work of some and that of others. It was in recognition of the unwieldy nature of such a multitude of relationships between people and functions that organizing as a managerial function came into being, some say with Moses when he appointed "able men" to lead the Hebrew children in more manageable groupings "of thousands, of hundreds, of fifties, and of tens." Now we have full-blown theories of organizing; we have arguments about the relative merits of flat versus tall organizations, about the need for open as opposed to closed systems, and about humanizing man-machine interfaces. Let there be no doubt about it, the physical and psychological structure of an organization is important, especially for sustained collaboration.

A truly collaborative system involves many relationships—managers with subordinates, workers with workers, job interfaces, and more—and these must be facilitated. If the structure of work and working relationships is such as to allow, indeed help, acting on collaborative opportunities, collaboration will occur. On the other hand, if relationships, information flow, and functions are so spread out as to hinder collaboration, the structure will make collaboration less probable. Managers must recognize that they work with neither just a technical system nor just a social system, but with a system in which technical and social characteristics and capabilities must be melded for optimal results. As Professor Albert Chernes of the University of Loughborough in Leicestershire, England, has written, organizational objectives are best met ". . . by the joint optimization of the technical and the social aspects, thus exploiting the adaptability and innovativeness of people in attaining goals . . ."[9] This is why the competence process demands a

[9] Chernes, A. "The Principles of Sociotechnical Design," *Human Relations,* 1976, Vol. 29, No. 8, pp. 783-792.

sensitivity to and conscious management of the organization's *support structure,* such that it serves, by design, collaborative objectives.

The need for melding technical and social dynamics into a support system for collaboration is an insight not easily achieved by many managers. But when it is, magic begins to happen. Take the case of Lew Veraldi, a corporate vice president and one of the top engineers at Ford Motor Company. In January of 1980, faced with Ford's mounting financial losses—soon to be $1.5 billion—Veraldi set protocol on its ear by managing for collaboration in the design of Ford's 1986 flagship, Taurus. John Holusha, of the New York Times, Detroit Bureau, tells the story:

> Traditionally, automobiles in Detroit have been developed sequentially, with little communication between the design, engineering and manufacturing groups. Designers prepare dozens of sketches of new possible models, and the most successful are transformed into full-size clay models. Once a design is approved by top management, it is turned over to the engineering departments, which develop and test each of the thousands of parts that go into a car. The finished specifications are turned over to the manufacturing staff so that it can prepare the assembly lines for mass production. As one engineer put it, 'We would wrap the plans for a new car around a rock and toss it over the wall to manufacturing. If it didn't come flying back within a few weeks, we assumed they could build it.'
>
> But Detroit has learned that there is a difference between just making something and making it

right. Many European and Japanese cars are designed for ease of assembly, since frustrated workers frequently make mistakes if a part is difficult to attach or adjust.

With this in mind, Veraldi has invited manufacturing and assembly experts to attend the scores of design meetings. This is the first time these groups have come together and some of the suggestions are novel—for Detroit. At one gathering, engineers from the company's assembly plant in Atlanta recommend that each side of the car be made of a single piece of metal, rather than welded together from a dozen or more pieces as they are in older American plants. Making one side out of one piece, they argue, will eliminate the errors that inevitably creep in during welding, help produce a more solid feel when the door is closed, and make a better actual fit. (Ultimately, each side of the car is made out of two pieces because the company does not have a stamping press big enough to create a whole side. Under the old system, the idea would have never been raised.)

Another time, Veraldi takes the design team to the Atlanta factory, to meet with the assembly-line workers. One worker asks that all the bolts used in the design be the same size. 'That way,' he explains, 'I won't have to spend time switching tools.'[10]

By managing around logistical barriers, recognizing the func-

[10] Holusha, J. "Ford Puts its Future on the Line," *The New York Times Magazine*. New York: The New York Times, December 1, 1985, pp. 94-106.

tional interdependence of designers, engineers, manufacturing, and assembly-line workers, Veraldi brought all the ingredients together in a truly collaborative effort. Did it work? In his own words, after getting the heads of all the engineering groups together, Veraldi typically understates both his own role and the innovations flowing from the process: "It was in June '80 that we went from a concept to a program. We put a stake in the ground and said, 'We've got a car!'"

Veraldi recognized a basic fact of the competence process: In support of collaboration, an organization's support structure must first reflect an awareness of and response to the need for *accessibility:* people should have access to those managers and co-workers with whom they are encouraged to collaborate; information flow—be it memos, reports, plenary sessions, or performance feedback—must be managed to include those who need and can add to pertinent information; and the fact of functional interdependence must be reflected in the logistics and work flow procedures of the organization. In addition, interpersonal supports are required; managers must personally work to get people involved and encourage their efforts. Such conditions serve to translate a philosophic commitment to collaboration into action.

A support structure for collaboration can be characterized as follows:

- Managers take the lead in creating openings for people to collaborate and provide ongoing encouragement and help toward this end. A rule of inclusion prevails.

- A two-way communication system assures

people of receiving the information they need for their work and of having opportunities to feed back pertinent information and ideas.

- Functionally related jobs and interdependent people are located in such a way as to insure access to one another.

- A norm of open critique is promoted as an ongoing support to the process and test of its efficacy.

Such a structure facilitates collaboration by removing physical and psychological barriers. It frees people to act upon the invitation extended by management to collaborate and allows them to be more responsive to problem situations at both the task and interpersonal levels of work.

With an eye toward the extent to which the physical and psychological structure of one's organization facilitates collaboration, we might ask the following questions:

How is information flow structured in the organization? Is information flow governed by the needs of those who do the work and given directly to them—or is it routed according to rank or position?

How do managers treat candid expressions of opinion? Do they work at creating opportunities for people to express themselves and encourage them to speak out—or do they discourage such attempts by ignoring, ridiculing, or perhaps censuring those who make suggestions?

How are working relationships structured in the organization? Can people contact co-workers and managers whose work affects their own—or are functions and people so spread that it is impractical or even impossible to confer or exchange suggestions?

These are some of the questions which bear on the structure of the organization. As they are answered, they can reveal whether collaborative objectives are being served or a more traditional control-oriented approach to organization prevails. In general, the more functional the structural arrangements, the more supportive the interpersonal transactions, and the more responsive to the informational needs of workers are the communication systems, the more supportive of collaboration the social and technical structures may be said to be. Systems within which information is coveted by management or collaboration is served by the suggestion box are not systems which are sensitive to the issues and dynamics of collaboration. To achieve a structure which is truly supportive of participation may require a rethinking of structural priorities and, indeed, the adoption of collaborative criteria as guidelines in organizing working relationships.

Managerial Credibility[11]

Managerial credibility is a factor which exerts tremendous influence on the amount of trust people have in the

---

[11] Major issues in Managerial Credibility are well developed in:

Argyris, C. *Interpersonal Competence and Organizational Effectiveness.* Homewood, Illinois: Dorsey Press, 1962.

Blake, R. R. & J. S. Mouton. "Managerial Facades." *The Managerial Grid.* Houston: Gulf Publishing, 1964.

Hall, J. "Interpersonal Style and Corporate Climate: Communication Revisited." In J. A. Shtogren (Ed.), *Models for Management: The Structure of Competence.* The Woodlands, Texas: Teleometrics Int'l., 1980.

Luft, J. "Of Human Interaction." Palo Alto, California: National Press Books, 1969.

workplace. Particularly in relationships with those in authority, the trust factor affects candor, spontaneity, and willingness to take full advantage of opportunities to collaborate. This is why the issue of managerial credibility may be considered to be a critical support to the dimension of collaboration.

People accept at face value the intentions and commitments of those they believe in. If collaboration—colored as it is by many implicit intentions, commitments, and action steps—is to work, managers who sponsor it must be prepared to work toward the establishment of personal credibility. They can do this by allowing those who need decisions to make them, by allowing those with on-the-job expertise to function as experts, and by insuring that productivity—not form or procedure—is the main objective. They can enhance credibility by consciously providing follow-up on collaboration through tracking mechanisms which can readily reveal the status of a given idea or suggestion, by instituting a feedback process which will keep people informed about events they have helped set in motion, and by being personally secure and honest in their decision to undertake collaborative practices in the first place. Such actions on the part of management afford opportunities for those affected by decisions made in collaboration with others to verify managerial intent. If intent can be verified on the basis of concrete results, trust is enhanced and managerial credibility is secured.

If management seeks opinions, asks for suggestions, or encourages employee collaboration, it is assumed that managers want such inputs and intend to do something with them. This is not necessarily the case. Many managers believe that the act of collaborating per se is its own reward and go no further. Others have the mistaken notion that people can be manipulated so that they will easily come to accept as their own ideas originated by management. Such managers, over time, lose their credibility. It becomes apparent to all at some point that very little is to be done with the ideas, opinions, or suggestions recruited by management—that there will be no follow-up: "Why ask what I think should be done if you have no intention of using any of my ideas?" A lack of credibility can stop the collaborative process in its tracks.

While credibility must be earned, this is not a difficult task. Often common sense and a frank manner will suffice. For example, John Hutchinson of Ford Motor's Design Staff recalls how uncertainty and suspicion were overcome by the Vice President, Don Kopka.

> We started having these meetings to identify problems. They didn't want George and me in there at first; they wanted us to come up with our list and they with theirs. So, they took minutes and everything, but they didn't really believe the message was going anywhere. They didn't quite trust anybody, like this was all a big smoke screen.
>
> But about a week later, Don had an opportunity to come down and meet with them himself. He said, "Hey guys, I want you to know we're really serious about what you are doing. I am aware of what is occurring in your organization. I am provided with a copy of the minutes and I read them very carefully. I intend to act on what you're telling us." Boy, their eyebrows went straight up.

One of the ironies of managerial credibility is that, unlike many other instances, the autocratic, direct, bull-of-the-woods manager usually has few problems. People know where they stand with such managers; they may not like it, but they are clear and they sense they can believe what they see and hear. Most problems of credibility come from *indirect* managers—often those who are "people" persons—who don't really trust people and try to use collaboration as a tool to maneuver or placate. A case in point comes from a friend of mine who, having been recently elected to the vestry, was astounded to learn how her parish priest operated.

> Our rector set up a long range planning commission—the first our parish had ever had. Bemoaning the lack of lay leadership, he appointed ten people to serve on the commission. I was pleased and flattered to be selected, and although the task assignment fell somewhere between vague and non-existent, I think each of us welcomed the challenge and the opportunity to play a part in the development of a long range plan.

> It wasn't long before we began to sense that there may be hidden agendas—that perhaps there already *was* a plan (to build a new church)—that we had actually been gathered together not to *formulate* a plan, but to *agree* to one and to sell it to the rest of the parish.

> Well, we decided to conduct an all-day workshop in which the laity brainstormed and defined short-term needs and long-term desires in six areas of church life—service, worship, education, evangelism, pastoral care and stewardship. With parish input about those areas and our research into the growth patterns of our community and

parish, we felt that the plan—whatever it turned out to be—would pretty much write itself.

The workshop was a huge success—attended by about ⅓ of our adult membership. Despite the priorities arrived at, the music program was mysteriously expanded—the choir director's time and salary doubled, a piano and additional music purchased, even though no funds were actually available. The reaction was, "Why are we beating our brains out attending meetings, trying to plan and prioritize when they've obviously already decided music has the highest priority!" And two months later, a special fund drive was necessary to obtain funds to pay the utility bills.

When I was elected to the vestry I noticed the same things happening with other groups. A commission would present an action plan, the vestry would approve it, and it would just disappear when the rector had to "think about it."

For me, the whole thing came to a head a couple of months ago at budget time. Through long hours of meetings the finance committee wrestled with the numbers and eventually mailed their budget proposal to each vestry member for consideration before the budget approval meeting. That budget proposal included one salary increase—for the education director whose duties had doubled in the past year. It was not balanced and did not provide for any expansion funds and it was up to the vestry to finalize it. Well, when the vestry meeting began, the finance committee chairman announced that he, the rector and the senior warden had met that afternoon and "fixed" the proposed budget. It included salary increases—some as high as 10%—for the entire staff (including the rector and his assistant)—and was balanced by cutting back on maintenance, education, outreach, and worship.

I don't quite know what to do. I can quit my appointment on long range planning and save myself the embarrassment of telling parishioners their input is valued; but I have two more years to serve on the vestry and I was *elected* to that position because, I assume, at least some people believed I would serve them well. The only thing I'm sure of is that the parish is in a hell of a mess!

The abuse of trust often occurs where it is least expected. And it can stop the process cold in its tracks.

Managerial credibility is, in many respects, the most critical component of the collaborative process for it signifies whether or not anything can be expected to happen. This condition of support for the dimension of collaboration might be summarized thusly:

- Past experience verifies that people can take management's word at face value.

- When people are asked to make decisions, their ideas are incorporated in work decisions and policy review; if asked only to recommend, this fact is clearly conveyed to them at the time.

- Work experience is valued and people expect to have influence on issues germane to their work.

- Management routinely provides feedback on employee suggestions, thus enhancing its credibility and lending substance to opportunities to collaborate.

- There is a logic to the workplace. Management resists being caught up in counterproductive precedent or political game-playing which direct attention from the objective of competent accomplishment.

We can put managerial credibility to the test by asking questions such as these:

What do people really expect to happen as a result of giving management their ideas and opinions? Do they believe that their ideas will be given genuine consideration—or do they suspect little effort and few actions as a result?

How are rules and policies treated by management? Is policy open to evaluation and revision by those whose work it affects—or is it treated as sacred, set in concrete, and therefore difficult to update or streamline?

How does management choose its "experts" for work planning and design? Is an "expert" a person who knows the most about a particular job by virtue of experience—or is it only someone with formal training in work planning and design or simply anyone with enough authority to make decisions stick?

Questions like these help focus on the extent to which managers are mired in traditional views as opposed to the realities of the workplace; they provide a check on the consistency of managerial action with managerial intent. Verifiability is a core issue. The more managers may be described, on the basis of past experience with them, as reinforcing the rational order of work processes while remaining true to their words, the more trusting people will be of opportunities to collaborate.

By pursuing a collaborative course, management serves notice that it wants people ". . . to be creative in work and social relations and to use well whatever potentialities"[12] they have. Collaboration is the first step in promoting that healthy productive outlook that predisposes people to join together to do, in fact, what they are capable of doing. There are elements in each set of requisite conditions which serve to color what people *expect,* both from their work and as competent human beings at work. The conditions for collaboration signify that people are valued, that they are deemed competent, and that doing well what needs to be done is a common goal among managers and those who are managed.

But, in the competence process, there is much more going on than an enhancement of outlook. Collaboration is but the beginning, the trigger; it prepares the soil. Having achieved this, managers must move on to sow and cultivate the seeds for commitment and creativity—to turn a potential for commitment into actual commitment; to

[12] English & English. *Op. cit.,* p. 411.

convert a capacity for creativity into creative output. These are the keys to competent performance after all and, as we shall see in the next two chapters, there is yet a substantial amount of work to be done in achieving widespread commitment and creativity.

V

Conditions for Commitment

Collaboration, we have said, creates a potential for commitment but does not insure it. In examining the second dimension of the competence process, it is helpful at the outset to recognize both how collaboration and commitment are related and how they differ: when we speak of collaboration, we are talking about activity that is augmented by feelings; when we speak of commitment, we are talking about feelings that are augmented by activities. Collaboration triggers a chain of psychological events. From the doing of collaborative tasks, people experience important feelings of personal worth and hope for the future. But these feelings must then be acted upon to be sustained and truly internalized. Action is central to maintaining the committed state.

Commitment: The Alternative to Alienation

Commitment has been characterized as ". . . an intangible but indispensable plus" in the pursuit of organizational goals.[1] This view appears to correspond with the conven-

---

[1] Blake, R. R. & J. S. Mouton. "Managerial Facades." *The Managerial Grid.* Houston: Gulf Publishing, 1964.

tional feeling among managers that commitment is some magical happenstance, a serendipitous bonus of some sort, which enhances both outlook and effort toward objectives. Most managers appreciate and value commitment insofar as the work of the organization is concerned; but they misunderstand its personal significance. Some see it as a commodity to be purchased by bonuses or special incentives; others see it as something to be artificially stimulated by contests and invigorating motivational speeches. It is managerially naive to employ such superficial means to so fundamental an end as commitment. In the competence process commitment is viewed as much more than just an organizational plus. It is personal and it is an absolute necessity. Commitment is the sole source of vitality and vigor in the workplace and, in the competence process, it is the major means to *health*.

Earlier, in Chapter II, we proposed that people work in order to be healthy. Through work, we said, people are best able to express many of those skills and attributes which make each of them unique. In work they are most able to influence and have impact on the world in which they live. Through work people achieve and sustain a feeling of movement, that stimulation and sense of growth that is basic to the life process. And, as Freud wrote, it is through work that people gain for themselves ". . . a secure place in a portion of reality, in the human community."[2] As portrayed, work is an important part of the condition of normalcy. But work will serve few of the requirements for either normalcy or health if it is devoid of commitment. Indeed, if commitment is ignored, discounted as a nice but unnecessary morale factor, or simply mismanaged, both normalcy and health will be impaired.

[2] Freud, S. *Civilization and Its Discontents*. New York: W. W. Norton and Co., 1962.

Albert Camus, the Nobel essayist, wrote that "without work all life goes rotten. But when work is soulless, life stifles and dies." Commitment is the soul of work. It is the sense of purpose that guides one's activities; it is the meaning that justifies one's investment of self; it is the feeling of responsibility that defines one's role and reason for being; and, when shared, it is a common bond which holds people together in ways that transcend differences and personal gratification. Commitment fuels existence.

To default on commitment is to opt for its unhealthy alternative, *alienation*. Alienation is one of the major social maladies of the twentieth century and, in the workplace at least, it may be traced in large part to the way work is organized and managed. Robert Blauner provides this insight:

> Alienation exists when workers are unable to control their immediate work processes, to develop a sense of purpose and function which connects their jobs to the over-all organization of productivity, to belong to integrated industrial communities, and when they fail to become involved in the activity of work as a mode of personal self-expression.[3]

Managing for commitment entails providing the very supports so notably lacking when alienation prevails. This is why, in the competence process, commitment is viewed as a necessity; it is the only healthy alternative to estrangement from self and others. And providing the means to commitment is the hard job of management.

[3] Blauner, R. *Alienation and Freedom*. Chicago: University of Chicago Press, 1964.

The Manager's Role: Delivering on Collaborative Promises

The basic issues underlying the state of commitment are these: having been made by their inclusion in a decision-making process to feel that their ideas and opinions count for something, people must actually be free to act on their ideas; they must actually be able to take actions consistent with the substantive thrust of their collaboration. Having glimpsed a heightened sense of purpose from opportunities to share in planning, people must actually be able to spend their time and energies on issues and tasks that serve that sense of purpose. And, having achieved an initial sense of partnership and cooperation, people must find that the system promotes and rewards cooperative effort and mutuality among people. The way management attends to these logical extensions of collaborative practices will dictate whether or not the potential for commitment is realized. But, before managers can serve commitment, they must come to grips with both their personal and organizational anxieties about control.

The task of managing for commitment will not always be an easy one for managers. Often they must contend with organizational and peer pressures to the contrary. We are faced with another managerial paradox for, more often than not, when managers deny to those they manage the means to commitment, it is because they have been encouraged to be more preoccupied with control and predictability. Yet commitment is the most potent control mechanism operating in human affairs. The strong sense of personal ownership and responsibility, identity, and purpose that characterize the committed state give meaning and direction to one's activities. People go where their commitments lead them; they invest energy, overcome obstacles, and risk rejection to pursue that sense of purpose which literally defines their being. As a source of guidance and as an organizing principle in human behavior, personal commitment is much more potent than managerial directives, job descriptions, or rules and prohibitions.

Managers may serve either commitment or alienation, health or illness, in the workplace. Their choices are important. The effects of their practices know few boundaries; whether with white collar or blue, professional or unskilled worker, the effects of mismanaged commitment are the same. Without commitment there will be little health or creativity. Therefore, managers must address the conditions for commitment head-on if widespread competence is the goal.

We take, as our requisites for commitment, conditions *opposite* to those which characterize alienation: conditions of impact rather than impotence; of meaningful tasks instead of busy work; and connectedness not separateness.

Figure 1. Conditions for commitment.

It is through these that managers may serve health in the workplace. As shown in Figure 1, the dimension of commitment is translated into policy and action by attention to conditions of *impact, relevance, and community*. These are the key elements of sustained commitment which would be uppermost in the minds of managers concerned with competence. As each is discussed in greater detail, the manager may experience a sinking sense of deja vu for many have encountered these issues before in their management, only to violate the tenets of commitment.

Impact[4]

Perhaps the quickest way for commitment potential to be nipped in the bud is for people to discover that, frequent collaboration notwithstanding, they cannot cause anything to happen—to hear from their managers about the many barriers to implementing agreed-upon decisions. Variously known as the "my hands are tied" or the "but we've always done it this way" or the "sorry, that's not my job" syndromes, unimaginative management of the commitment phase of the competence process can make it virtually impossible for people to have any impact on the organization and how it functions.

It makes little sense for management to encourage collaboration if people have little control over procedures and work design in their part of the organization. Indeed, a collaborative boomerang may be set in motion and do

---

[4] The power dynamics and their effects which are implicit in the Impact condition have been well treated in:

Blake, R. R. & J. S. Mouton, *Group Dynamics: Key to Decision Making.* Houston: Gulf Publishing Co., 1960, pp. 5-9, 27-49, 97-112.

McClelland, D. *Power: The Inner Experience.* New York: Irvington Publishers, Inc., 1975.

more harm than good; not only might the original purpose be defeated but the situation might actually become worse because of the added tensions of frustration and hostility. If people are led, on the basis of collaboration, to expect that they can make changes, improve, or manage more creatively their own work processes only to find that such decisions are made by people external to their workplace—by efficiency experts or those in the home office or people at higher echelons—they will feel misused. They will lose interest quickly and, as frustration grows, they may become counter-committed, intent on beating rather than improving the system. Managers who insist on having the final word may be better served by avoiding collaboration in the first place.

The essential issue in building commitment is one of insuring a *personal impact.* For this condition of commitment to exist, management must make sure that people, having shared in planning how best to get a job done, can have an *impact* on what happens next. For feelings of potency to enhance and sustain commitment, people must receive affirmation of their causal role in the work process. They must be accorded the power to do what they have been asked to decide needs doing. It is in this condition that the sharing of power, symbolically begun in collaboration, becomes formalized in operations.

And interesting things begin to happen to productivity when people are assured of personal impact. We know the effect on productivity and morale factors when the full-participation group at Harwood began to control its own work processes. Other documented instances confirm the principle. In the Rade Koncar manufacturing plant in Zagreb, Yugoslavia, a worker-producer self-management plan was set up in 1945. From 890 employees in 1946, the company grew to 7,946 by 1966, and today plays a leading role in producing heavy equipment for nuclear and transformer power plants.[5] And at the Weyerhauser Company's Washington plant, an "I Am" program—short for "I am manager of my own job"—was implemented with 300 employees. Workers were reported as more enthusiastic about their new jobs and productivity improved substantially according to executive reports.[6] Although but a fraction of the total process, providing the means to personal impact has rather quick effect on both morale and productivity it would appear.

Bruce Ingraham, a salesman for a paper supply company, in talking to his wife:

> You know what gets me about this new job? They let me make decisions! Right on the spot! I use my own judgment. I just solve the problem and that's it. No hassle, and I'm giving better customer service than I've ever been able to do before. My sales are up 37% over last quarter!

> Mr. Akers didn't let you do that?

> Are you kidding? We had to run a 'policy check' every time a problem came up. It made me look foolish . . . like I was stalling or something. (Laughing) Maybe that's why Akers and Associates has lost its five biggest accounts to *us*!

---

[5] Mladen K. *Self-Management in the Enterprise.* Medunarodna Stampa Interpress, 1967.

[6] Rush, H. M. F. *Job Design for Motivation.* Report from the Conference Board, 1971, pp. 55-60.

One can sense a feeling of personal impact in Bruce's words and his commitment—even pride—is evident.

On the other hand, I am reminded of a personal experience while building a new home. Three weeks after moving in, the air conditioning in the master suite still did not work properly. I waited patiently for Sam Walker, the 62-year old service man for Bates Engineering, the contractor for the job. Sam arrived right on time, as usual. "Mr. Hall, this is the fourth time I've been out in two weeks!" he greeted me. "I know it, Sam, and I'm really sorry; but the unit doesn't work!" I said a little defensively.

"I know it doesn't. It never has and it's not going to. What I want you to know, Mr. Hall, is I *know* what's wrong with it. I've been in this business 22 years and I *know* air conditioning. The unit is too big for the space it services . . . it keeps shutting down too soon, before it ever has a chance to take the humidity out of the air. I told the boss, too much tonnage!"

"So, what do we do?" I said. "Mr Hall, I'm embarrassed. I keep coming out here when I know what the problem is. I can't say this to just anybody, but my boss won't let me fix it! He said we'd have to tear out and put in a smaller unit. It would cost a bundle, so he wants me to jerryrig some additional outlets and dump some air somewhere else. But that won't fix it and you don't get what you paid for. I've got to tell you 'cause I'm tired of looking like a damn fool. But if word gets back I told you, I'm fired!"

So much for uncaring people who don't want to work anymore. Give me a hundred Sam Walkers!

We can learn from both type experiences. We can learn

that if we want committed workers, impact must be managed in such a way that people are empowered to act in accordance with agreed upon objectives. The following circumstances summarize the key ingredients of a high impact situation where those who do the work have direct influence on events in the workplace.

- People control their own personal operating procedures and guidelines.

- Collectively, those who are charged with doing the work for the organization determine the best way of doing it, jointly determining who will do what and desired work priorities and pacing.

- People have direct influence in design decisions and production goals where their own work is concerned and have access to the decision process on more general issues affecting them.

- Management provides for a sustained sense of personal power and a feeling that individuals can cause things to happen, that they can influence both what is done and what will be done in the future.

- People are trusted to use their best judgement in responding to problems and have the freedom to make decisions at the point of impact.

These are all facilitative to doing one's best and give substance to the intent of collaboration. Commitment will grow with each successful impact on the system.

When we begin to consider the issue of personal impact, we may find that we are striking at some fundamental tenets of formal organization theory. Traditional practices have followed a rigid chain-of-command rationale and those who are managed have been encouraged to be the passive and submissive recipients of directives. Impact changes all this and redistributes power according to a new rationale: those who need the authority to do their jobs are the ones who will have it. In light of the following considerations, we can gauge the current status of impact in our own organizations.

How much control over their own work priorities and production pace do people have? Are day-to-day pacing and priorities for personal work pretty much set by those who do the jobs—or does management rely on devices like time-and-motion studies or efficiency planning for each person's job and then make it a part of its Standard Operation Procedures?

How much freedom do people have in laying out the scope and resources required for their individual jobs? Are design decisions made by those who must do the work so that experience and knowledge are well-utilized—or is design responsibility controlled by management or third party "experts" working under the auspices of those in authority?

How much local control do people have over how things are done in their respective parts of the organization? Do people govern their internal work procedures, organize themselves, set their own ground rules, and make decisions as needed in their part of the organization—prescribe the specifics and insist on the right of review for how their part of the organization is to function?

These questions bear on the issue of impact, the extent

to which people are actually able to influence both what they do and how they do it, and the sense of mastery they can derive from their work. An implicit theme in conditions of impact is freedom of choice. Generally speaking, the greater the sense of choice people experience in a given situation, the more impact they will feel they have and the higher will be their level of commitment to the decisions governing their work and to the work itself.

More often than not, when managers equivocate on issues of power, it is because they themselves feel constrained by their positions of authority and accountability. Managers sometimes feel that they are *required* to exercise all the power vested in them by virtue of their managerial role. It is helpful to recognize that, in the organizational manpower chart, there is seldom a prescribed manner for utilizing managerial authority, only an implicit statement of the amount of authority which goes with a given position. Managers have discretion and the creation of conditions of impact falls within the range of acceptable options. The manager concerned about commitment will choose that option. If the manager's colleagues or superiors lag behind in their concern for commitment, the manager must work all the harder to see that those things which can be controlled internally are, in fact, done so by those whose commitment is at stake. Most often, managers can at least set the tone of those conditions which will prevail from their positions downward in the organization. This can suffice to serve both personal impact and commitment—particularly if the work people are asked to do has meaning and can be seen to contribute to both personal and organizational objectives.

Relevance[7]

Perhaps more than in any other dimension of competence, there is in commitment an inherent sense of logic. A number of implicit sequential connections underlie the commitment process: people expect their talents to be appropriately used; they expect to spend their time on important tasks or, at the very least, on jobs that need to be done so that the organization can attain its objectives. They expect this in return for being willing to give their best. Not so much a quid pro quo arrangement as a factor of coherence and consistency is at stake. And it is this sense of logic which is easily and often violated to the detriment of commitment.

Peter Drucker has said that, for the manager, the key to making people more productive is to make sure that they can do the work they are being paid for.[8] Drucker is not talking about capability when he uses the phrase "can do." He is referring to opportunity and the fact that, to quote directly, "In today's organization, the impediments to people doing their work are growing much too fast." Many of these impediments are created by management and they consist of irrelevant tasks which neither serve the ostensible objectives of the organization nor allow people to feel that what they do is important. Irrelevant tasks undermine the sense of purpose so critical to commitment; they spawn frustration, resistance, and stifle motivation.

---

[7] Relevance, at its core, is a motivational issue. I recommend three books in particular for a more in-depth study of the dynamics of relevance:

Herzberg, F. *Work and the Nature of Man.* Cleveland: World Publishing 1966.

Maslow, A. *Motivation and Personality.* New York: Harper & Row, 1954. Harper & Row, 1954.

Foulks, F. K. *Creating More Meaningful Work.* New York: AMA, 1969.

[8] "A Candid Talk about Training with 'The Man Who Invented the Corporate Society." *Training HRD, October,* 1977.

Some of the irrelevancies of work are due simply to poor or insensitive managerial judgment. Linda Sanders' predicament is a case in point.

> I'm the best executive secretary he's ever had . . . and he admits it! I coordinate all his meetings without a hitch. His correspondence is flawless. I'm a world champion on the word processor. I come in early. I stay with it however long it takes. I don't care about 'office hours!' So, you ask what's the problem? The problem is he wants me to type his wife's recipes for her church bazaar cookbook! What's that got to do with anything? *She* doesn't work for Amtech and I sure as hell don't work for her!

Linda obviously has some feelings . . . that she has been misused . . . that her skills—ones she takes pride in—are not really appreciated . . . resentment. Mr. Moody, her boss, might wonder what all the uproar is about, but it is unlikely he would come up with the real explanation: an infringement on commitment.

If irrelevance were always a matter of local mismanagement, salvaging commitment would be an easier task. But some irrelevancies are imposed from without, by some anonymous authorities; invariably, these are "defensive" irrelevancies, designed to protect someone—a boss, an agency, a whole profession—from charges of malfeasance. All of us have been distracted from our work by bureaucratic requirements at one time or another, but there are vital segments of our society in which vitality and commitment are undermined daily by irrelevant demands.

Mary Russell teaches 11th grade World History. She knows the effects of irrelevancy.

> I'm working on my curriculum guide for this year. It's the third one in three years. Same class. Same subject, but the T.E.A. requires that every teacher prepare one for every class every year. It takes me 200 hours to do one. No one looks at it. I don't use it in teaching my classes. It just gets filed. I guess somebody somewhere thinks its important, but if you ask me and the other teachers, we'd tell you it doesn't have *anything* to do with teaching.
>
> How do I *feel* about it? Well, for one thing I'd rather spend the 200 hours on preparation for class. (I don't know what the teachers in elementary school do. They've got four or five different classes to do guides for.) Mainly, I'm insulted! I resent the implication that everything I do in class has to be documented. I'll tell you one thing: morale at my school is at an all time low because of this. Some of my friends have just about decided that somebody else can teach the kids, not them anymore!

Some of our teachers are caught up in a classic approach-avoidance because of imposed irrelevancies. They love their work, but they are less and less willing to pay the price of nonsense which irrelevance exacts. We even find forced irrelevancies in the practice of medicine. L. J. Macatee, M.D., and Chief of Staff at Burdette Tomlin Memorial Hospital relates the following all too common experience:

> An admission note is required in the chart of every hospitalized patient.

Translated from "medicalese," the note I had written read something like this:

"This fifty-one year old white female is admitted because of abnormal uterine bleeding which started over two weeks ago but which has become alarmingly heavy during the past 48-72 hours resulting in her admission for D & C for both diagnostic and therapeutic reasons."

The above note was dated on a Monday afternoon when the patient was admitted. The D & C was scheduled for mid-morning Tuesday, which was the earliest available time slot short of calling in the emergency on-call OR crew which in my professional opinion would not have been justified by the circumstances.

Early on Tuesday morning I was informed that P.R.O. (Professional Review Organization) had disallowed this patient's admission. The various P.R.O.'s in this country are funded by the U.S. Government and are paid to "watchdog" the use of hospital facilities.

It is difficult to know how much detail is appropriate to tell this tale.

Suffice it to say that additional data of history, physical findings, and laboratory results satisfactorily justifying the need for this patient's hospitalization had been accumulated and recorded in a manner which would unquestionably satisfy any sincere reviewer with reasonable diligence in uncovering the information.

The position of the various P.R.O.'s, however, is expressed by the philosophy of "guilty until proven innocent" thereby placing the onus of responsibility on the physician to collect and document the information for the P.R.O. reviewer in such a way that the written criteria of the P.R.O. are met. The first line P.R.O. reviewer, by the way, is not a physician nor a specialist peer, but a registered nurse using a bureaucratically generated "cookbook" of medical practice criteria.

P.R.O. denial of the admission means that the hospital will not be paid for this patient's care by whatever third party payor (government or private insurance) might be involved nor can the patient be billed. The significance for the physician's fee is lessened by the fact that there is as yet no law which forbids the physician from billing the patient for his services.

Nonetheless, on a busy Tuesday morning with an unexpected surgical procedure now scheduled in the midst of previously scheduled office appointments, hospital rounds to make, phone calls to return, and correspondence that must eventually be dealt with—fortunately, none of my patients was in labor—I find that I now must confront a hostile P.R.O. representative, not to ensure that the patient gets cared for but to attempt to ensure that the hospital can get paid. This, of course, was eventually accomplished, though not without a considerable investment of time and effort, and with a significant cost in terms of emotional energy. I would hope it would be clear to any reader that the tasks involved bear no relevance whatever to the mission of the physician which is primarily, yea, singularly, to care for the sick if illness cannot be prevented. All of these efforts were necessarily directed to combating a distrust of competence based on no proven justification nor even significant, real suspicion.

I've been asked to answer the question of what sort of feelings these kinds of events generate in my soul. I felt:

Frustrated, angered, insulted, angered, mistrusted, angered, persecuted, angered, overwhelmed with responsibilities and chores unrelated to my goals, angered, irate, and angered would be a short but appropriate list. These reactions grow proportionately to the frequency with which such goal-disoriented tasks claim a growing percentage of my efforts.

The effect is that hard work is made harder without any return on the investment. The involved patient's care is certainly not enhanced. Time which might have benefited another patient is wasted. I have no reason to believe that hospital utilization is actually improved.

The worth of any work is to a large extent the inherent personal value of a job well done. This perception is warped, and distorted by the frustration and anger which are integral to the experience. I did not devote myself to a career in medicine in order to pursue irrelevant work.

Accordingly, a number of my most conscientious

and competent colleagues have expressed to me that these events and others like them have driven them to a desire to abandon their commitment to the practice of medicine just as soon as social and family circumstances permit. I share these feelings in spades.

Apparently, in Dr. Macatee's profession function follows form! Dr. Macatee and many of his colleagues have had it. Mary Russell has nearly had it. For those who may not worry too much over a lathe operator or secretary being asked to do work that is not relevant, it is important to recognize just how widespread irrelevant work has become. It not only diverts energy, it can even work backwards to undercut sense of impact. Macatee, a physician, finds his decisions being overridden by a Registered Nurse with manual in hand. We can speculate on the effect of all this on doctor-nurse teamwork, but one fact is clear: forced irrelevance renders work not only soulless, but mindless! Managers interested in the nurturing of competence and the release of commitment must, sooner or later, come to grips with the erosion of spirit which irrelevance breeds.

When people are asked to spend a major part of their time filling out reports on what they have done, they have less time to do. When they are asked to meet in ad hoc committees to decide issues peripheral to their work— to manage the current fund raising campaign or to plan the company picnic— they have less interest in doing. And when their attention is focused by fiat on minor issues, busy work, while major problems go begging, their talents for accomplishment are wasted. Irrelevance breeds indifference, the enemy of commitment and productivity.

As the degree to which the tasks to be done and the skills

they call for are both pertinent to organizational objectives and meaningful in terms of personal goals, the condition of relevance serves to sustain the *sense of purpose* which is part and parcel of commitment. Irrelevant activities, meaningless tasks and insensitive systems of reward are the non sequiturs of organizational life. They violate the logic of the apparent reasons for working competently and they undercut commitment in the process. Therefore, the condition of relevance is accorded special status as a characteristic of work activities which is logically consistent with and pursuant to those goals to which people have commited themselves.

Management makes work purposeful and meaningful, both in its relation to the goals of the organization and the individual's personal need for competent performance, in the following ways:

- Management strives to see that people spend their time on "core" activities, in defining goals and working for their attainment.

- Management places major emphasis on organizational tasks which challenge and stretch people.

- People are encouraged to create for themselves more interesting and meaningful tasks.

- People are given both the latitude to plan for job accomplishment and the challenge of high standards to keep them emotionally involved in their work.

- Management provides an incentive system

based on the psychological needs of mature
people in addition to its basic economic and
fringe benefits.

Meaningfulness of one's activities, both personally and
organizationally, is a strong sustaining force for commitment.
Rewards consistent with the need for competence cement
the process. Relevance is the binding agent for each day's
activities and lends the coherence so necessary for ongoing
commitment. The following questions begin to reveal how
organizations measure up to the relevance test:

**Does the work people do draw on the skills and interests
in which they take greatest pride?** Is work geared to their
need to feel that they are making a unique and worthwhile
contribution to organizational objectives while doing things
they enjoy and find fulfilling—or is the work primarily
geared to superficial skills and simple objectives in return
for base rewards like gainful employment and dependable
income?

**How realistic and challenging are the goals people are
required to work toward?** Can people see the relationship
of their tasks to both their own capabilities and what needs
to be done organizationally so that they feel stretched and
energized—or are task goals set so low or aimed at such
peripheral objectives that people find them so boring that
they have little interest in accomplishing them well?

**How relevant to work objectives are the decisions
people are called on to make?** Do people make decisions
about those core aspects of their work bearing on execution
and quality—or do people decide only routine issues bearing on maintenance of the status quo and purely personal
matters like vacation times and other activities?

The answers to these and related questions reflect the degree to which people are allowed or encouraged to spend their time in activities which they see as germane to their work. They reflect the amount of challenge and sense of importance to be found in work. In general, the more people feel that their talents are being fully used and that their efforts contribute to the organization's objectives, the greater will be their sense of relevance and the more committed they will be to what they are doing.

The pursuit of relevance may require a more planful and genuinely collaborative approach on the part of management. A more logical task analysis may be needed to avoid that all too common fragmentation of tasks and activities which undercuts relevance. Many times the people themselves are in the best position to help in doing this, once again providing an opportunity for reinforcing relevance.

Community[9]

For relevance to become a shared experience, for the sense of personal challenge and contribution to become a collective feature of the organization, there must be a norm of interdependence and mutual reliance. As employed in the competence process, community refers to the sense of oneness or spirit of belonging and identification with the organizational group—its objectives and well-being. As such,

[9] For a more encompassing treatment of the issues important to both Community and its competitive alternatives, I recommend:
Gibb, J.R. *Trust: A New View of Personal and Organizational Development.* Los Angeles: Guild of Tutors Press, 1978.
Slater, P. E. *The Pursuit of Loneliness.* Boston: Beacon Press 1970.
Wright, J. P. *On a Clear Day You Can See General Motors.* Grosse Point Michigan: Wright Enterprises, 1979.

it is concerned with issues of interdependence, mutual respect, and sense of shared responsibility for one another's well-being. Community is reflected in a healthy and spontaneous mutual reliance and the security that comes from knowing that people can depend on one another.

Community is, in a larger context, the bedrock of mature societies. And like so many fundamental requirements of civilized functioning, it is difficult to achieve under the best of circumstances. People often seem torn between their more primitive urges for dominance and survival of the fittest and equally strong needs to relate to other people in ways that are collaborative and reinforcing to them as social beings. They vacillate, at once seeking out people to depend on while remaining vigilant to encroachments on their individuality; they magnify the ways in which they are different from others while working hard to be accepted and included by those same people. Community is hard-earned in society at large, but not necessarily so difficult within the organizational context.

For managers, the achievement of a sense of community may be easier because it turns on the doing of work. In many respects, managers control the means whereby many of the esteem and social needs of people might best be satisfied. It is in the doing of work that each of us is both different from, yet a part of, other people; where we can be both independent and interdependent. These possibilities in the workplace can be seized upon and emphasized by management in the service of community if management appreciates the role of community in sustaining commitment.

As a condition supportive of commitment, a sense of community is important because it is the mechanism whereby commitment becomes a shared widespread commodity. It takes more than one or two or a handful of committed individuals to make an organization function well. For widespread competence to be achieved, commitment itself must be so widespread that it is a defining feature of the organization. This may only be accomplished where there is a norm of mutual reliance, trust and dependability among people, where there is an abiding concern for the common good.

Some managers work for community intuitively, out of a personal hunch that it is a better way to go, and are often surprised by its impact. Hank Spencer, production supervisor, is such a man. One can hear the themes of community as he talks with the Plant Manager:

> I'll tell you what's remarkable, Mr. Williams. You see Bill Davis over there? Well, he's a milling machine worker, but he took it on himself to learn Joe Baker's job, too. So he could backstop for Joe when his wife went in the hospital. Andrews did the same thing with Daniels. Now all these guys know one another's work. I didn't do it; they did. I just told them it was like the Army, a buddy system, where we take care of one another. Now they rely on one another. They help each other. They're like good neighbors to one another, you know? I can't explain it exactly, Mr. Williams, but these six guys have more pride and turn out enough work for twenty!

Other managers—and this is the more typical case—have to overcome tradition and learn to experiment with new ways of working. They, too, are often surprised. John Hutchison, International Advanced Concepts Modeling Coordinator at Ford's Design Staff, reflects on some of the changes which have taken place since Division Management began to apply the competence process:

> We used to have a lot of problems with when somebody would be doing something unusual, a special task—say a really down and dirty one. Everybody would be pointing their finger at the individual, criticizing something, somebody, making fun and that kind of thing. Now they don't. A guy's respected for accepting that particular task and everybody knows it's a tough one. That's starting to show too. They need help, they're helping one another. I find that I don't have to be around to tell them, "Drop what you're doing and give him a hand." It's happening automatically. Just went through quite a change in switching people from one project to another and it was kind of a hodge-podge there for awhile. Didn't know which way to go. The clay modelers, they finally said, "Hey, no problem. Just tell one of the leaders that a couple of guys may be needed on this other job," and if it does come that time, they send someone there. So, it's a little easier.

> In the past, a lot of times, you know, you might have some people who have more equity in the job but they'd sure love to have the assistance. It used to be, "This is mine. I don't want anybody near it and I want to do the whole thing." They'd take it away. "I'm going in the corner and play with it." You know, so they get all the credit, etc. Now there's a lot less of that. When they see they need help, they don't mind asking, "Hey, give me a hand for awhile. And for the next day or so."

> People are feeling more responsibility, but they're also taking more initiative, their own initiative. They're working together . . .

How strange it is that management has traditionally worked to separate rather than unite, to encourage people to compete rather than cooperate, to be self-centered rather than concerned with the welfare of all. Many managers, in what seems to be an aberration of the ethic of free enterprise, have literally set in motion within their own organizations competitive dynamics appropriate only to the marketplace. They have willfully pitted parts of the same organization against one another; they have consciously created situations in which someone must win and someone must lose; they have devised special rewards for the fittest who survive; they have, at one and the same time, exalted "team players" and isolated people from one another by promoting a rugged individualism, answerable-only-to-management, work ethic. They have made work lonely and people more concerned with self and team than with the organizational community. In doing so, they have not only appealed to and exacerbated the baser side of people at work, but they have failed to recognize that interdependence—rather than prideful independence—is the most psychologically mature, and therefore most desirable, basis for productive relationships. Managers who exalt independence and competitiveness in their organizations deny to all—themselves included—both the means to greater maturity and a potent mechanism for commitment.

Scientific studies which support the beneficial effects of competition *within* organizations are not to be found. But opposing evidence is abundant. For example, at the Norsk Hydro fertilizer plant in Oslo, Norway, the idea was introduced that every worker should be able to get help from others when he needed it. The steps taken to implement a program of mutual reliance resulted in two noteworthy effects: at the social level, job satisfaction increased from 58% to 100%, security from 39% to 73%, and sense of responsibility from 42% to 96%; at the task accomplishment level, production costs decreased by 30% in the first six months of the new program.[10] Interdependence and opportunities for personal growth were the defining characteristics of the Norsk Hydro approach.

Surely, we can do as well. Community in support of commitment requires a more mature perspective of management. Community as an organizational characteristic occurs when:

- Management promotes by policy and practice a sense of interdependence among people.

- Management encourages and models mutual reliance and trust between both individuals and departments or teams.

- Management demonstrates that both the work to be done and the people who do it are essential to the health of the organization.

- Management reflects this value by demonstrating a strong concern for employee commitment through programs of collaborative decision making, goal-setting, and the like.

Community is achieved on the basis of norms and values

---

[10] Bregard, A., J. Gulowsen *et al.* "Norsk Hydro, Experiment in the Fertilizer Factories." Work Research Institute, January, 1968.

promoted by management. How managers provide for community in the workplace or fail to do so may be revealed by the following kinds of questions:

What kind of work ethic does management promote among people? Does management encourage people to help one another—or does it stress selfsufficiency, competitiveness, and reward only individual effort?

How essential are people made to feel? Are people made to feel that their individual skills and unique contributions are fundamental to the well-being of the organization—or are they made to feel that virtually anyone could do their jobs without seriously affecting organizational success?

What kind of organizational community is encouraged by management? Does management encourage people to be respectful and considerate of one another's rights by promoting a "we're all in this together" ground rule—or does it favor "political" tactics, play favorites, and allow a "chosen few" to profit at the expense of others?

Cooperation, mutuality, trust and essentiality are the ingredients of concern in assessing communality in organizations. If these are favored in responding to the above questions, management may be said to promote that sense of community which makes commitment a widespread commodity. And commitment in the service of competence must be widespread. This may require a reevaluation of management's traditional notions of "motivating" the system. Instead of trying to inject the organization with new energy, we will be better off trying to release the energy that is already present. But we should appeal to the higher instincts of people at work in the process. We must eschew elitism and appeals to the competitive spirit which divide rather than unite. Managerial practices which serve to contain commitment, to parcel out its potential to only a select few, oppose competence.

Yesterday's competitions are with us yet. No amount of good humor, while recreating the gamefields of youth in the executive suite, can dissipate the resentments, bruised egos, and outright hostilities which come from interpersonal and interdepartmental competition. Managers must recognize this if they choose competence as a goal. They must promote collaboration; they must help people achieve a blend of self and mutual reliance; in spirit and practice, they must advance the norm of caring, trust, and interdependence among people. A sense of communality will follow and commitment will be well served.

Commitment, as a dimension of competence, is primarily a *feeling* state; but it has implications for much more than morale and job satisfaction. It has direct bearing on task accomplishment. Commitment is a personal desire to contribute to the success of the organization by doing one's best in accomplishing the tasks for which one has accepted responsibility. Moreover, it is a need to do all this in a spontaneous, self-generated and self-directing way. As such, commitment is the psychological energy which powers the organizational system. It must be a shared commodity, touching as many people and tasks as possible.

In the competence process, the manager is encouraged to recognize the personal and organizational necessity of commitment and, in particular, to recognize that it is managers who most control the conditions which insure its presence. Most of all, management is encouraged to recognize that commitment is a characteristic of health; it is the uniquely human energy which fuels both existence and creativity. When the conditions for commitment are managed with these thoughts in mind, the manager can then expect people to be energized and poised for creative enterprise.

VI

Conditions for Creativity

If, as we have said, collaboration is the trigger and commitment supplies the energy, it is in the creativity dimension that the competence process begins to come together. It is in the creative *capacities* of people that the themes and dynamics associated with collaboration and commitment come to fruition. Creative output is the natural consequence of a healthy productive outlook coupled with a sense of ownership and purpose. And, when these latter effects are achieved, both the organization and those who do its work prosper.

Many managers, when they contemplate what should be done in pursuit of more creative output, fairly quickly invoke the magic phrases of "new technology" and "more capital investment." But most of the work of an organization—those day-to-day solutions to vexing problems, those spontaneous insights which lend perspective to priorities, and those small yet significant inventions of new procedures—involves a more mundane kind of creativity than that implied by technological advances and investment. Sustained creativity of a type to characterize an entire organization relies on old-fashioned human ingenuity.

While capital investments and technical know-how may

certainly help, neither can take the place of day-to-day human ingenuity. Even in the most sophisticated of circumstances, technology often fails or triggers more problems than it was designed to solve. John Glenn, orbiting the earth in the technological marvel of his time, still had to "fly by wire" to get Friendship VII safely back to splash down. And the management of General Motor's ultra- modern auto plant in Lordstown, Ohio, learned all too well in 1972 that technology and investment are not enough: their "perfectly efficient," highly automated system so ignored the human part of the equation that workers simply went out on strike in protest of the line speed and the robot-like tasks they were required to perform.[1] Neither technology nor money is the keystone of creativity; people are.

As managers charged with seeing that the organization's work is properly done, we are fortunate that, as Douglas McGregor has written, "The capacity to exercise a relatively high degree of imagination, ingenuity, and creativity in the solution of organizational problems is widely, not narrowly, distributed in the population."[2] Managers *need* creative people; and they *have* them in abundance. The question, as it has been throughout this volume, is whether or not managers *do* anything to aid the expression of creative capacities.

Traditionally, managers have availed themselves of but a fraction of the human talent represented in a typical workplace. The competence process is designed to remedy

[1] Lee, H. C. "Lordstown Plant of General Motors." In F. E. Schuster (Ed.). *Contemporary Issues in Human Resource Management.* Reston, Virginia: Reston Publishing, 1980, pp. 265-272.

[2] McGregor, D. *The Human Side of Enterprise.* New York: McGraw-Hill, 1960, p. 48.

this; the dimension of creativity, through its supporting conditions, is aimed at releasing and facilitating that creative talent which one can expect from people who have participated in planning and become committed to doing their tasks in the best way possible. Managers can turn creative capacity into creative output if they appreciate and manage the reservoir of talent available toward that end.

Creativity in Perspective

It is important in the competence process to keep the notion of creativity in proper perspective. We are not talking about those quantum leaps in imagination that set creative geniuses apart from the rest; we do not expect symphonies or laser beams any more frequently than they have appeared in history. But we do expect novel insights, innovations, and new uses of old resources. We expect people, when they are committed, to rise to the challenge. We expect the unexciting but fundamental kind of creativity and care described by Studs Terkel's stonemason, Carl Murray Bates:

> The toughest job I ever done was this house, a hundred years old plus . . . this doorway had to be closed. It had deteriorated and weathered for over a hundred years. The bricks was made out of broken pieces, none of 'em were straight. If you lay 'em crooked, it gets awful hard right there . . . It took a half day to measure with a spoon, to try to get the mortar to match. I'd have so much dirt, so much soot, so much lime, so when I got the recipe right I could make it in bigger quanti-ty . . . I even used soot out of a chimney and sweepin's off the floor . . . the boss told the lady

it couldn't be done. I said, 'Give me the time, I believe I can do it.' I defy you to find where that door is right now. That's the best job I ever done.[3]

If managers never see this kind of creativity, it is usually because they are inclined to view people as basically uncreative, and therefore have not done anything to encourage innovation or to reward creative effort. They may even promote policies which discourage and punish creative problem solving.

Yet widespread competence requires personal ingenuity and creative problem solving, not on the part of but a few highly placed individuals but across the board, everywhere there are problems to be solved before work can be competently done. The point is that creative problem solving, innovation, and imagination are well within the capability of most organizational personnel. No one has a monopoly on either the talent or the capacity for novel insights, although many organizational leaders behave as if this were the case. When we pause to consider the fact that few people know as much about doing a particular task or using a particular tool as the people who spend a major portion of their time doing such tasks and using such tools, it is presumptuous to doubt that those same people are capable of solving work-related problems in a creative fashion. It is up to management to insure that they are allowed and encouraged to do just that. Through the conditions they create, managers must stimulate creativity.

[3] Terkel, S. *Working*. New York: Avon Books, 1975, p. 21.

Providing a Context for Creativity

To the extent that managers are responsible for the internal environment of organizations, they influence creativity. They provide the contexts within which creativity may or may not become manifest. Environmental supports have been found to be a significant influence on the creative process. For example, we know that for optimal results a problem solver should have adequate financial support, facilities and assistance for experimentation, opportunities to communicate with colleagues, and free choice regarding tasks, methods, and approaches to the problem.[4] Such supports may not always be seen as appropriate for wide distribution in an organization. But the capacity for creativity is itself widely distributed among human beings much as other traits are; if, as a work function, there is a widespread need for creativity, then it must be deliberately stimulated and nurtured by management.

The stimulation of creativity is an important managerial function. So important that the American Psychological Association addressed itself to creativity in organizations at its 1984 annual convention. At a symposium on corporate creativity in Toronto, speakers addressed the social and organizational factors influencing creativity. They concluded that we can have creativity in our organizations if management is creative enough to implement it.[5]

Managerial ingenuity would certainly be welcomed, but the manager can also take some very practical and straight-

---

[4] Skolnik, Y. & A. H. Fried. "Creativity." In B. Wolman (Ed.), *International Encyclopedia of Psychiatry, Psychology, Psychoanalysis & Neurology.* New York: Aesculapius Publishers, Vol. 3, 1977, pp. 424-426.

[5] Bales, J. "Freedom, Support Boost Creativity." *Monitor.* Washington, D.C.: American Psychological Association, November, 1984, p. 28.

forward steps to encourage, facilitate, and reward creative problem solving on the part of those people who do the organization's work. In the creativity dimension of the competence process we are particularly concerned with those conditions which bear on the work itself and influence how creatively it may be accomplished. As depicted in Figure 1, the prime conditions in support of the creativity dimension are the *task environment,* the *social context* which determines the ambience of the workplace, and the prevailing *problem-solving process.*

Figure 1. Conditions for creativity.

Task Environment[6]

It is pretty much agreed by management and its personnel alike that work needs to be structured, that tasks and

---

[6] Little work has been done on designing creative task environments, but three readings pertaining to Task Environment and its management are:

Argyris, C. "Organizational Entropy." *Intervention Theory & Method: A Behavioral Science View.* Reading, Mass.: Addison-Wesley, 1970, pp. 56-87.

Blauner, R. *Alienation and Freedom.* Chicago: University of Chicago Press, 1954.

Tuan, Y. F. *Space and Place: The Prospectives of Experience.* Minneapolis: University of Minnesota Press, 1977.

objectives need definition and that priorities need to be set. How much and what kind of structure, however, are often points of departure between those who do the work and those who supervise it. The manner in which work processes are structured, physically and psychologically, and the priorities and situational considerations according to which people must do their jobs serve to define the *task environment* of an organization. And task environment has a direct impact on creativity.

Teresa Amabile, of Brandeis University, reported at the APA symposium in Toronto on her study of R & D managers in North America and Europe.[7] "People will be most likely to produce creative work," she said, "when they feel motivated primarily by their own interest in the work itself, by the challenge and satisfaction it provides, and not by factors imposed by other people." Amabile went on to stress that there are identifiable environmental stimulants to challenge, satisfaction and creativity—all under the control of management.

The most important environmental stimulant to creativity in her study was freedom in one's work. Conversely, the most important obstacle was constraint on one's work—"lack of freedom, autonomy, and self-direction." Stimulants identified included abundant resources with which to get the job done, challenge and encouragement—regardless of how things were going. Major obstacles in the environment, on the other hand, included lack of resources and poor project management, time pressures—not having time to explore problems sufficiently—and organizational factors such as inappropriate rewards, competitive pressures, and management disinterest. Amabile's findings emphasize both

[7] Bales, J. *Op. cit.*

the importance of task environment in stimulating or damping creativity and the role of managers as the creators of task environment.

As a condition clearly amenable to managerial control, the task environment governing work may be either of a type to facilitate creativity or to render it virtually impossible. When managers press for standardization of every possible feature of the work, when they maintain rigid controls over the resources needed for doing a job, when they punish departure from approved procedures, they emphasize conformity as a work priority. In the process, they blunt creative effort and discourage individual attempts to improve on existing technology. When people are told that their adaptive efforts must conform to the preconceptions and controls of management, there will be little creativity. People get the message that the boss wants predictability not excellence, a smooth-running department not the trial-and-error discords of exploration and discovery. On the other hand, if managers display a faith in the creative capacities of people by encouraging reliance on individual standards and spontaneous allocations of resources, by encouraging experimentation and rewarding innovativeness, they will often encounter a windfall of creative input.

Some corporations, like 3M for example, routinely encourage creative inquiry, and have for years. As the word spreads, others pick it up with exciting results—both productivity and morale are impacted. Ron Presley works for a large printing firm on the East Coast:

> I'll tell you the truth. It's been a joy to work here this past year. Management heard about some of the things they do at 3M and decided to give it a try. We are encouraged—can you believe it—

encouraged—to spend part of each hour *experimenting*. You know, playing around with better ways of doing things—even tinkering with new product ideas. Some of us have been doing this work for twenty years and we know some shortcuts—and some possibilities—you wouldn't believe. Only now, management says go ahead. Do something. They give us the time and the tools we need and if we hit on something, great! But if we don't, it's no big deal. It's just a joy. That's what it is!

Faith and a dash of courage on the part of management can sometimes make all the difference.

There are numerous ways available to the manager for making the task environment more conducive to creativity. The task environment may be altered such that there is more inherent challenge to work processes. For example, at the Corning Glass Works in Medfield, Massachusetts, management explored the beneficial effects of benchwork as opposed to piece rate production.[8] Assembly line techniques were abandoned and instrument assembly workers were allowed to assemble entire electrical hot plates as well as to schedule their work as a group in meeting weekly objectives. Rejects dropped from 23% to 1% and absenteeism from 8% to 1%. Irwin Mintz, President of the fast growing JBM Electronics Company, made his own creative use of such a boon to creativity. "When I was working for someone else, everything was rules, company politics—I was stifled. I knew if I ever owned my own company things would be different. I can't afford to pay the big salaries of my competitors, but even if I could, I'd still

---

[8] *U. S. News and World Report.* July 17, 1972, p. 50.

offer the extras . . . I can't compete with a McDonnell Douglas in salary, so what I offer is a feeling of accomplishment and rewards." For example, it would be cheaper for JBM to use an assembly-line process in making computer programming boards, but in the interest of employee satisfaction each worker assembles the entire board. Mintz says, "I could reduce costs as much as 30 percent if I wanted an assembly line process, but I'd lose my people. Besides, I would never operate this place any other way."[9]

On the other hand, the layout of the task environment may be changed to make needed resources more available. This may involve taking steps which may not, of themselves, seem particularly creative. I am reminded of the supervisor who, after some persistence on the part of a group of assembly-line workers, authorized the relocation of a tool crib to make it more accessible. It cost $1,500 to do this; and it paid for itself in increased production during the first 24 hours. The assemblers knew their time was better spent in doing the job than in going after their tools. The point is that the task environment may be altered in simple ways and yield disproportionately high benefits when managers are willing to look for more creative structures which serve rather than hinder getting the job done.

While the specific measures will differ according to the nature of the work to be done, in general a task environment supportive of creative effort will be a *free-flow* task environment in which the major emphasis is on getting the job done in the best way possible:

- Work standardization is more a matter of personal preference and judgment than of policy.

9 "Workstyle." *Inc.* January, 1986, p. 46.

- People exercise, where possible, control over the kinds of work they do, organizing themselves in whatever manner they feel will most effectively accomplish the organization's objectives.

- People have ready access to those resources they need to do their jobs, even for experimenting with doing things in what may be a better way.

- There is relatively little time consciousness on the part of management or workers beyond that associated with meeting normal objectives.

- Coordination of all of the above is a matter for work-group determination.

- There is freedom to try and fail, and try again.

Such a free-flow and unconstrained task environment allows people to focus more directly on their work and encourages them to bring their best efforts to bear, increasing the probability of creative output. Insight into the prevailing task environment and the degree to which it supports creativity may be gained from answering the following kinds of questions.

How are work assignments made? Are work assignments amenable to a self-selection or group coordination process wherein people's interest influence the tasks they will do—or are assignments made solely by managers on the basis of personal intuition or mechanical, nondevelopmental, selection and placement procedures?

How might the work be characterized? Is the work structured to allow the solving of problems and adapting to spontaneous events so that people must think their way through their tasks—or is the work so simplified and routine that it can be standardized and fit to a single way of doing things?

How accessible are the resources people need to do their best work? Do people have direct access to not only the tools, time, materials, and funds they need for doing their jobs but to resources for experimentation as well— or is it a chore for people to get what they need to do their work because of red tape or accounting procedures that stand in their way?

These are the kinds of questions managers might ask themselves in reviewing the task environments of their organizations. In general, the more the environment supports and facilitates the doing of work, the more it allows people to learn and develop, the more creative freedom people will feel they have. By the same token, the more difficult and rigid the task environment makes the doing of work, the more it constrains opportunities for self-expression, the less creativity people will feel allowed or encouraged to express. The more experimentation is encouraged and the less punitive the reward system, the more creativity there will be. And the more widespread will competence become in the process.

The task environment requires managerial attention. And managing the task environment in support of creativity will require an openness on the part of the manager to new ways of doing things. Usually the insights and novel approaches which can enhance creativity will come from those who deal daily with the task environment and are most familiar with the constraints it imposes on them. The thoughtful manager has but to listen.

Social Context[10]

The quality of what the listening manager hears will depend on the quality of life, the social context and ambience of the workplace. It is a well-established psychological fact that the presence of other people may enhance one's performance on a variety of tasks. This effect, known among behavioral scientists as social facilitation, is a potent force for creativity when properly managed. Social facilitation acts as a stimulus; combined with the benefits accruing from opportunities to interact with other people, to try out ideas and receive feedback and critique, it can lead to heightened awareness and excitement in the workplace. Because of this, the social dynamics which characterize and define the social context within which work is to be done are every bit as important to creativity as the task environment.

The social context, however, is often ignored by managers; its potential for facilitating work and countering boredom tends to be particularly overlooked by managers preoccupied with efficiency and increased production. The paradox is that the social context of work affects productivity directly. As the prevailing system of social norms and priorities governing the workplace, the social context defines the manner in which people can relate to one another in doing their work. It determines whether or not work will be socially stimulating. Such dynamics underlie excitement or boredom,

---

[10] Some of the issues implicit in managing for a more creative social ambience are well addressed by:

Gibb, J. R., G. N. Platts & L. E. Miller. *Dynamics of Participative Groups.* St. Louis: J. S. Swift, 1951.

Jacques, E. *Work, Creativity, and Social Justice.* New York: International University Press, 1962.

Rohlen, T. P. *For Harmony and Strength: Japanese White Collar Organizations in Anthropological Perspective.* Berkeley: University of California Press, 1974.

extended effort or apathy, and the urge to create or the urge to escape. All of these in turn impact both the quantity and quality of production.

The individual manager plays a pivotal role in setting the tone of the organization. His or her personal practices sow the seeds of ambience. Richard Wright, head of the advanced product development (APD) group at Mead Corporation, reported to the Toronto symposium that "management by walking around" is the most important means of encouraging innovation and creative thinking, while minimizing fear of failure. The manager routinely mingling with the troops "encourages frequent informal meetings in the hallways, maintains good communication and helps to build a group culture so important in maintaining positive group identity," he said. Wright's group at Mead developed a reputation as a strange bunch who had fun and got results. This was because of social context factors like handling conflict in such a way that it is acceptable to disagree with the boss or anyone else. "If the boss is always right, there's no advantage to disagreeing. But if the boss is sometimes wrong and admits it, and there is a clear and unequivocal commitment to sharing responsibility within the group, then there is no benefit to be gained by keeping quiet when you disagree," Wright said.

Being "absolutely honest"—a critical factor in establishing a creative ambience—and sharing all that is known are vital to open communication, a major element in Wright's list of social stimulants to creative effort. "Confident that others in the group will critique ideas honestly," he said, "employees are free to try new things, and even to fail."[11]

---

[11] Bales, J. *Op. cit.*

Wright zeroed in on the way personal practices—of the manager and other members of the work group—work to establish norms of behavior. There can be norms of sharing and caring, of fun and achievement, or norms of fear and defensiveness. More than any other condition in the competence process, creating a social context for creativity depends on personal skills—on the part of everyone—in relating effectively to fellow human beings. . .assuming the opportunity exists at all.

For reasons best known only to themselves, many managers create social contexts which are the interpersonal equivalents of sensory deprivation. Either ignoring or rejecting out of hand the facilitative effects of social stimulation, these managers have created workplaces that are lonely and frustrating, places where isolation, apprehension and vulnerability are the dominant emotional tones. In some managers' departments, people are censured for talking to one another, workers may only leave their work stations at mealtime or to go to the bathroom. No one is allowed to help another in his work. Such managers and the social contexts they promote take the fun out of work. They depress individual thought processes; people become sluggish and resentful. Heather Lamb, a telephone operator, knows the feeling of such isolation:

> (Laughs.) I'm a communications person but I can't communicate. I've worked here for almost two years and how many girls' first names do I know? Just their last name is on their headset. You might see them every day and you won't know their names . . . You have a number—mine's 407. They put your number on your tickets, so if you made a

mistake they'll know who did it. You're just an instrument.[12]

Any kind of creativity becomes improbable under such conditions.

The social context for work requires thoughtful and sensitive management in support of creativity. First there must be recognition of the fact that people have a need to interact with one another in the workplace; virtually every study of the sociology of work has found that people value opportunities to exchange ideas, share work experiences, and simply talk with one another in the course of their work. Research shows that this is so whether we are talking about unskilled laborers or research scientists.[13,14,15] Moreover, it has been shown that the most valued interchanges are those which concern the work which is being done, not topics which disrupt or supplant the doing of work, such as the latest ballgame, fishing trips, or what one's children are doing lately.

Such social dynamics tend to be spontaneous and, although anticipated with pleasure, are essentially unplanned; they occur because of what people are doing— because of their common interests and overlapping tasks. They may occur at certain times of the day in conjunction with the doing of various tasks which allow discussion— while the mail is being opened or while the OR is being

[12] Terkel, S. *Op. cit.,* p. 66.

[13] Pelz, D. C. "Some Social Factors Related to Performance in a Research Organization." *Administrative Science Quarterly,* Vol. 1, 1956, pp. 310-325.

[14] Van Zelst, R. H. "Validation of a Sociometric Regrouping Procedure." *Journal of Abnormal and Social Psychology.* Vol. 47, 1952, pp. 299-301.

[15] Walker, C. K. & R. H. Guest. *The Man on the Assembly Line.* Cambridge: Harvard University Press, 1952.

prepared for surgery—or as a result of the layout and logistics of the workplace. The sensitive manager, rather than blocking such opportunities, should be alert to these dynamics and encourage, indeed provide for, their occurrence. These are often creative moments during which important problems get solved.

And, again, we must stress the fact that the manager is personally important in setting the tone, the overall ambience of the workplace. Authentic and spontaneous rather than formal behavior on the part of the manager facilitates social dynamics; friendliness rather than aloofness makes for an enjoyable ambience; and praise and encouragement make for a healthier ambience than do censure or "perfectionism." In short, at a time when the depersonalization of work is a major malady in organizations, managers must themselves be the focal point for *re*personalization if the social context is to serve creative enterprise.

In general terms a creative social context is a reality when managers promote a *spontaneous and dynamic* context, one in which the importance of social factors for effective task accomplishment is both recognized and provided for:

- Management is highly visible and involved.

- Creativity and innovativeness are encouraged by management and those making such contributions expect to share in the benefits realized.

- People are encouraged to share freely ideas and opinions and to seek out feedback and comments from others.

- Feedback is valued as a developmental tool.

- Management actively promotes an ethic of candor and mutual responsibility in the service of effective feedback.

- Fun and playfulness are encouraged as a healthy complement to creative social effort.

Such a social context for the doing of work capitalizes on the positive features of social stimulation for task accomplishment. The resulting shared excitement and cross-fertilization of ideas makes work enjoyable and enhances the probability of creativity. Whether work is fun and stimulating, whether one can look forward to going to work each day, and whether the people one works with may be thought of as dependable and supportive—all these bear on the issues of creativity. Whether the ambience of a workplace is of a type to serve creativity may be determined by the way the following questions can be answered:

How does management treat spontaneity, playfulness, and humor in the workplace? Does management encourage people to relax and enjoy one another, to be authentic and to share camaraderie, such that fun and good humor are basic to the work process—or does management view such interaction as small talk, frivolity and a waste of time and encourage people to be more dignified and formal, more "professional" in their work?

What purposes do candid feedback and critique serve in the workplace? Is feedback used as a developmental tool for all so that people actually work at obtaining critiques and reactions from others—or is it viewed as solely a management vehicle for evaluating and controlling people such that it is to be avoided as much as possible?

How does management treat personal experimentation or originality? Is management pleased by attempts at innovation even when they fail and does it encourage people to look for better ways of doing their work—or does any sort of departure from established ways of doing things bring displeasure or even become possible grounds for disciplinary action?

The social context of work, the ambience of the workplace, is the product of an amalgam of values, expectations and practices. In general, those conditions which acknowledge and incorporate the healthy effects associated with social facilitation will enhance the probability of creative output. These require not only support of self-expression but the judicious use of candor, critique, and feedback processes to advance the cause of creativity. When people can look to the workplace for camaraderie and stimulation, when co-workers are seen as interested and dependable, when honesty and openness prevail, and when it can be expected that one can both share personal competence and draw on that of others, the social conditions for creativity exist as well. On the other hand, practices which stifle the interchange of ideas, punish originality, keep people subdued and under wraps, or insulate people from one another will discourage creative social dynamics and undermine the expression of competence.

An essential point, worth making again, is that managing the social context for creativity entails doing what one can to promote work as fun. There is an element of play— almost child-like spontaneity, exuberance, risk taking and experimentation—inherent in the creative process. Managers must work to insure that this element characterizes the workplace if they want creative output. If they then add to all this appropriate problem-solving processes, creativity will become manifest.

Problem Solving[16]

The solving of organizational problems typically involves more than a single person. People meeting informally, scheduled committee sessions or the foreman and one of his hourly workers—these tend to be the settings for problem solving. The manner in which people, collectively, approach problem-solving tasks is another core issue in competence. The task environment can be ideally managed and the social ambience can be stimulating and full of excitement, but unless the problem-solving processes employed are geared to creativity, novel insights and innovative thinking will not find their way into final solutions. Process—the way in which people work together, how talents are meshed, and the standards of agreement embraced—is the sluice gate of creativity. Depending on the form it takes, the problem-solving process can either close off creativity to a mere trickle or encourage a major flow of originality and emergent solutions.

There are two factors at work in problem solving. The first is a task factor; the information, knowledge and expertise most germane to the problem at hand are all important task considerations. This is the facet of problem solving which typically receives major attention. The second factor, of equal importance to creative problem solving, is a procedural one. The decision rules employed, the inclusion or exclusion of pertinent people, the management of opinion differences,

---

[16] Recommended reading for managing problem-solving processes for creative outcomes are:

Hall, J. "Managing for Group Effectiveness." In J. A. Shtogren (Ed.), *Models for Management: The Structure of Competence.* The Woodlands, Texas: Teleometrics Int'l., 1980.

Janis, I. L. & L. Mann. *Decision Making: A Psychological Analysis of Conflict, Choice, and Commitment.* Riverside, New Jersey: The Free Press, 1980.

Likert, R. & J. G. Likert. *New Way of Managing Conflict.* New York: McGraw-Hill, 1976.

and other social dynamics make up the problem-solving process. And there is reason to believe that process skill is a more important influence on creative outcomes than task skill. In spite of ample evidence to this effect, process is a relatively ignored facet of problem solving in general.

Managers and subordinates alike err in the preoccupation with substantive task issues to the neglect of process when in a problem-solving situation. There is a seductive quality to the "facts," the concrete information which makes up the substance of problems; most people derive a certain amount of comfort from dealing with known or verifiable quantities which afford some logic and structure to problem-solving deliberation. When the pressure is on and stakes are high, task issues will preempt in importance the more subtle yet powerful effects associated with process. For creativity to be achieved, people must develop both an awareness of and sensitivity to process dynamics—those which blunt creativity and those which serve it well.

We know, for example, that poor problem solving is seldom traceable to a lack of expertise or substantive resources.[17] More often than not, when a group of people fails at problem solving it is because they have employed decision processes which *prevented* all available resources from either being expressed or effectively brought to bear on the decision task. At the same time, we know that groups may produce decisions which are creative, even when they lack expertise, if they employ good decision processes.[18]

---

[17] Kelley, H. H. & J. W. Thibaut, "Experimental Studies of Group Problem Solving and Process." In G. Lindzey (Ed.), *Handbook of Social Psychology.* Cambridge: Addison-Wesley, 1954, pp. 746-747.

[18] Hall, J. & M. S. Williams, "Group Dynamics Training and Improved Decision Making." *Journal of Applied Behavioral Science,* Vol. 6, No. 1, 1970, pp. 39-68.

In my own research I have encountered a situation in which groups of hospitalized neuropsychiatric patients, despite their limited task resources, significantly outperformed groups of business executives because they had learned to employ more sensitive and sophisticated decision processes.[19] For our purposes, two points are made by this research: process is a critical factor in creative problem solving and people—even those with severe psychological handicaps—can learn to use creative processes.

Managers must demonstrate an appreciation of the importance of problem-solving processes to the creativity dimension and monitor and teach, initiate and provide for the use of competent processes. They achieve this primarily through their own practices. If differences of opinion are squelched, if innovative ideas are ignored or punished, if only "experts" are allowed to make input, if most problem solutions must be accommodated to the policy manual, little creativity will occur. Such a process is ritualistic, more concerned with form than with the problem per se. By the same token, if managers favor compromise, if they are willing to lower their sights in order to avoid conflict, if people are encouraged to pass off to others the difficult problems, then creativity will be diminished as well.

A sensitivity to group processes coupled with an appreciation of the creative potential of differences of opinion, however, can often lead to both innovative decisions and broad support. Managers can learn such a sensitivity and appreciation and, through their own practices, promote the norms and interpersonal skills necessary for creative problem solving. The Directors of EPARCO's New Jersey group had undergone some management training in group decision

19 *Ibid.*

making just prior to being faced with a major decision about the location of a new refinery in Europe. The choices seemed pretty clear-cut except for one director. The CEO might have gone with the majority position. Instead, he said:

> Okay guys, we've hit a snag. I thought we were pretty much in accord on this one, but Steve has an entirely different opinion on the problem and that's why I've gotten us all together. As far as I'm concerned, this is everybody's problem and we're gonna solve it to everybody's satisfaction. We're all experts here as far as I'm concerned, so don't anybody hold back. And another thing—I don't care what the manual says. *We* are going to solve this one and, frankly, I think we've got a chance to do something really creative. Steve has approached this one entirely different from the rest of us—a whole different set of criteria.
>
> So, the way I see it is we can sure take the time to rethink our approach. Maybe we'll end up where we started, but maybe not. We're talking about big bucks, so let's get it right. Steve, let's start with what you've been thinking . . .

The upshot of this approach—one characterized by a genuine give-and-take of opinions, resistance to premature closure, and an examination of conflict rather than suppression of differences—was a certifiable consensus. Steve's unique—some later described it as "off the wall"—attack on the problem prompted a reevaluation and clarification of location criteria. The final choice was different from anyone's original position but, when implemented, it saved the company several million dollars in future labor, transport, and time-to-delivery costs.

For creativity to be realized, problem-solving processes must be managed in such a way as to remove constraints on imagination; conflict must be recognized for what it is—a necessary precondition to creativity—and managed accordingly; common problems must be managed for common acceptance; and the rewards for trying must be far greater than the costs of failing. Managers facilitate such processes when they work for the following conditions:

- Management promotes an experimental, hypothesis-testing approach to problem solving.

- People are encouraged to think and recommend freely, unconstrained by "worst case" apprehensions.

- Conflict is valued as a vehicle for stimulating novel insights and new perspectives on the problem.

- Management expects people to be challenged by problem situations and encourages those involved to approach them with open minds and high expectations.

- On common problems, a collaborative process is promoted wherein both commitment and innovative solutions are attainable.

Such an approach encourages abstract thinking among people, prevents premature closure on less acceptable decisions, and reinforces feelings of personal impact. As a primarily goal-oriented function, this problem-solving process enhances the probability of high creativity.

As a core issue in competence, the problem-solving processes advanced by management often determine the bottom line of creativity. Whether the processes are such as to facilitate creative problem solving may be revealed in the way the following questions are answered:

How are common problems resolved? Does management promote a broad-based decision rule such as group consensus which will serve the concerns of all—or does management favor a unilateral or majority faction decision rule for the sake of expediency and purposes of retaining control?

What objectives are most emphasized in solving day-to-day work problems? Are people encouraged to avoid anticipating the system and conforming prematurely so that a given problem can be solved primarily on the basis of doing what needs to be done in the best way possible—or are people required to approach problems within fixed boundaries so that they can only be solved on the basis of precedent and accommodated to existing policy?

How are conflicts managed during problem-solving sessions? Are disagreements treated as an indication that not all considerations have been explored and taken as opportunities for looking deeper for different, perhaps novel perspectives—or are disagreements simply squelched or smoothed over in order to save time and avoid hurt feelings?

What management expects of people in the way of problem-solving competence, the overriding considerations that govern the acceptability of solutions, and whether or not the seminal relationship of conflict to creativity is appreciated, all affect the process employed in problem solving. Add to these the individual and collective decision-making rules employed and the thrust of managers' personal norm-setting influence, and processes become defined. In general, the more people are encouraged to be open to novelty and experimentation, tolerant and sensitive to conflict dynamics, and consensual in their approach, the more creative will be their output. Neither unilateral decision making nor compromise serve the creative demands of widespread competence.

The strength of such a dynamic process for problem solving lies in the fuller utilization of available resources which it fosters. While the conventional view of creative problem solving is that of the solitary genius, working alone and drawing on some mystical internal reserve, such is seldom the case in the world of work. Most creativity in organizations flows from transactions between people. In its most common sense, collective creativity tends to be a function of group dynamics; and it is because of this group property that the processes of problem-solving become important and require conscious management. If individuals worked in a vacuum, if their ideas affected no one else, or if the acceptance of others were not a factor in implementation, perhaps process would not matter. But the case is not so simple. We must plan for interpersonal dynamics in group settings if creativity is our aim. And so doing, we enhance the probability of creative outcomes.

It bears repeating that it is in the creativity dimension that the competence process begins to come together. Collaboration and commitment come to fruition in creative output. Themes set in motion earlier in the process are embellished and addressed to task accomplishment in the creativity dimension. In providing for a collaborative system, we were concerned with the physical and psychological structuring of relationships among people; in managing creativity, we have addressed the physical and psychological structuring of work because, without a logistically sound task environment and availability of resources, the benefits of collaborative relationships are short-lived. By the same token, in creating conditions for commitment, we were concerned with norms of mutual reliance and essentiality. But unless these are buttressed by norms of authenticity and candor, spontaneity and fun, neither interdependence nor problem solving will be of a type to encourage creativity. Earlier we spoke of credibility, candor and communality; these are precursors to both the consensual use of resources in problem solving and the creative management of conflict. All of these themes are important in terms of both organizational performance and individual needs for competence.

Creativity itself is more than a problem-solving device; it is an element which defines humanness. No other species enjoys the gift of creative capacity. As Berelson and Steiner have written, "Animals adjust to their environment on its own terms; man maneuvers his world to suit himself, within far broader limits."[20] This is the gift of creativity and the key to organizational and individual adaptability. It is also the key to health, progress and peace . . . not only in our factories and service organizations, but in society.

There is, among human beings, a *need* for creative outlets—for opportunities to solve problems, to use one's ingenuity, to verify oneself through innovation and adaptation. The competence motive is best exercised and satisfied through creative accomplishment. If, as managers

[20] Berelson, B. & G. A. Steiner. *Human Behavior.* New York: Harcourt, Brace & World, 1967, p. 199.

and leaders, we fail to provide the conditions for creativity we not only lose its contributions to our organizations, we do damage to the species and to our society. *For the opposite of creativity is destructiveness.* When one's creativity is blocked, there is a very real risk that the unused, frustrated energy will be redirected in destructive acts. Erich Fromm has written:

> . . . the life-destructive forces in a person occur in an inverse ratio to the life-furthering ones; the stronger the one, the weaker the other, and vice versa. This fact offers a clue to the understanding of the life-destructive energy; it would seem that the degree of destructiveness is proportionate to the degree to which the unfolding of a person's capacities is blocked. I am not referring here to occasional frustrations of this or that desire but to the blockage of spontaneous expression of man's sensory, emotional, physical and intellectual capacities, to the thwarting of his productive potentialities. If life's tendency to grow, to be lived, is thwarted, the energy thus blocked undergoes a process of *change* and is transformed into life-destructive energy. *Destructiveness is the outcome of unlived life.*[21]

When we see sabotage in our factories or vandalism and crime in our streets, we must ask if they are the result of a blockage of productive energy. (It is interesting that crime rates have gone down in those ghettos where certain buildings and walls have been set aside for painting—murals and the like—by ghetto youth.) And we must ask what role we play.

21 Fromm, E. *Op. cit.,* p. 218.

I'm not suggesting that any of us should set out to save society—only that, as leaders, each of us can influence a bit of it. We play a pivotal role and we are in a position to choose creativity over destructiveness. If, through our policies and practices, we affirm creativity, we will be able to use the resources afforded by our environments, do good work, and achieve full expression of that competence which breeds growth. As managers, we should remember that only with growth is there survival.

VII

Turning Point: The Process in Perspective

We have reached a point of transition. Having developed the underlying considerations and rationale as well as the framework and managerial action requirements of the competence process, we will soon turn to proving the process. The test of an idea is not whether it jibes with conventional wisdom or how much it appeals to one's sense of rightness or personal need for change. The truth and practical applicability of an idea must be verified; the premise must be put to the test in such a way that we can have confidence in both its message and its consequence. Testing the competence process— both through scientific research and practical application—will be the subject of the remainder of this volume. But before we undertake such a change in direction and tone, there are some implicit themes which need to be made more explicit and some implications which need to be explained in more direct terms.

In the preceding chapters the focus has been on the concepts, principles, and conditions relating to widespread competence within an organization. We have introduced a number of new terms and hopefully a few new thoughts. Before moving on to the next section which puts the competence process to the empirical test, it seems appropriate that we pause just long enough to put the process in perspective, to look at it from several different angles. First, it is worth looking back in review of the key ideas upon which the process as a whole is based. Next, the perspective needs to be turned in such a way that we can visualize competence dynamics in an organization once the process has been implemented; by viewing the process in motion, managing for competence will seem less arduous and piecemeal a task than it might have appeared as the competence process was developed over several chapters. In turn, the role of the manager—why the individual manager is deemed the prime mover in the process—needs perspective. Finally, the issue of competence needs to be moved to the foreground so that we can look beyond to its raison d'etre, to productivity in the workplace; performance—doing what needs to be done—is, after all, the driving force behind the development of the competence process.

Competence in Retrospect: A Practical Review

In the first three chapters we explored competence issues ranging from the traditional view of human capacity for work to the premise of widespread competence and how it can be brought to bear on organizational goals. Although the following capsule descriptions do not do full justice to the scope and depth of the matter, they may serve to recap our thesis and provide useful reference points for further thought.

The Manager as Prophet

One of the most potent yet subtle mechanisms operating

in human affairs is the self-fulfilling prophecy. The fact that one individual's expectations can, in effect, set limits on another's performance should be a key consideration in organizing and managing work. Nowhere are personal prophecies of performance more evident than in manager-subordinate relations. Unfortunately, managers have traditionally organized work as if they expected less than competent performance, and it is little wonder that workers have not been able to produce up to their capacity. Should managers do an about-face and base their practices in prophecies of competence, their subordinates will demonstrate unprecedented levels of resourcefulness and accomplishment—because they are demonstrably competent.

The Personal Side of Competence

We *learn* to perform competently for the sake of survival; but we *value* individual competence as a personal expression of continued biological and psychological growth. For our purpose, the thrust of Robert White's thesis is that managers should not be hesitant to expect high levels of competence in the workplace. All of us—managers and workers—have been developing our ability as creative problem-solvers and producers since the day we were born. We continue to hone our skills and seek new opportunities to apply our talents because of our personal needs to be good at what we do. We are pleasure seekers in a practical way— we feel good when we do well. Creativity and a commitment to doing what needs to be done are characteristics which define the essence of human nature. When we behave competently, we feel good about ourselves.

A Context for Competence

There is a basic assumption that individual competence is the rule not the exception, but a corollary assumption is that very little of this reservoir of talent will be expressed if the means to competent performance and its intrinsic rewards are denied to the individual. Individual competence requires a supportive context if it is to be fully expressed. In organizations, the work that is done and the policies and practices of management define the context within which competence may or may not be expressed. Managers must provide for the expression of competence; they must provide a work context which will allow for the natural predisposition for productivity to become manifest. To do so does not call for motivating subordinates by pushing and prodding them or dangling rewards before them as if bribery were the only way to get them to work. Neither does it call for a benevolent form of laissez-faire supervision.

Creating a context for competence is the hard job of those in authority and it is largely a matter of paving the way for a natural process to unfold—for competence to be expressed in the carrying out of organizational tasks. Managing for collaboration, commitment and creativity will insure such a context. When this is accomplished, it fosters a healthy productive orientation—a set of positive feelings the individual has for work and coworkers when it becomes apparent that management values competence and will see that it is supported. If instead managers place roadblocks in the path of competence, subordinates will become frustrated and alienated. They become less willing to be productive because they are barred from both the means to and rewards of competence.

The Basic Premise

The competence process is an alternative approach to management founded in a recognition of the unheralded but nevertheless proven fact of widespread human competence. The objectives of the process are threefold: to activate managerial prophecies of competence; to promote a healthy productive orientation; and to insure conditions supportive of a widespread, collective expression of competence. The competence process relies on three dimensions of organizational life, as these are revealed in the policies, practices and priorities of the workplace. Initial attention must be given to collaboration, to establishing a role of partnership between manager and subordinates. The function of collaboration is to reaffirm the fact that management wants people to give their best; it is a symbolic mechanism for engaging individuals in the business of the organization at the same level of commitment and creativity they display in their personal activities. In short, collaboration makes work personal, makes the individual an owner of the corporate enterprise, and denotes that the prospects are good that competent performance can result in feelings of efficacy and worth. For this salutary effect to be sustained, the dimensions of commitment and creativity must be consciously and purposefully managed.

The three major dimensions—collaboration, commitment and creativity—and their nine supporting conditions which comprise the total context for competence are shown in Figure 1. The conditions are comprehensive in that they reflect psychological and physical aspects of the workplace— the way managers and subordinates feel about each other, what they expect from their work and how relationships and tasks are structured.

Figure 1. The competence process: Basic dimensions and supporting conditions.

While viewing the competence process as a whole in Figure 1, a manager may begin to feel overwhelmed by the complexity of developing nine discrete conditions. However, in the process as shown here the emphasis is on the *development* of conditions for competence more than on *maintaining* competence conditions once they are in place. The most difficult phase of managing for competence is setting the process in place; once in place, competence gains a kinetic energy of its own.

Competence in Place: A Well-knit Fabric

Visualizing how competence unfolds—how collaboration yields a potential for commitment which in turn yields potential creativity and culminates in that state of adaptive fitness we call competence—is useful for capturing the step-by-step approach managers must follow to create conditions for competence. But this linear process is transfigured to a dynamic system once the rudimentary conditions have been established. There is an inherent system of integrity and logic in the competence process which works to reinforce the interdependencies among dimensions and their supporting conditions. These internal dynamics—involving primarily systems of values and rules of logic—simplify the manager's task of maintaining a productive environment.

What may have appeared to be a certain redundancy in the competence process—a recycling of themes and values within and between dimensions—is in fact a system of vertical integrity and lateral logic which, as threads in a fabric, tie the process together in a well-knit and functionally durable way. The metaphor of competence as a social fabric is revealing of the vertical and lateral themes of the process which interlock and reinforce one another. Each dimension of competence—collaboration, commitment and creativity —depends for its strength on the vertical continuity and consistency of values characterizing its supporting conditions. By the same token, there are logical bridges across the supporting conditions of the three competence dimensions which produce a lock-stitched quality. Figure 2 depicts this vertical and horizontal integration.

Values: Key to Vertical Integrity

First and foremost, the dimensions of competence possess a consistency of values and mutually reinforcing practices. Attention to one supporting condition for a particular dimension will automatically evoke a concern for those other conditions upon which it depends for reinforcement or expression. For example, *management values* in support of collaboration are reinforced—verified, if you will—by a genuinely collaborative *support structure.* By the same token,

COLLABORATION   COMMITMENT   CREATIVITY

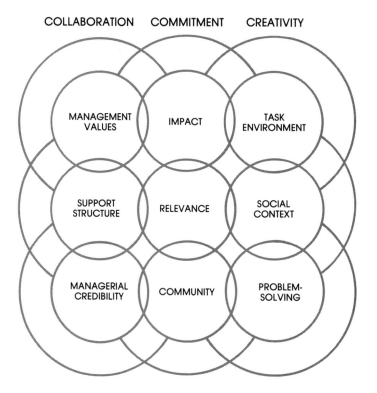

Figure. 2. The fabric of competence.

management values are further reinforced by *managerial credibility; credibility,* in turn, takes its structure from *values* and finds a major context for expression in *support structure.*

Perhaps an example from the automotive industry can illustrate the interplay and cross-referencing properties of dimensional supports. One of the salaried workers in the Transmission and Chassis Division of a struggling auto firm was interviewed in early 1985.

You ask if things have gotten any better. Well

. . . yes and no. I mean, who can say? We started off with them telling us how important we are . . . you know, wanting our ideas and suggestions 'cause we're the real experts . . . that sort of thing. And most of us bought into it. We had a lot on our chests . . . and a lot to offer. Some of us didn't really know what to think at first, but we said, "What the hell! Give it a try!"

So, we really begin to get into the employee involvement program management set up. And we liked it. There was some good stuff; you know, how to do things better and faster, good stuff. But the next thing we knew—or maybe it was about the same time, I don't remember exactly—they wanted us to cooperate with some cost-saving programs . . . said it was a matter of survival. So, we ended up giving up our cost of living increase, cutting back on some health benefits, and some other stuff.

Then we find out that some of the management is more concerned with *how many* groups are operating than they are with the ideas that come out—like keeping score or something. That was the first thing. But what really frosted me—and a lot of other guys—was after telling us how we're all in this thing together and getting us to go along, give up our living increases and everything—they give top management *bonuses!* I mean millions of dollars! So . . . I don't know . . . who do you trust? Right?

Clearly the values espoused, the practices and policies condoned, and the good faith of management are all intertwined and must stand the test of day-to-day reality if a collaborative system is to be achieved. As St. James said, good words are no substitute for good deeds. For collaboration, and for all dimensions, there is an inherent integrity that must not be violated if the resulting fabric is to do its job.

The same system of vertical interlocks is found in the two remaining dimensions of commitment and creativity. For example, *impact* and *relevance* are interwoven conditions for commitment. The likelihood of work being meaningful and relevant without a sense of personal impact and internal control is remote. As we saw with Mary Russell and Dr. Macatee, commitment depends on a productive interplay among the elements of impact, relevance and community. Forced irrelevance undercuts a sense of personal impact and, as with Macatee, can promote conflict to the detriment of community. Similarly, in the creativity dimension, *task environment* requirements necessarily set in motion considerations of the *social context;* the efficacy of physical and psychological structuring of work is directly affected by the social dynamics which characterize the workplace. The work group must not only be able to interact freely but, indeed, must value the opportunity to do so in a collaborative manner. Like so many threads weaving up and down, the conditions which support collaboration, commitment and creativity have a vertical integrity which gives them coherence and strength.

Logic: Key to Lateral Connections

Just as the dimensions of competence possess a basic integrity among their supporting conditions, there is a lateral logic *across* dimensions. For example, *managerial credibili-*

ty directly influences *community* and the norms under-lying ambience and *social context;* the influence of managerial candor and trustworthiness, while primarily a collaborative force, is an important source of normative values and exemplary behaviors in the creation of both a sense of community and a rewarding social ambience. Likewise, *impact* and *relevance* in support of commitment exert direct influence on the *problem-solving* process; it is the sense of personal power and shared purpose which make the outcome of creative problem-solving seem so important to individuals. Quite simply, the personal stake which comes with commitment makes people justifiably concerned with how creatively common problems are to be solved.

Managers may take a certain comfort in the internal dynamics of the competence process just described. Because of these internal connections a managerial action taken to support one condition of competence is likely to contribute to—indeed, evoke a concern for and help satisfy—another. In other words, maintaining a context for competence is easier than it may have first appeared. The competence process guides gently and, once set in motion, possesses its own energy for staying in motion. Managing for competence will still take effort, but in time the fabric will take shape and, if managers are resolute, come to cloak all who labor.

The Manager as Prime Mover

We have placed by far the major burden for widespread competence on the shoulders of the manager. If it seems that we have singled out managers for attention and taken them to task for misjudgment, misunderstanding and mismanaging—it is because we have. But there is a reason. Professor Jerry Harvey—psychologist, humorist, and resident iconoclast at George Washington University—tells the story of his old Army sergeant who, when accused of unfairly calling on the same conscientious recruits to do the hardest jobs, would reply,

> Well, the way I see it, you whips the hoss that pulls the load. If I've got me a brace of hosses and one of 'em's ridin' loose in the harness and the other's strainin' at the bit, when I want to go faster I'm gonna whip the one that's rarin' to go.

We have singled out managers because they are the ones who pull the load.

Managers have the hard job. Those in positions of authority—and our generic use of the term *manager* should not obscure the fact that we also mean teachers, principals, administrators, elected officials and parents—those with formal influence are the obvious caretakers of competence. They structure and provide the contexts for work. Only rarely might those with little authority or influence dictate how things are to be done in an organization. When they are able to do so, it will usually be from an unhealthy and adversarial rather than collaborative posture. Realistically, it seems that only managers are in a position to set in motion the healthy dynamics of the competence process.

The fact that most managers have managed in ways that are inconsistent with the values and objectives of the competence process does not necessarily mean that they would not like to do so. More often than not, managers mismanage, not because of personal shortcomings or evil intent, but because they operate from *faulty premises*. Managers have not defaulted on competence because power corrupts so much as because accountability intimidates. Most managers inherit the policy structure, precedents and priorities which govern their work. They, too, know what it means to feel constrained in work, to be faced with choices between doing their best and doing it according to the Manual; managers know what it means to be barred from personal feelings of efficacy and worth. Managers have bosses too. The Catch-22 is that, faced with a choice between managing as they themselves would *like* to be managed or as they *are* managed, they pass down to those they manage ineffective and counter-productive practices lest they be accused of mismanagement.

As we have said, the competence process is an alternative, a choice point, for managers who wish to break the self-reinforcing cycle of mismanaged competence heaped upon competence mismanaged at the next level down. Each manager may exercise the option that, from his or her position downward, competence will be valued and a context will be provided for its expression. When this choice is made, the manager, the worker, and the organization as a whole prosper in unexpected ways because productive output increases along with quality of life in the workplace. And these are the primary goals of the competence process.

Productivity: Competence Manifest

For six chapters, issues of competence have been our singular focus of attention. It is now time to shift our attention away from competence per se and look to its more apparent consequences, to what some consider to be the most critical problem we face today—*productivity*. For years we have watched its rate of growth slow as if entropic laws— the irreversible tendency to decay—were in full effect. Advances in technology and additional capital investment have done little to offset the decline. In my view the solution to problems of production is not likely to be found in these areas of material resources but in the area of untapped human competence. If we can harvest but a fraction of the unique individual capacity to do, now lying fallow in the shadow of oppressive or ill-informed managerial practices, we can yet increase productive output and secure for ourselves and others more abundant lives in the process.

Productivity is the yardstick of both our corporate and national health. For ease of measurement, economists use a simplified definition centering on output per labor hour. Although such a measure of productivity may work for enterprises which produce tangible goods, those that provide services or perform support functions need other criteria and standards. Customer satisfaction, personnel turnover, labor grievances, number of merit scholars, or costs of hospital room care may be better indicators of an organization's ability to attain its goals. But there is more to productivity than measuring it. No matter how productivity is defined, conditions for competence should, if our thesis is accurately conceived, be the determining factor.

Our thesis receives tentative support from a study covering the past decade—the period of dramatically declining productivity between 1967 and 1977—after what Bradley Graham[1] called the "golden growth" days following World War II. Robert P. Quinn and Graham L. Staines, of the University of Michigan's Institute for Social Research, did a survey of job conditions for the U. S. Department of Labor in 1977.[2] They were able to compare their responses

[1] *Graham, B. "U. S. Productivity: Golden Days Over." The Washington Post,* September 10, 1978.

[2] Quinn, R. P. & G. L. Staines. *The 1977 Quality of Work Survey.* Ann Arbor: Institute for Social Research, University of Michigan, 1978.

from the 1977 survey to those from a similar study made in 1969. In their survey, Quinn and Staines asked several questions about specific aspects of a worker's job; interestingly enough, some of these bear directly on issues of inherent significance in the competence process. The results are thought-provoking.

During the same time frame that productivity was declining most noticeably, key features of work with direct implications for the expression of competence were also found to be in decline. Consider the following in light of the conditions for competence which we have claimed as critical:

- I am given a chance to do the things I do best: *down* 25.0 percent.

- I have an opportunity to develop my own special abilities: *down* 25.9 percent.

- I am given a lot of freedom to decide how I do my own work: *down* 19.8 percent.

- I have enough information to get the job done: *down* 17.3 percent.

- I am free from the conflicting demands that other people make of me: *down* 43.0 percent.

- I have enough authority to do my job: *down* 17.2 percent.

- The work is interesting: *down* 13.5 percent.

The Quinn and Staines survey was not a study of productivity per se and they do not venture a connection between the decline in certain job conditions and the concurrent decline in productivity. But there may be a connection between the core aspects of one's work and productivity—indeed, just such a causal relationship has been the central theme in our development of the competence process.

I submit that we do not have a problem of productivity. *We have a problem of mismanaged competence which shows up in low productivity and worker malaise.* To solve the problem requires a redefinition of the problem itself and of management's role in the manager-worker-productivity equation. Required is a new perspective on productivity: it is a measurable symptom, nothing more, of how available competence is managed. This means that whether or not a high level of productivity is achieved is as much the manager's responsibility as it is those who make the product or deliver the service. Managers must be productive too.

Any equation for productivity must, in my view, include managerial productivity as well as some of the more conventional considerations. The manager's place in achieving productivity is portrayed in the following formula where productivity is seen as a function of both the context created by the manager and individual competence:

$$Productivity = f \left\{ \begin{array}{cc} Context\ Created & Individual \\ By\ Managers & Competence \end{array} \right\}$$

Several aspects of the equation require emphasis. Productivity, for our purposes, is only a measurement tool, a symptom; individual competence is a fixed commodity, only its expression is subject to change. The fact that remains is that the context created by managers—whether or not it is one which provides for a healthy productive outlook and the expression of competence—is the only variable which can be manipulated. Thus, how competence is managed becomes the critical factor in productivity. Clearly, at least from a hypothetical point of view at this point, the fate of our economic institutions, and by extension our social institutions, lies squarely on the manager's shoulders.

Productivity based in the management of competence is our transition point. We must move beyond the hypothesis that productivity depends on managers and the kind of context they create for competence. The key issue at this juncture is whether or not there is a clearly demonstrable relationship between conditions for competence and performance in organizations. That is what the rest of this volume will resolve—whether productivity, measured by a variety of criteria in a variety of settings, truly is a function of the context a manager creates to facilitate the expression of individual competence.

Part Two

Proving the
Premise

VIII

Opportunities for Competence: The Key to Productivity and Health

It was Kurt Lewin who said, "Nothing is so practical as a good theory."[1] It has been well over forty years since Lewin first offered this sage observation; and, because the idea that what we believe affects what we do made sense to a lot of practical-minded realists, Lewin was able to persuade many people to be more trusting of scientific thought. One of the ironies of science is having to struggle and amass empirical support to have an idea accepted, only to find a bandwagon effect where *any* idea is accepted, virtually without question. Today we are faced with a plethora of "theories" about effective management. As managers with very practical concerns and accountability for the well-being of our organizations and the people who populate them, we must exercise a certain amount of caution before we buy into new explanations or fanciful depictions of what we might do differently. With today's pop-psychology, neat packaging of ideas, and pseudoscientific "anybody can play" game of behavioral theorizing, I feel a need to amend Lewin's premise: nothing is so practical as a good *validated* theory.

---

[1] Marrow, A. E. *The Practical Theorist.* New York: Teachers College Press, Columbia University, 1977.

It is helpful to remind ourselves that a theory, by definition, is ". . . a general principle, *supported by considerable
data,* proposed as an explanation of a group of phenomena;
a *statement of the relations believed to prevail in a
comprehensive body of facts.*"[2] (Italics mine.) Not all
"theories" of management meet these requirements. Not
all reflect an affinity for either data or even for scientific
accuracy. Propositions which are not supported by data and
do not lead to a testable specification of relations are, quite
simply, not theories. They are hunches, personal opinions—
sometimes informed, sometimes not—or, all too often,
only provocative restatements of conventional wisdom
designed to appeal to the need for common sense explanations of complex phenomena. Managers should be wary of
unsupported prescriptions for managing because our
organizations and people are simply too important to
entrust to unvalidated premises.

To validate—to *specify* relationships among factors, to
predict outcomes and then to *demonstrate* with some degree
of confidence that such relationships and outcomes do in
fact exist—is the sine qua non of developing any proposition that even smacks of a prescription for management. As
we said at the outset, it *matters* how our organizations and
communities are managed. Managers are entitled to—
indeed, they must insist upon—supporting data and verification of premises from those who would advise them on how
to manage their organizations. We often accept on faith—
because of our own misplaced trust in the studied eloquence
of others—new ways of doing things. I would not have
anyone accept the tenets of the competence process on faith
alone. As it turns out, no one has to. The competence

---

[2] English, H. & A. English. *A Comprehensive Dictionary of Psychological and
Psychoanalytical Terms.* New York: Longmans, Green and Co., 1958.

process demands verification and this is a straightforward undertaking. The process is based on an explicit set of assumptions leading to an equally explicit proposition: Individual competence abounds. Given a context supportive of both the capacity and need to do what needs to be done, a widespread expression of competence can become the defining feature of our organizations. And organizations characterized by competence will be productive.

These are testable assertions and putting the premise to the test is the most critical step thus far in the development of the competence process.

Verifying the Premise

Testing any process requires basic research. This is hard work, sometimes frustrating and sometimes exhilarating. It is in such work that the social scientist has the most fun. Validation research of the type required for the competence process is not unlike calling the daily double at the local race track, complete with having to play the odds. The researcher must predict the outcome of the investigation within statistically significant limits for it to mean anything. At the same time, designing and conducting such research is often like solving a good mystery. The inductive and deductive reasoning required in devising an appropriate test of a premise provides its own kinds of private suspense for the researcher.

There is a public relations function to basic research as well. Recruiting people to participate in research may be the hardest task of all; not everyone wants to talk about performance or evaluate themselves, and yet research requires cooperative people willing to risk assessment. And finally, data analysis and drawing conclusions call for a special statistical expertise and philosophic posture. Steps must be taken statistically and inferentially to insure that, if one errs, errors of methodology or judgment will be on the conservative side; it is better in science to understate the case than to reach unwarranted conclusions.

So, in beginning the research necessary for verifying the competence process, we had an opportunity to be gamblers, sleuths, P. R. reps, tacticians, technicians, and social scientists all at the same time. For the researcher, this is anything but a sterile experience, and it is one which must be shared with the manager if the verification process is to be fully appreciated.

We began with basic predictions, moved next to the development of appropriate measurements and design of the research project. During this time we recruited organizations to participate and, finally, collected sufficient data over a two-year period to allow us to begin the hard task of analysis and summation. Each of these was a special step in the process, designed in its own way to put the competence process to the test.

Basic Predictions

Productivity, we have said, is a function of the combined effects of (1) individual competence and (2) the context provided by management for the expression of competence. In our equation, individual competence is taken as a fixed commodity. Only the managerially-created context for competence can vary widely. As context varies, so will productivity. This is why, in Chapter III, we said that we should look to management when things go wrong in our organizations; performance is not *uniformly* bad, even in the same organization. There are pockets within the least productive or organizations where things go quite well and people perform competently. There are also pockets in the best of organizations where things go badly and people are unproductive. The key is context.

If we were to compare productive or high performing units with comparable but unproductive, low performing, units from the same parent organization we would expect them to differ on the dimensions of competence if the competence process holds true. Our research plan involved such a comparison and our basic prediction was as follows:

> *High performing, productive units will be characterized by significantly greater competence dimensions—i.e., by more conditions in support of collaboration, commitment, and creativity— than will their low performing, unproductive counterparts in the same parent organization.*

If high performing units are found to differ from low performing units on the dimensions of competence by a magnitude greater than we can expect by chance, the premise may be accepted. A context for competence, as portrayed in the basic process, may be said to be a defining feature of productive organizations. Making predictions, however, is the easy part of the verification process. We need dependable measures and a research sample from which we can generalize.

Measuring the Context
for Competence

Warren Bennis, in a thoughtful essay on the meaning of organizational competence, observed that the problem of measurement, until it is solved, seriously qualifies the notion of an organization as an adaptively fit entity.[3] This same qualification applies to the notion of a context for competence. That is why our first priority was one of developing reliable measurement procedures. This is a time-consuming, often neglected, but critical step in validation research.

Over a six-month period, we constructed a survey in which we focused on organizational conditions; we studied practices and values—the context for competence created by management—which people can observe or infer, and which we have posited as the major supports to competence. We asked about the work ethic promoted by management; we surveyed people about their involvement in decisions; we asked them to describe the ambience of their workplaces and many other aspects of their organizations.

By asking questions similar to those raised earlier in this volume, we produced an exceptionally dependable 40-item survey, the *Organizational Competence Index.*[4] The survey allows people to describe competence conditions both as they actually are in their organizations and as they, the respondents, ideally wish them to be. We were interested,

---

[3] Bennis, W. *Changing Organizations.* New York: McGraw-Hill, 1966, p. 55.

[4] Cronbach's Alpha test of reliability was employed in developing the *Organizational Competence Index.* Responses from 159 people yielded an Alpha of .928. This result was cross-validated with a second group of 120 people, yielding an Alpha of .924.

for obvious reasons, in prevailing conditions; but we were also curious about those conditions people would prescribe for themselves, given the opportunity. The latter, we reasoned, could shed light on both the veracity of the competence motive concept for the workplace and, to the extent that actual and desired conditions were discrepant from one another, provide information about productive orientation and its related feelings. Armed with appropriate tools for measurement, we then sought to evaluate the competence process across organizations of varying size and mission.

Obtaining a Representative Sample

One of the most noteworthy traits managers have in common is a belief that they are different. Many managers equate their practices with the technology and objectives of the organization they serve. Some are quite adamant about the fact that a manufacturer of hard goods is not subject to the same managerial practices as a research and development group or school system. Not only do the objectives and technologies of such organizations differ, they reason, but so do the *people* who comprise them. Different organizations require people of differing skills—from the most basic to the most complex—and different aptitudes— from the dullest to the brightest—and one just does not manage people so different in the same way. Any widespread presumption of uniqueness among managers has direct implications for the general utility of the competence process.

On the face of it, the presumption of uniqueness is a convincing argument; but if it is valid the competence process is not. The competence process rests on a recognition of similarities. It is founded in a belief that we are all variations on the same grand theme and, just as uniformities among people allow physicians to practice good medicine, so may human similarities allow managers to practice competent management. People are people, and whether they work in a pajama factory in Marion, Virginia, or in a fertilizer plant in Oslo, Norway, they are able to do what needs to be done; moreover, they *need* to perform competently so that they might feel good about themselves.

But this is mere philosophic discourse and we are concerned at this point with empirical validation of the competence process. If the argument of uniqueness is a valid position, the competence process should not generalize. Differences in collaboration, commitment, and creativity should not separate high from low performers in different kinds of organizations.

To control for this assumption, and in the process to strengthen our test by including diversity of work and size, we decided to employ what statisticians call a matched-groups design: we would compare comparable units—those doing the same kind of work, relying on the same kinds of people—from the same parent organization; these units would be *matched* on work and objectives, but *differ* on productivity. We looked for organizations of truly diverse pursuits and in each organization we asked that two comparable units—plants, department, teams, regions, etc.—be made available to us for study. One of these, we asked, should be a good producer, an identified *high performer*, while the other should be minimally productive, a known *low performer* engaged in the same or comparable activities pursuant to the same organizational goals.

We were able to enlist the aid of nine different organizations, ranging from supermarket and fast food chains to research and development teams, a government agency, and a school system. The people in these organizations should be applauded, for they were willing to confront the hard questions of competence. As the following descriptions will reveal, the nature of the work, the age and educational levels of the people involved, and the unit size of organizations differed greatly. Our point of inquiry was whether the competence process could account for performance differences between otherwise comparable parts of organizations like the following:

A national supermarket chain. Most of us are familiar with the jobs characterizing a retail grocery. In two zones in the same state, we surveyed people from 23 different stores. Stockers, check-out clerks, sackers, and zone and store managers from both the high and low performing areas were asked to describe their respective stores, as they are and as they might ideally be. Males outnumbered females by a 3:2 ratio; management personnel typically had some college education while hourly workers had, for the most part, completed high school. Ages ranged from 17 to 54 years, and most hourly workers were union members.

A nationwide fast-food chain. Again, most of us have eaten in a fast-food restaurant and know something of the work involved in preparing and serving meals. Two districts were studied, each comprised of approximately 40 restaurants, and both salaried and hourly workers were surveyed. Waiters, cooks, area and restaurant managers were asked to describe the conditions in their respective places of work, as they are and as each person would like them to be. Males outnumbered females in this organization by a 4:1 ration; management personnel had some post-high school study while hourly personnel had generally completed high school. Ages ranged from 19 to 40 years.

A major petrochemical company. In this organization, the nature of work and professional backgrounds shift substantially from those encountered in the two former organizations. Three divisions comprised of a field force of 60 people selling industrial raw materials were studied. Field sales personnel and sales managers were asked to portray the prevailing conditions in their respective divisions and as they would like them to be. Males outnumbered females by a 5:1 ratio and all personnel had completed college, with some possessing master's level degrees. All were salaried personnel and the age spread was from 26 to 42 years.

An electronics engineering and manufacturing firm. Cross-sectional slices of two large divisions, each comprised of several thousand people, were studied. People surveyed were engaged in engineering, manufacturing, marketing and management with males outnumbering females by a 10:1 ration. Both divisions operated under the same general management and in the same plant, but functioned as individual profit centers. Only salaried personnel were involved in the study and these people had an average of 4-6 years of college and represented an age span of 27 to 61 years.

A technical equipment manufacturing firm. Two capital-intensive heavy equipment plants manufacturing identical products were studied. One plant of 10,000 people had been unionized since the turn of the century; the other, only ten years old, was non-union and employed 1,000 people. Both management and supervisory personnel, all salaried, were surveyed; 60% to 70% of these had technical college degrees while the remainder had some college study. The age range of this all male group was from 30 to 64 years.

A major bank. Two of seven sections involved in electronic data processing in the main bank were studied. Non-union computer programmers and analysts, all with at least a Bachelor of Science degree, were surveyed. These were salaried personnel, predominately male by a 4:1 ratio, who represented an age span of 25 to 60 years.

A research and development firm. Two small R & D teams, all male, working on engineering problems related to space exploration were studied. All were salaried professional engineers with five or more years of college. These were non-union groups working under the same general manager but for different supervisors. Ages ranged from 24 to 59 years.

A school system. Bilingual teachers and administrative staff personnel in two compensatory elementary schools were studied. Of primary interest in this instance is the fact that the criteria used to designate high and low performing schools were student achievement test scores. All subjects were college educated and females outnumbered males.

A government agency. Two departments in a government research laboratory were studied. The laboratory employs 4,000 people, 12% of whom are female, and is primarily engaged in pure and applied research. The eight department heads were asked to rank-order all departments except their own in terms of their productivity. The department receiving the highest productivity rating was considered high performing and the department receiving the lowest rating was designated the low performer. Individuals surveyed were salaried, predominantly male, and predominantly advanced degreed.

Service, manufacturing, sales, financial, and R & D—as

portrayed, the organizations studied insure diversity of work, education, age, mission, and size and allow for a test of the general applicability of the competence process. Given a means for distinguishing high performers from their less productive counterparts, the design is complete.

Appraising Performance

We purposely avoided spelling out or suggesting performance criteria because we wanted each organization to identify its high and low performing units on the basis of *its own standards*. This was another source of design strength; the competence process could be evaluated in terms of the practical concerns of each participating organization. The supermarket, fast-food, and electronic manufacturing organizations chose profit criteria; the technical equipment manufacturer and bank chose production rates; the chemical and R & D firms chose morale, labor grievances, turnover, and dependability; and the school system chose student achievement test scores; and the government agency chose peer ratings. We felt that allowing organizations to assess performance according to their own priorities, when combined with the different organizational types, unit sizes, and job scopes included in our study, would allow us to gain a more realistic and practical evaluation of the competence process, as well as results which could be generalized irrespective of organizational type.

So it was that we worked with eighteen organizational units and compared the nine units identified as low performers with their nine high-performing counterparts on our three competence dimensions—that is, on the extent to which each was characterized by the nine support conditions for collaboration, commitment, and creativity. In all, we obtained survey data from 576 people regarding current conditions as compared with those to be desired in their respective places of work. And, in the process, we put the competence process to the most stringent test we could devise. We predicted our outcomes in advance; we invested our energies; now we were prepared to let the chips fall where they may.

Results: Competence and Productivity

The competence process, as we have said, is three dimensional. This means that it is all three dimensions which, together, account for organizational performance. Neither collaboration, commitment, nor creativity alone can reveal the competence level of an organization. Competence is a fabric; to be complete, collaboration needs follow-up in commitment and, in turn, commitment requires a creative outlet. Because of this, the data collected required a technique of analysis in which the *combined and simultaneous effects* of all three dimensions could be assessed and related to organizational performance.

I mention this because researchers and managers alike have too often ignored the fact that a given organizational event, such as productivity, is caused by multiple influences. We have tried to account for organizational phenomena by attending to one causal factor at a time, placing the whole burden on a single consideration in trying to explain complex events. This is an oversimplified view, but it is one which is frequently found in studies of organizational performance: job satisfaction as a predictor of productivity, managerial style as a means to corporate excellence, the effect of climate on absenteeism; the list is endless.

We need to be mindful of the fact that we live in a world of multiple causation, where any given event is usually the result of the simultaneous operation of several factors. And our research efforts must reflect this awareness. Certainly this is the case with the competence process and productivity. Competence forces, although interdependent, are functionally different influences; and it is how they combine and interact that determines the performance of an organization. The importance of this for the manager is that, proceeding as we did, we discovered heretofore unknown relationships between performance and those organizational conditions which managers control.

Competence Results in
High Performance

We found such large differences between high and low performing units on the dimensions of competence that they could occur by chance only one in 10,000 times.[5] *High performing organizations are characterized by significantly stronger conditions for competence than are low performing organizations.* Our premise is verified. Productive organizations, as compared with their less productive counterparts, are those with the greatest supports for collaboration, commitment and creativity.

At the risk of oversimplifying the dynamic interplay among dimensions, in Figure 1 we have presented a bar graph of the scores on Collaboration, Commitment, and Creativity conditions for both high and low performers by organization. The average score for all groups is given as a

---

[5] See Table II of the Statistical Appendix for a summary of the data analysis leading to this conclusion.

reference point and organizational profiles are plotted around this grand mean.

Two points are apparent from the data. First, different types of organizations are characterized by different levels of the conditions for competence. Could this be a reflection of managers' presumptions of uniqueness? If so, the efficacy of such a position is challenged by the second apparency: with few exceptions, all three competence dimensions are greater for the most productive of organizational pairs, irrespective of type of organization. Out of a total of 27 pairs of raw scores—three pairs each per the nine organizations—23 are as predicted. Anomalies show up in the relatively lower creativity score of the high performing supermarket zone, the slightly lower commitment scores of the high sections of both the fast food chain and banking organization, and the essentially equal collaboration scores for banking. While these are minor differences—from one to six points—they are departures from predicted results. We live in an imperfect world, it seems; but it is reassuring to realize that, given 23 "hits," we could expect only 1.35 by chance alone.

The major thrust of the data is captured by the statistical analysis showing that, overall, the combined and simultaneous effects of collaboration, commitment, and creativity constitute a significant point of departure between productive and unproductive organizations.[6] This overall relationship of productivity to the three dimensions of competence is portrayed in Figure 2. From this depiction we can clearly see that organizational performance varies as the conditions for competence vary. We take these findings as verification of our premise that productivity is a function

[6] See Table II of the Statistical Appendix.

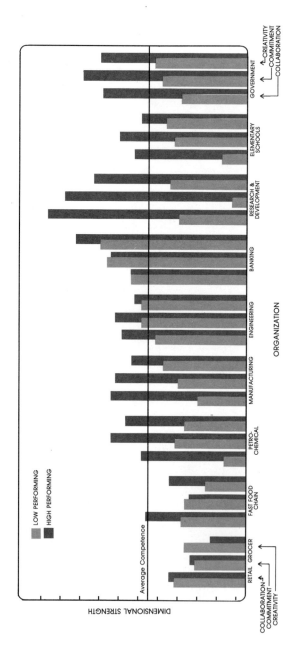

Figure 1. A comparison of the dimensions of competence in matched low and high performing organizations.

of the combined effects of individual competence and the context afforded for its expression. Providing a context for competence is not only the job of management, it is in their best interests to do so. One must wonder why, in low

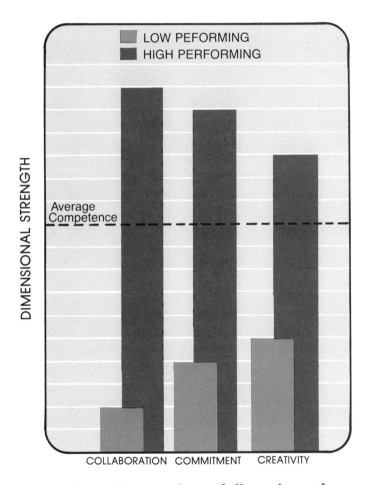

Figure 2. Overall comparison of dimensions of competence in low and high performing organizations.

performing organizations, managers have failed in so fundamental a task.

Performance and the Managerial Enigma

The manner in which conditions for collaboration, commitment, and creativity are related to productivity appears so clear cut that we can legitimately wonder why managers of low performing units have not discovered it for themselves. Given the fact that other units in their organizations are performing well under different conditions, why haven't managers of unproductive units profited from others' experience? Perhaps managers in the same organization do not talk to one another. Perhaps competition for the same position undercuts collegiality and inhibits the sharing of managerial insights. Or it may be that managers simply think they are doing a better job of supplying appropriate support conditions than they actually are.

As part of our analysis of results, we compared managerial and subordinate depictions of existing conditions in both low and high performing organizations. We suspected that managers—as those who set in motion and monitor prevailing conditions—might perceive these differently than those on the receiving end, people whose work is directly affected by such conditions. Allowing for the effects of good intentions on the part of managers, we anticipated that they might be inclined to overestimate how good things were in their organizations; and, if anything, we thought this tendency might be more pronounced among managers of unproductive workplaces than among those of more productive units. We were wrong on all counts.

Managers of high performing units differed from their subordinates by *under*estimating supports for collaboration, commitment, and creativity. For whatever reason—whether managers of productive workplaces expected more of themselves or were more sensitized to the importance and therefore more critical of support conditions—subordinates reported more supports for competence than did managers themselves. The upshot was that in high performing organizations managers were doing a better job than they knew.

This was not the case in low performing organizations. Managers of unproductive workplaces neither overstated nor underestimated conditions in their organizations. They were in virtual agreement with their subordinates about prevailing supports for collaboration, commitment, and creativity. In short, managers of low performing units knew exactly what they were providing in the way of a context for competence.

This finding takes us back to the original question: given the relationship of conditions for collaboration, commitment, and creativity to productivity, why would managers with production problems knowingly provide fewer of the supports found to characterize the more productive parts of the same parent organization? Why would they purposely create a context for work so different from that found in higher performing but otherwise comparable places of work?

These are difficult questions to answer without imputing motives to managers and putting words in their mouths. But I am persuaded that, more often than not, managers feel that low productivity *requires* different management. Many managers take poor performance as a direct reflection of the innate lack of ability and basic unwillingness of people to perform well. Good productivity is equated with competence and low productivity is equated with incompetence. And, when performance falls off, managers respond by turning the screw a little tighter. They become more directive and less collaborative, more preoccupied with control and less concerned with commitment; they push for more standardization and less creativity. They do this, I think, because of a belief that unproductive people will only respond to such management.

This is, of course, one of the ways in which counterproductive prophecies get fulfilled in organizations. Managers, themselves frustrated and disappointed, begin to curse the tree for the quality of its fruit rather than seeing to the soil in which it must grow. Latent managerial values and assumptions come to the surface. I have known bright and decent managers who, in trying to explain why things go wrong in their organizations, will resort to explanations like, "Well, you *know* what kind of people would take a job like *this!*" or "At this time of night, you don't expect to get the *best* people." or "Let's face it; if they could do any better, they wouldn't be *here.*" These are familiar themes to most people. As an amalgam of prophecies of pessimism and presumptions of uniqueness, they reflect the belief that a context for competence is just not appropriate in a lot of instances.

I wonder what such managers would say if they were privy to the aspirations of those they manage, if they knew the conditions desired by the people they describe? I wonder if low performance would, in their minds, still call for stricter management and fewer conditions of competence?

Performance and the Competence Ideal

Mindful that many of the conditions of work which prevail in an organization are beyond the control of those who must do the work, in collecting our survey data we asked people to describe those conditions which they would most *prefer* to characterize their workplaces. People were given free rein in doing this; they could opt for existing conditions, conditions less competent than those currently in effect, or conditions more in accord with a context for competence.

Information about the conditions people would prefer to characterize their places of work bears on several issues simultaneously. For example, it strikes at the core issue of the competence process: a belief that people *want* to perform competently, to do their best and, so doing, to gain feelings of efficacy and self-worth. The viability of the competence motive is revealed in the conditions of work people desire for themselves and others.

By the same token, insight into preferred conditions has implications for the general applicability of the competence process and the notion that people in unproductive organizations are somehow different, that poor performance requires conditions other than those associated with competence. And, finally, preferred conditions—when compared with existing conditions—may tell us something about the productive outlook of people, the degree to which they can realistically anticipate that the prospects for doing their best and attaining the rewards of competent performance are good. The compromises people feel forced to make by prevailing conditions may best be appreciated in the light of those conditions which would free them up, those they would deem ideal. The difference between "what is" and "what ought to be" directly affects one's productive orientation; the greater the discrepancy, the greater the implied compromise and the less hopeful and productive one's outlook will be.

So, in many respects, data about preferred conditions are just as germane to the goals of the competence process and the issue of productivity as are data about existing conditions. We found that people had clear-cut views on the conditions which should characterize their organizations. And we found that people are ready for competence, irrespective of organizational type or current level of organizational performance.

The people in our study categorically desired conditions for greater competence in their work settings. People desired an improvement of conditions of such a magnitude as to be expected by chance fewer than one out of 10,000 times.[7] The data clearly show that people in general, irrespective of type of organizational work, aspire to a *competence ideal.* In Figure 3 are portrayed the competence ideals desired by members of low and high performing organizations.

A readiness for greater competence is clear in the competence ideals of both groups. High and low performers do not differ significantly in the level of conditions they desire. In fact, those who would claim that unproductive people are "different" or that performance crises are not amenable to the competence process will find little support for their views in these data. Indeed, the competence ideals so clearly depicted for low and high performers alike reaffirm the uniformity of the competence motive in the

---

[7] See Table III of the Statistical Appendix for a summary of the data analysis for actual and ideal scores.

workplace and underscore the basic premise that poor performance is rooted in a managerial blocking of the expression of individual competence.

The data are consistent with the belief that people work in order to be healthy; the competence ideal reveals that they are consciously aware of those conditions which would best serve the cause of health. And implicit in each

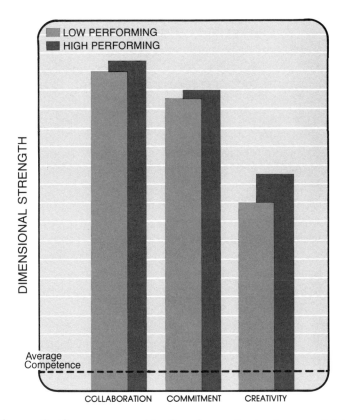

Figure 3. Competence ideals of people in low and high performing organizations.

conscious ideal is a potential for disappointment, a benchmark for measuring how well a given organization affords people the means to health in the workplace. Herein may be found the elusive link between productivity and morale.

Productivity and Morale: Signs of Health in the Workplace

Productivity and morale are the perennial problems of organizational life. As managerial concerns, they vie for equal attention because trouble in one area is usually accompanied by difficulties in the other. It seems that they should be related to one another in some understandable and direct way. But this is seldom the case. Both managers and theorists have tried to force a marriage between performance and morale, but the relationship has been tenuous at best.[8,9] There was a time when both groups believed that happy people were productive people. But all of us have known harmonious fun-filled workplaces that are minimaly productive and, by the same token, some highly productive organizations in which drudgery and hostility prevail.

The notion that happiness is a requisite of productivity has pretty well been discarded as we have come to know more about the issues involved.[10] More recently, as they have begun to pay attention to mental health factors in the workplace, some managers and theorists have reversed the logic: productive people are happy people, they say. But this

---

[8] Brayfield, H. H. & W. H. Crockett. "Employee Attitudes and Employee Performance." *Psychological Bulletin*," 52, 1955, *pp. 396-424.*

[9] *Vroom, V. Work and Motivation.* New York: Wiley, 1964.

[10] Likert, R. *New Patterns of Management.* New York: McGraw-Hill, 1961.

notion also misses the mark and, indeed, finds only sporadic support in either research or actual practice. In the present research, for example, we found that people in productive organizations differ from those in less productive units only in the greater feelings of pride which they report. Simply being more productive than one's co-workers or people in another department is not enough to account for the dynamics of morale.

And yet, managers and workers alike are justifiably concerned about the issue of morale. Morale factors influence the quality of life in the workplace and, very likely, outside the workplace as well. In addition, more often than not, the symptoms of poor morale impinge on productivity and the organization's capability to function. Absenteeism, labor grievances, waste, pilferage, and poor quality—all signs of unrest and low morale—certainly affect how well people do what needs to be done. We can agree that morale is important; as managers, however, we need to *understand* morale so that we can do something constructive about it and avoid the tremendous human and economic toll poor morale exacts.

Part of the difficulty in managing morale competently stems from the way we have tended to think about it. We have been inclined to equate morale with happiness versus unhappiness, with satisfaction versus dissatisfaction, with loyalty versus disloyalty, or with productivity versus its lack. Such factors are but indicators; they are but reflections of a more fundamental consideration: the essential health and related emotional overtone of the workplace.

Competence and Health:
A Different View of Morale

William Glasser, M.D., a noted psychiatrist and author, has described the healthy person as one who is *involved* with others, *committed* to a personally meaningful set of standards and course of conduct, and *working* at tasks whose accomplishment will yield feelings of personal worth and self-respect.[11] As criteria of health, these characteristics are much more closely related to the conditions of competence than to productivity per se. Indeed, given Glasser's observation, the dimensions making up the competence process may well be taken as conditions of health which, in turn, influence both productivity and morale. It may be that many of us have assumed a relationship between productivity and morale not because they each vary as a function of the other but because they *both* vary as a function of the prevailing context for competence.

If people work in order to be healthy as we have maintained, actual achievement of health—and the consequent level of what we have typically called morale—will vary as a function of the conditions of work which characterize the organization. We have already seen that productivity varies as conditions for competence vary; it may be that the same realtionship holds true for the emotional complexities which make up morale and reflect health in the workplace.

Within organizations productivity is a *relative* characteristic; some parts function better than others, usually as a result of prevailing conditions. But the organization as a whole may or may not afford a context sufficient for good

---

[11] Glasser, W. *Reality Therapy.* New York: Harper & Row, 1965.

health and high morale, even in its relatively more productive segments. Evidence of this fact may be found in the Figure 1 depiction of low and high performing units from seven totally different organizations. Closer scrutiny will reveal that, while high performers *within* organizations are characterized by relatively more conditions for competence, there are substantial differences in conditions *between* organizations—so much so that the high performing units in some organizations have fewer of the supports for competence than do the low performing units in different organizations.

If our thesis is correct that health—whether it is defined as morale, satisfaction, or happiness—will vary as conditions for competence vary, we should find greater differences between the emotional tones of different organizations, irrespective of performance, than we found between just low and high performing groups per se. As part of our research strategy we decided to test for this possibility. We included a survey of the emotional tone of the workplace, a very dependable six-item questionnaire entitled *Personal Reaction Index.*[12,13] *PRI* data were available for 390 subjects in seven of the nine organizations—all except the school system and the government agency. As an index of those sentiments which we equate with health and positive productive orientation—involvement, satisfaction, responsibility, commitment, frustration, and pride—the index has been found to be a good measure of subordinate reactions

---

[12] Hall, J. *Personal Reaction Index.* The Woodlands, Texas: Teleometrics Int'l., 1974, 1980.

[13] Reliability, as determined by Cronbach's Alpha, was found to be .81 with 255 people. This result was cross-validated with a second sample of 203 people in which Alpha was found to be .80.

to the interpersonal practices of managers,[14] to their overall managerial style,[15] and a good index of the level of achievement attained by managers.[16] For our purposes of relating health and emotional tone to organizational conditions, subordinate reports from the *PRI* are particularly pertinent to the issues of concern.

When we compared subordinate reports between organizations we found that conditions, not relative performance, were the major determinants of feelings of competence and health.[17] As the competence profiles in Figure 1 would lead us to expect, there were such vast differences between the emotional tones of organizations that they could be expected less than one time out of 10,000 by chance alone. In general, *the more supports to competence found in an organization the more positive and healthy the emotional tone of the organization was found to be.*

From a practical standpoint this finding means that the stockclerks, checkout personnel, cooks, waiters, and electronic data processors in our study are experiencing lower commitment and greater frustration, for example, than are the sales people, R & D engineers, and manufacturing personnel. Not because they are cooks and stockclerks, or engineers and manufacturers, but because of the conditions characteriz-

---

[14] Hall, J. "Communication Revisited: Interpersonal Style and Corporate Climate." In J. S. Shtogren (Ed.), *Models for Management: The Structure of Competence.* The Woodlands, Texas: Teleometrics, Int'l., 1980.

[15] Hall, J. "Management Synthesis: An Anatomy of Managerial Style." In J. A. Shtogren (Ed.), *op. cit.*

[16] Hall, J. & S. M. Donnell. "Managerial Achievement: The Personal Side of Behavioral Theory." *Human Relations,* Vol. 32, No. 1, 1979, pp. 77-101.

[17] See Table IV of the Statistical Appendix for a summary of the data analysis for this study.

ing their organizations. It appears that, irrespective of relative performance and regardless of the fact that they might share the same competence ideals, people working under fewer conditions for competence garner fewer of the emotional rewards of work than people in organizations where the expression of competence is encouraged. This cursory result suggests that both healthy and unhealthy outlooks among people—both good and poor morale—may be tied to *opportunities* for competent performance rather than to actual performance per se. Opportunities for competent performance translate as conditions for competence. This leads to a testable hypothesis: morale factors—as revealed in those positive feelings characterizing a healthy productive orientation—vary directly as conditions for competence vary.

Predicting Healthy Productive Orientation: Feelings of Involvement, Commitment and Pride

As an initial test of the idea that one's feelings and productive orientation vary as conditions for competence more or less characterize the workplace, we tried to predict subordinates' feelings of involvement, commitment, and pride on the basis of their collaboration, commitment and creativity reports from the *Organizational Competence Index*. Essentially the research rationale was that, if the work-health-morale premise was viable, knowing something about the nature of prevailing conditions should tell us something about the likely level of morale among people. We set the data up in a predictive model for analysis; each person's *OCI* scores were used to predict his or her *PRI* scores.

We found that levels of collaboration, commitment and

creativity had a direct bearing on feelings of involvement, commitment and pride. *The greater the conditions for competence ascribed to their organizations, the more involved, committed, and proud people described themselves as feeling.* The strength of the positive relationship between conditions for competence and a healthy productive orientation was great enough to be expected by chance fewer than one out of 10,000 times.[18] The implication for managers is that they influence morale, for good or ill, by the conditions they provide. We conducted a second analysis to verify this implication.

Because of differences in competence supports between and within organizations, we wanted a more straightforward test of the notion that morale factors vary as conditions for competence vary. To test more directly the effect of competence conditions on morale factors we needed a "pure" case design. We therefore decided to work with a sub-sample of the 390 people studied in all and addressed ourselves only to those 253 individuals who uniformly reported either (1) few conditions in support of collaboration, commitment and creativity, (2) moderate levels of each, or (3) strong supports for each. After grouping people on the basis of these reports into a Low, Moderate, or High Competence group we then looked at their reported feelings of involvement, commitment, and pride from the *Personal Reaction Index.*

Our findings are portrayed in Figure 4. In all cases, highly significant differences were found to exist between involvement, commitment, and pride scores as a function of differences in competence levels. Results from this approach

---

[18] See Table V of the Statistical Appendix for a summary of the canonical analysis of data for this study.

served to reaffirm the strong influence competence conditions have on basic productive orientation.[19]

Now, in terms of their practical implications for employee
morale, these findings may be summarized rather simply.
Managers may, through their policies and practices, influence
for the better the overall emotional tone of the workplace
by insuring the conditions for competence. Put differently,
managers may directly influence morale factors simply by
taking steps originally intended to increase their organization's productivity, so long as they keep in mind that both
are related to health. We have the prospects for a managerial
bonanza! By upgrading the conditions for collaboration,
commitment and creativity, managers do a unique service
for those they manage and the organization as a whole by
working for both better productivity and higher morale
through better health in the workplace.

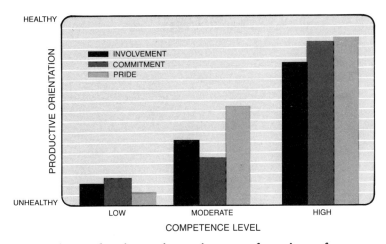

Figure 4. Productive orientation as a function of competence supports.

[19] See Table VI of the Statistical Appendix for a summary of this data analysis.

Predicting Unhealthy Productive Orientation: Feelings of Alienation, Dissatisfaction and Frustration

The alternative to good morale born of health is poor morale born of illness. Low morale, that dysfunctional array of feelings and resentments, dissatisfaction and frustration that mark unhealthy productive orientation among people, was addressed as well. Frederick Herzberg has cautioned us that dissatisfaction is not just the opposite of satisfaction; it is a distinct emotional state in its own right and, along with frustration, may be traced to deficits in the work setting.[20] Our work-health view is consistent with that of Herzberg's in that we approach dynamics of frustration and dissatisfaction as *discrepancy* phenomena: that is, as being linked to the difference and inherent conflict between "what is" and "what might be" insofar as competence dimensions are concerned.

The implications of this view of health in the workplace give new meaning to the idea of "low morale." As a symptom of impaired productive outlook and negative feelings based in discrepancies between actual and preferred conditions, poor morale in the workplace shares many of the characteristics of the clinical illness known as *reactive depression.* As a painful and debilitating reaction to a sense of personal loss, reactive depression is situationally induced. Loss or deprivation of environmental supports can trigger feelings of hopelessness, despair, anger, lack of control, and little self-worth. Usually of a temporary nature, if prolonged by continued loss and deprivation, these feelings eventually take on neurotic overtones, or worse. To the extent that we as managers deprive or take away the

[20] Herzberg, F. *Work and the Nature of Man.* Cleveland: World Press, 1966.

conditions for competence—which we are not equating with conditions for health—it may be that we do much more than encourage low morale. We may actually promote illness—depression, alienation, and despair—in the workplace.

This trend of thought would lead us to predict that, given a person's need to be competent, the greater the discrepancy between existing competence levels and the *desired* level, the more frustrated and thwarted one's competence needs become. If, in our organizations, we place limits on the capacities of people to interact effectively with their work environments—if we block their opportunities for learning and behaving competently—we deny them their *feelings of efficacy*. So doing, we sow the seeds for those very frustrations and dissatisfactions—the predilections for illness—which come back to haunt us as absenteeism, turnover, wastage, labor grievances, and poor performance.

To test this notion we focused on the magnitude of discrepancies between reported levels of collaboration, commitment, and creativity and those levels desired by people. Using the resulting Actual vs. Desired discrepancy scores for the three competence dimensions, we found substantial support for the thesis that poor morale is traceable to a sense of loss, to the degree that "what is" differs from "what might be." *The greater the discrepancy between existing levels of competence conditions and the levels desired, the greater the feelings of both frustration and dissatisfaction among people.* Once again, these results could be expected by chance alone less than one out of 10,000 times.[21] But as in the past, we desired a more straightforward test of such a provocative result.

---

[21] See Table VII of the Statistical Appendix for a summary of the canonical analysis of these data.

To provide a "pure" case test of the premise that Actual-Desired discrepancies exert major influence on morale, particularly as deprivation-like constraints on health, we again worked with a sub-sample of people. We selected for study four groups of people: those 25% with the smallest Actual-Desired discrepancy scores on collaboration, commitment and creativity and those falling in the next three quartiles. Using this procedure we were able to compare the growth or decline of satisfaction and frustration as a function of four broad levels of Actual-Desired discrepancy.

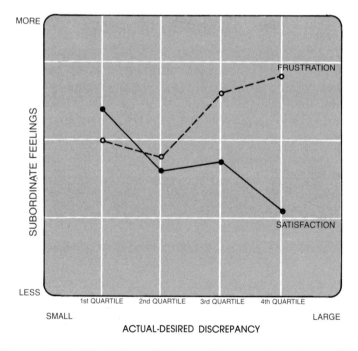

Figure 5. Satisfaction and frustration as a function of the Actual-Desired discrepancies of competence supports.

Our results are portrayed in Figure 5. The relationship of both satisfaction and frustration to deficits in the workplace can be clearly seen. When the discrepancy is small between "what is" and "what might be" in the way of supports for collaboration, commitment, and creativity, satisfaction is the dominant feature of the workplace. Some frustration is present, as it likely always will be, but it plays a minor role. But as we move just to the next quartile—to people reporting only slightly larger discrepancies— frustration moderates and satisfaction decreases. Frustration begins to become the dominant emotional theme in the workplace. This trend continues through the fourth quartile, to people reporting substantial Actual-Desired differences, until frustration combines with dissatisfaction to characterize the workplace. These data, with differences again greater than chance by a 10,000 to one margin,[22] dramatically capture the volatility of morale factors and their sensitivity to a managerial blocking of competence needs.

Managerial practices affect health; the evidence is clear. In their report on work in America, the Special Task Force to the Secretary of Health, Education and Welfare reported that, in several studies of aging in several different cultures, the strongest predictor of longevity was work satisfaction.[23] In a similar vein, heart disease has been linked to such work-related risk factors as job dissatisfaction, low self-esteem, occupational stress, and several other deficits in the work environment. Mental health problems—alcoholism, drug abuse, suicide and delinquency, to name a few—are traceable in part to one's work situation. Arthur Kornhouser has

[22] See Table VIII of the Statistical Appendix for the summary of the data analysis for this study.

[23] *Work in America*, Special Task Force to the Secretary of Health, Education and Welfare. Cambridge: The M. I. T. Press, 1973.

summed up the same work-health dilemma as portrayed in our Actual vs. Desired data thusly:

> . . . Poorer mental health occurs whenever conditions of work and life lead to continuing frustration by failing to offer means for perceived progress toward attainment of strongly desired goals which have become indispensable elements of the individual's self-identity as a worthwhile person. Persistent failure and frustration bring lowered self-esteem and dissatisfaction with life, often accompanied by anxieties, social alienation and withdrawal, a narrowing of goals and curtailing of aspirations—in short . . . poor mental health.[24]

Kornhauser might well have been describing the consequences of frustrated competence and serving notice to managers of the enormity of their responsibilities.

So it is that the conditions for competence which managers create account substantially for performance and health in our organizations. According to the data, conditions for competence do double duty: They serve both health and productivity at the same time.

When we consider the enormous costs associated with low productivity and illness in the workplace, the dual role of the competence process takes on added significance. By

[24] Kornhauser, A. *Mental Health of the Industrial Worker.* New York: Wiley Press, 1965.

comparison with the costs of various programs used over the years to upgrade morale and the variety of attempts to increase production by retooling, automating, motivating and the like, the competence process is virtually free. As a social technology of productive relationships and health on the job, the competence process requires no new machinery or personnel—no expansion or reduction of either technical or intellectual resources. It requires only that managers begin to manage as though competence were a fact of organizational life.

If Peter Drucker is correct, managers might be well advised to begin the competence process now. In a 1977 interview, Drucker made this sobering observation:

> If you ask me what major objective I would set for any business I know of today, it would be: It must be able, five or eight or ten years from now, to do twice the amount of actual business it does now without a penny of additional capital and without a single additional employee . . . in other words, be able to increase the productivity of the money it has now—actually, double it—and (sic) must double the productivity of the people it has now. I think this is absolutely essential.[25]

Our data indicate that Drucker's objectives are not only realistic but, as he himself observed, already being met to varying degrees within some organizations. The more productive organizations in our research were not spending more money or relying on more people than their unproductive counterparts. Managers were simply managing different-

---

[25] "A Candid Talk about Training with 'The Man Who Invented the Corporate Society.'" *Training HRD.* October, 1977.

ly. They were attending to the conditions for competence.

As the organization's recognized decision makers and formulators of policy, managers may be said to control the costs of productivity and personnel because they control the expression of competence and the conditions of health that characterize their organizations. This fact points to the all important issue of managerial choice: managers may choose the direction their organizations will pursue. They may choose excellence or mediocrity, health or illness, growth or stagnation. Given the significance levels of our tests of the competence process, they may now make their choices with increased confidence in the outcome. Such is the purpose of the validation process.

IX

Principles of Competence

Performance and morale vary in organizations as conditions for competence vary. The competence process does double duty. The data are clear on this point. From a purely empirical point of view, support for the basic premise of competence seems ample.

We could have stopped our investigation of the competence process at the point when confirming data were well in hand. But had we done so, we would have overlooked some important characteristics of high performing, productive organizations that managers might find helpful as operational guidelines in setting the competence process in motion.

Roughly speaking, there are two general kinds of research in the social sciences. On the one hand, there is the highly-controlled *experimental* study (with its many variations) which is used to test specific hypotheses and predictions, or to compare the effects of different treatments or different conditions. For example, our use of matched groups from different organizations in comparing productive with unproductive units on the dimensions of competence illustrates this general approach. On the other hand, there is an approach to research in which controls are minimal and which is less stringent in many respects—but which may be more revealing and intriguing. There are neither hypotheses to be tested nor, necessarily, any planned comparisons to be made. Such an approach may be termed *exploratory* research and is simply a search for relationships among factors of interest—sometimes anticipated and sometimes not—which might shed additional light on previous results or point the way to new directions research efforts should take.

In seeking to refine the competence process, we adopted an exploratory posture. In addition to our sleuthing, strategic planning, public relations work and tactical operations, we embarked on what might be thought of as a fishing expedition. We recombined all the information we had from people about the dimensions of competence in their organization; we lumped all the data together irrespective of organizational type or level of performance. We then dipped into this data pool to see what might surface.

This assumption-free approach yielded evidence of three noteworthy relationships which we were then able to test in greater depth. So provocative were their implications, particularly as ground rules for setting the competence process in motion, that we adopted our findings as operational guidelines for managers contemplating the process and accorded all three the status of *Principles of Competence.*

The Principle of Isodynamic Balance: Competence Requires an Equality Among Forces

The first operating principle was suggested during our initial testing of the competence process. It may be recalled that, while comparing low and high performing organizations on the dimensions of competence, we took steps to control for differences between organizations. We did this by addressing ourselves only to the differences in competence dimensions between low and high performers in each organization; the effect was to minimize differences *between* organizations and highlight performance differences *within* organizations.

But the results of this analysis, in addition to confirming the prediction of interest at the time, also gave evidence of an unanticipated effect: *high performing organizations appear to be characterized by an equality of force among the dimensions of collaboration, commitment and creativity.* Although such a characteristic is certainly consistent with our Chapter VII depiction of the competence process as a fabric held together by values having vertical integrity and a system of lateral logic, there is no theoretical or statistical rationale for the finding that *dynamic balance* is a definitive feature of productive organizations.

The original premise of competence, stated simply, was that the more supporting conditions for the expression of competence in an organization, the more productive that organization would be. However, when we controlled for organizational differences, we found that the original premise was not stringent enough. For optimal competence, a condition of isodynamic balance must prevail.

Isodynamic versus Static Balance

Taken literally, the term isodynamic means "characterized by an equality of magnitude among forces." There are two practical implications of the fact that productive organizations are characterized by isodynamic effects. Certainly, as James North made clear in Chapter III in his depiction of life in a government organization, prevailing conditions act like forces on individual workers. They pressure, prod, channel, direct, inhibit and prevent; they exert tremendous influence on both the behaviors and feelings that characterize the workplace. Conditions for collaboration, commitment and creativity qualify as bona fide forces in the same sense of the word.

The unexpected finding that an equality of magnitude among the forces of collaboration, commitment and creativity is a definitive characteristic of more productive organizations means that managers must give all three dimensions *equal* attention. Put differently as an operational guideline, managers must consciously plan for and provide just as many supports for commitment and creativity, for example, as they do for the dimension of collaboration. Given the recent fascination with Japanese-style management—complete with quality control circles and employee involvement programs—and the consequent re-discovery of participative management, this finding has important implications for managers. Becoming "participative" is not enough. They must purposefully work for a system of influences which is both *balanced* and *dynamic.* The fact that people have opportunities to collaborate does not necessarily insure that they can use their own judgment at the work point, spend time on relevant tasks, or find fun and stimulation in their workplace. All three dimensions require explicit attention from management.

It is possible to achieve balance among support conditions without necessarily achieving a dynamic system. A dynamic system is one in which forces are characterized by continuous movement, increase and expansion; such forces are indicative of the energy level of the organizational system. On the other hand, the forces in an organization may be static albeit in balance. When collaboration, commitment and creativity forces are characterized by a state of static balance, the system of influences on work and morale is characterized by a lack of movement, little animation or progression. According to one definition particularly appropos to present purposes, a static system "exerts force by reason of weight alone without motion." An organization heavy with procedures and prohibitions, oppressive managerial practices, and constrained by short-sighted priorities must use all its energy in simply maintaining itself. Little is left for the doing of meaningful work.

Both the supply and channeling of energies in a static system are substantially different from those in a dynamic system. And it is not surprising that productive organizations in our study are essentially isodynamically balanced while their less productive counterparts are static and, more often than not, characterized by imbalance. Again, managers are the key factor: If they work to create conditions which expand and push outward, they serve the expression of competence; if managers work to create or maintain conditions which press inward and constrain, they promote stress and prevent the expression of competence. In either event, the result of managerial practices will be revealed in organizational performance. This fact affords us a simple diagnostic device for portraying the performance potential of our organizations in terms of isodynamic effects.

Portraying Competence Graphically

Whether an organization is characterized by movement, increases, and an expansion of its energies or by "weight," lack of movement, animation or progression has obvious implications for its adaptive fitness. Adaptivity, by definition, demands both useable energy and a readiness for action, neither of which is likely under static conditions. For this reason, for the sake of long term survival, it should be helpful to managers to be able to gauge quickly and easily the amount of dynamic balance characterizing their organizations.

The principal of isodynamic balance leads to a quick assessment of competence. The isodynamic state characterizing optimal competence might be portrayed graphically as an equilateral triangle: representing, in effect, the adaptive energy field of the organization; such a plot is determined by the organization's three forces of collaboration, commitment and creativity, and takes on a three-sided character in which each side is defined by one of the competence forces. As the three forces become more nearly equal in magnitude —more isodynamic—the triangular field will become more equilateral. Therefore, in graphic terms, the isodynamically competent organization could be plotted as a large equal-sided triangle while the less competent organization would plot either as smaller, as a scalene—a non-isodynamic triangle with one or two shorter sides denoting impaired forces—or as both. Such a technique affords an easy and quick depiction of an organization's overall potential for the expression of competence.

In Figure 1 we have plotted the profiles of our high and low performing organizations from Chapter VIII. As may be seen, when we plot the average collaboration, commitment and creativity scores achieved by nine high-performing organizations, an essentially equilateral, isodynamically balanced plot results. By way of comparison, the scores for the nine low-performing organizations not only reveal lower magnitudes on the dimensions of competence but plot as a non-isodynamic scalene triangle.

As an operational guideline, the principle of isodynamic balance calls attention to the fact that managers cannot ignore any facet of the competence process if they expect to achieve high levels of competence within their organizations. Operationally, the isodynamic principle suggests that managers may *not* assume that commitment will become manifest simply because collaboration requirements have been satisfied. Nor, by the same token, may they assume that people will behave creatively simply because there are good supports for commitment. The forces of collaboration, commitment and creativity must be managed in such a way as to maintain a dynamic balance among them. That is, for every increment of collaboration added there should be an

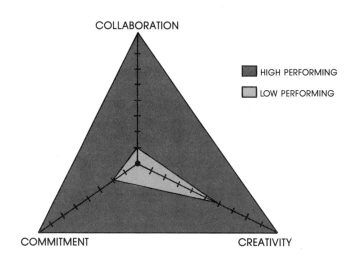

Figure 1. A comparison of the balance among competence dimensions of low and high performing organizations.

increment of commitment support added and, in turn, an increment supportive of creativity.

Managers must give simultaneous attention to all three forces and consciously plan for the maintenance of an isodynamic balance if widespread competence is to be achieved. It is clear that isodynamic balance is related to performance. Violations of the principle, we found, are also related to morale.

The Isodynamic Principle and Productive Orientation

Collaboration, commitment and creativity are *psychosocial* forces; that is, they are factors which influence how individuals *perceive* the organization, how they *feel* about their roles in the workplace and, moreover, how they will *interact* with both the organization and one another. Given the psychosocial significance of our competence dimensions, we might expect the effects of either isodynamic balance or the various forms of non-isodynamic imbalance among forces to be especially evident in morale data. People should, if the principle is valid, *feel* differently under balanced as opposed to imbalanced conditions; their productive orientations should become more positive the more closely prevailing conditions approximate an isodynamic state.

To test this notion, we again went fishing. We dipped into the data pool and located the competence data of some 253 individuals who, irrespective of actual organization or performance level, reported different combinations of collaboration, commitment and creativity. From these data we "created" different organizational groupings, each reflecting a different mix and balance state among reported levels of collaboration, commitment and creativity. This allowed us to pursue a "pure" case analysis like those reported in Chapter VIII.

In this instance, we wanted to study the effects on productive orientation of prototypical organizations characterized by different forms of imbalance. We constructed eight groupings: one group characterized by high scores on all three dimensions, another by low scores on all three, three groups low on one dimension but high on the remaining two, and three groups high on a single dimension but low on the two remaining forces. Having grouped our data into eight organizational prototypes, we were then able to look at the morale factors likely to be associated with such organizational conditions. We compared the *Personal Reaction Index* reports of people from the eight different prototype organizations.

When we analyzed people's *PRI* data in this light, we discovered that the differences in productive orientation accruing from differences in balance among competence forces were of such magnitude as to be expected by chance fewer than one out of 10,000 times.[1] Two effects associated with balance-imbalance were isolated by our analysis, each with important implications for managing the competence process. Of the two dimensions found to discriminate among organizational prototypes, the first was essentially a productive orientation dimension, with which we are already familiar. The second was a bipolar index of feelings of *complacency vs. anxious accountability*. Depending on the state of balance or imbalance characterizing an organization, people may experience either a sense of complacency or of frustrated responsibility in their work; this along with

[1] See Table X in the Statistical Appendix for a summary of this analysis.

a given productive outlook. As the data portrayed in Figure 2 reveal, both one's productive orientation and complacency-accountability vary as a function of (1) *amount* of balance-imbalance among the forces of collaboration, commitment and creativity and (2) the *type* of balance-imbalance created by different combinations of forces.

Figure 2. **Differences in productive orientation as a function of differences in balance among competence dimensions.**

In Figure 2 we are first interested in the productive orientation dimension and at what point along the dimension our various organizational prototypes fall. In creating each prototype, we looked for forces falling above and below the grand mean for each dimension of competence. This "average competence" cutoff served as a competence threshold; that is, as the point above or below which a force might be considered to serve competence or not.

Conditions for collaboration, commitment and creativity are designated respectively as 1, 2 or 3—their order in the competence process as developed. Each of the organizations has been identified according to the particular force or forces which are above the competence threshold and, therefore, most operative; low, below threshold, forces are designated by zeros. We can readily see from the plotted results that organizations in which all three forces are below threshold—group 000—are characterized by unhealthy productive orientations while isodynamically competent organizations—group 123—are characterized by the most healthy observed levels of productive orientation. We can see that productive outlook becomes healthier as systems become more isodynamic; that is, as the number of strong operative forces increases so does the overall health of one's outlook.

At the same time we can see that some dysfunctional effects on morale are associated with the *particular* forces that are more or less operative. That is, as captured by the vertical complacency-accountability dimension, feelings differ according to the particular forces operating. For example—if we take the midpoint on the complacency-accountability dimension as the desired range—we can see that any time there is an imbalance due entirely or in part to an over-emphasis of conditions for creativity, feelings of anxious accountability, a sense of frustrated responsibility, are likely to characterize the workplace. Prototypes 003 (where creativity alone receives operational support), 023 (where creativity and commitment are emphasized), and 103 (reflecting collaboration and creativity supports) are all higher than the midpoint on complacency-accountability. Undue emphasis of, that is imbalance due to, creativity prompts anxiety and what appears to be a futile sense of being personally accountable without all the support necessary.

On the other hand, collaborative imbalance—whether due to collaboration forces alone as in prototype 100 or collaboration plus commitment forces as in 120—serves to promote a sense of complacency. These are all potential boomerang effects the manager should be sensitive to in planning for competence. The key to both healthy outlook and a desirable melding of concern for performance and comfort is, of course, to be found in the state of isodynamic balance as portrayed by prototype 123.

These results not only dramatically portray the effects associated with various violations of the Isodynamic Principle, they also confirm that such imbalances can affect morale as well as performance in our organizations. This is an important consideration in planning programs of organizational change. For example, many managers—perhaps prematurely enamored of participative techniques—may find that such practices alone violate the principle of isodynamic balance. The result is an organization like 100 in Figure 2 where productive orientation is essentially unhealthy. In the same vein, we have conducted a survey of the practices of some 484 organizational consultants, only to find that the vast majority are placing major emphasis on conditions for "participation." Consultants, by their own reports, are inclined to violate the balance principle and promote 100-type organizations with their attendant unhealthy productive outlooks.

The manager contemplating the competence process is forewarned by the principle of isodynamic balance. The way managers organize the field of competence forces in their organizations has several implications for how people experience their places of work and consequently feel about both their productivity and themselves. The study summarized in Figure 2 is immensely important to the competence process. Not only do the results provide strong empirical support for the Isodynamic Principle, but they call attention to the potential pitfalls associated with non-isodynamic conditions.

* * *

The Principle of Isodynamic Balance calls attention to important operational requirements in both the achievement and maintenance of widespread competence and to the need for a balanced perspective. We should remind ourselves that the balance we speak of is dynamic—one in which forces are actively operating, above threshold, promoting change of the type required for adapting to changing demands, and ever expanding the energy field of the organization. This contrasts with the static balance which all too often characterizes organizations, where below threshold forces turn inward such that there is no movement or change. While static balance promotes organizational entropy, where the energy invested in the system cannot be taken out and made available for work, our data show that isodynamic balance is a feature of competence and one directly amenable to managerial influence. For this reason, the objective of isodynamic balance is the reigning principle in the achievement of widespread competence. Next we shall consider ways in which this principle may be unwittingly violated by managers.

The Polarity Principle: Forces For and Against Competence

Closer study of the plots in Figure 2 will show that the eight organizational prototypes arrange themselves in three separate "bands" relative to productive orientation. Groups 000, 100, 003 and 020—each with either no or only *one* operative, above threshold, competence force—are clearly associated with the least healthy productive orientations reported by people. Groups with *two* competence forces operating—120, 103 and 023—are associated with healthier, albeit only moderately so, productive orientations. And group 123—the only prototype in which all *three* competence forces are above threshold—is just as clearly associated with the healthiest productive orientation reported. The most straightforward conclusion to be drawn from these data is that healthy productive orientation increases as the number of above threshold conditions in support of competence increases. On the surface, this amounts to a restatement of results already treated at some length in Chapter VIII. But there is a reverse logic implicit but less apparent in the data: productive orientation *decreases* rapidly as the number of *below* threshold conditions increases. This is because *below* threshold forces *oppose* competence.

The issue is one of directionality. And, while the point may be implicit so far in our development of the process, we need to make it explicit as a guide to starting and maintaining the competence process. The "0" forces in our prototype organizations are not so much inoperative as they are forces operating *counter* to the expression of competence. The point is that, in working with competence forces, we are working with *bipolar* influences.

There is a tendency, when talking about forces, magnitudes, and the like, to think in terms of weak vs. strong or low vs. high. So it is that managers might describe their organization as having "strong" creativity forces but as rather "weak" on collaboration, for example. The language is convenient—we have used it ourselves. But such a depiction not only fails to capture the essence of the effects noted in Figure 1, it serves to obscure an important feature of competence forces. In dealing with those conditions which underlie the achievement of competence, we are concerned with *polarities:* at some point, going down a hypothetical scale of magnitude, a given competence force ceases to exert simply a *weak positive* influence on competence and comes, instead, to exert a *negative* influence, actually to *oppose* the achievement of competence.

The opposite of a strong force for competence is not a weak zero force for competence but a *strong force against competence.* The opposite of conditions in *support* of collaboration are conditions which *prohibit* collaboration. In the absence of forces *for* commitment, we are likely to find forces *against* commitment; and if supports for creativity seem lacking, we may discover in their stead forces which *suppress* creative enterprise. The Polarity Principle of organizational competence addresses the counterplay among the forces of collaboration, commitment and creativity and their *net* effect on competence.

We can illustrate our point by citing a sample item from the *Organizational Competence Index,* the survey according to which people were asked to describe conditions—both Actual and Desired—in their workplaces. In Exhibit 1 are three capsule descriptions of conditions bearing on collaboration. People are able to characterize their organizations in terms of a single description alone or as some combination of elements from all three. Capsule A is clearly collaborative; described are practices and policies which encourage the involvement of people in making work-related decisions. Capsule B is less straightforward; described are practices and values which are pseudo-collaborative, with involvement receiving lip service but few real supports. Capsule C, on the other hand, is not merely noncollaborative, it is proscriptive; it describes conditions which prohibit, indeed punish, involvement. To think of the conditions portrayed in Capsule C as simply "weak" supports to collaboration would not only be to misstate the case, it could lead to a serious diagnostic error. Such conditions *oppose* collaboration; they are the opposite of conditions which support collaboration.

Exhibit 1
Sample item from the Organizational Competence Index.

How do individual managers treat expressions of opinion in your part of the organization?

A	**B**	**C**
Our managers work at creating opportunities for us to express what we are thinking and feeling, encouraging us both to speak up and to help one another do so; not only do managers support us in the process, but they make it a point to open up as well.	Our managers are usually willing to hear what their people have to say and will often take the time to listen when people have ideas or comments; usually managers are good listeners and people feel better for having had a chance to speak their piece.	Individual managers are intolerant of expressions of opinion, suggestions, and the like from their employees; people who volunteer their thoughts have been known to meet with ridicule, reprimand, or to be simply ignored.

AS IT IS ➡ ○ ○ ○ ○   ○ ○ ○ ○   ○ ○ ○ ○

AA A A$_B$ A$_C$ BB B B$_A$ B$_C$ CC C C$_A$ C$_B$

AS I WOULD LIKE IT TO BE ➡ ○ ○ ○ ○   ○ ○ ○ ○   ○ ○ ○ ○

Managers must be mindful of the fact that they are dealing with polarities when they plan conditions for competence. Because, as Chris Argyris has cautioned us, traditional values and practices in organizations tend to run counter to the conditions for competence, managers must be vigilant for signs of counterforces. They may, in the typical organization, take nothing for granted. What is perceived as a weak force for competence will more often than not be a moderate to strong force in opposition to competence. The Polarity Principle encourages the manager to focus on this possibility and, through a polarity analysis, to determine the directionality of prevailing conditions. This may serve to avoid the pitfalls of managerial neglect in planning for competence.

Polarity and Managerial Neglect

The major operational significance of the Polarity Principle lies with the issue of what might be called *managerial neglect.* While there certainly are managers who actively oppose collaboration and openly seek to thwart feelings of community or squelch innovativeness, it has been my experience in talking with managers about their organizations and their personal practices that many of the barriers to competence in organizations are traceable to managerial sins of omission. Neglected and unmanaged forces drift away from competence and take on negative valence. The level of competence when this occurs will be lower than it could be if all forces were positively directed, if conscious provisions were made for operationalizing specific supports for collaboration, commitment and creativity.

It is not enough, if widespread competence is the aim, to emphasize only one or two forces in a positive way; those forces left unattended will likely have negative valence and serve to offset—if not override entirely—the positive benefits accruing from better managed competence forces. Because traditional theory and practice—very likely the organization's very historical roots—encourage negative drift, sporadic or incomplete attention to forces *for* competence will not suffice to wipe out the effects of years of counter competent values and practices. Unmanaged collaboration, commitment and creativity forces can easily become countervalent, negatively accelerated forces in opposition to competence.

The Polarity Principle, therefore, may be stated thusly in three parts: (1) competence forces are bipolar influences; when positive they facilitate the achievement of competence, when negative they oppose the achievement of competence; (2) unattended or neglected forces will, because of historical factors characterizing the organization, tend toward negative drift and serve to cancel out some of the effects of any positive forces present; and (3) the level of attained competence will be a function of the combined strength of positively accelerated forces relative to the combined strength of negatively accelerated forces—of the ratio of positive to negative accelerators.

A Case in Point

We can illustrate the essential message of the Polarity Principle from a case in history. When Al Marrow and Harwood acquired a plant in Puerto Rico and began to introduce participative management practices, the workers began to quit. Interviews revealed that, given their past experiences, workers were shocked and frightened. If management needed *their* ideas, management must not know what it was doing. Better to get out now. Even with sincere supports for worker participation, the historical neglect of employee commitment and creativity—with all its negative drift—was not easily overcome. The data in Chapter VIII tell a similar story. If, rather than describing the 18 organizations in our study as "weak" or "low" on certain forces and "strong" or "high" on others, we characterize them in terms of positive or driving—above threshold—forces and negative or restraining—below threshold—forces for competence, we can reconstitute the data in terms of the Polarity Principle. When we do this a definite pattern emerges pertaining to performance.

In Figure 3 is a graphic summary of a polarity analysis of low and high performing organizations. The influence of different polar combinations on performance is readily apparent. The Polarity Principle, in effect, is adhered to in high performing organizations and violated by low performers. Seven of the nine high-performing organiza-

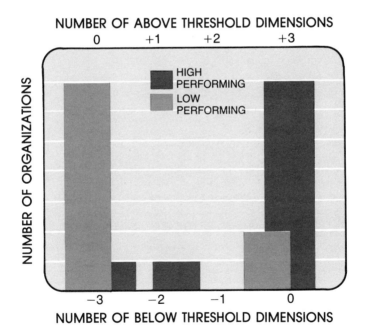

Figure 3. A polarity analysis of low and high performing organizations.

tions—78%—are characterized by above threshold, positively accelerated, forces for collaboration, commitment and creativity. Only two low performers share this distinction while most by far—78%—are characterized by below threshold forces which oppose collaboration, commitment and creativity.

Testing the significance of this pattern of polarities revealed significantly more positive acceleration for high performance than for low performance. These results could be expected by chance alone fewer than one time out of 1,000. We are willing on the basis of such results to conclude that a defining feature of productive organizations is a positively accelerated field of competence forces, while unproductive organizations are characterized by a field of forces which oppose competence.

* * *

In practical terms the Polarity Principle is meant to alert managers to questions such as, for example, how much competence can be expected if a strong program for employee involvement is implemented but nothing is done to insure internal control over operating procedure? Or how beneficial to competence will strong feelings of community and mutual reliance be if no one is open and candid, if harmony and caring are sought at the expense of creative conflict? Or, moreover, what good is relevance if there is no access to the various resources needed for doing one's best work? The Polarity Principle would answer the same in all instances: productive orientation may vary from poor to moderate and net productivity will be less than possible whenever there is negative acceleration, irrespective of the particular conditions or competence dimensions found to be in opposition.

In alerting managers to some competence pitfalls, we are trying to underscore the operational fact that the achievement of competence requires conscious and informed planning, planning based on an understanding of the various ramifications and interdependencies inherent in the process. Perhaps this notion is apparent in the guidelines aimed at maintaining an isodynamic balance; but if it is not self-evident within the context of isodynamic requirements, the Polarity Principle should serve as a reminder.

The competence process, to be successful, requires that nothing be left to chance. Organizational conditions and their role in the competence process require thoughtful management; left unattended or taken for granted those very forces most germane to competence may, because of history and mythology unique to the organization, become countervalent and constitute potent but unapparent barriers to the achievement of competence. Change is difficult and the organization is not a tabula rasa upon which the manager may write without regard for the past. Recognizing the inherent polarities of competence forces and managing in such a way as to promote their positive effects can do much toward avoiding the polarity pitfall.

The Principle of Proper Sequential Management: Collaboration is the Wellspring from which Commitment and Creativity Flow

In both the Principle of Isodynamic Balance and the Polarity Principle, we found performance and morale factors to be intertwined. Adherence to both principles was seen to have salutary effects on both the productivity of the organization and the productive outlook of its people; violations of either principle, on the other hand, were found to be associated with an impairment of performance and morale alike. By way of contrast, our third principle of competence relates primarily to performance.

As we continued our exploration of relationships among competence forces and performance or morale effects, we were repeatedly struck by what seemed to be a salient and somewhat ironic characteristic of low performing organizations: more often than not, conditions for creativity seemed to receive the most emphasis, even in below threshold cases. From a cursory view it looked as if managers were, in effect, *bypassing* both collaboration and commitment—those dimensions primarily concerned with social-emotional, morale-related, factors—and going straight to the task-related issues of the problem-solving process, and the task environment which serve the creativity dimension.

We had already noted that, as discussed in the Principle of Isodynamic Balance and portrayed in Figure 2, an emphasis on creativity at the expense of either collaboration or commitment was detrimental to morale; reports of both anxious accountability and less healthy productive outlooks seemed to be more prevalent when creativity conditions received primary attention. There appeared to be "noise" bearing on both performance and morale which, in turn, was related to *sequencing* effects; that is, performance and morale effects seemed to vary according to the *order* in which the dimensions of competence received attention. When we took a more studious look at the data in this light, we found evidence of our third operating groundrule: the *Principle of Proper Sequential Management.*

PSM: Managing in Sequence

The Principle of Proper Sequential Management—PSM—concerns the *order* in which the dimension of competence must be attended. It is of particular importance while initially setting the competence process in motion; and it addresses the disruptions associated with improper sequencing which are likely to occur before the process is in place, complete with its own kinetic energies. We can't be sure, but early-realized effects may account for Harwood's difficulty in Puerto Rico. Of prime importance, PSM emphasizes that competence is a *process,* a chain of events to be set in motion and managed to fulfillment. It deals with the realm of social relations and feelings and the "mind set" which these can create among people trying to make sense of the organizational environment.

The central theme in the notion of PSM was stated earlier as the foundation of the competence premise . . . *collaboration is the wellspring from which commitment and creativity flow;* and . . . *creativity is an outgrowth of commitment and both, in turn, are by-products of collaboration.* While the notion of sequencing is implicit in these phrases, we had not—quite frankly— thought of the ordering of conditions as a potent consideration. This was because we were caught up in the development of a premise rather than the realities of managerial practices in the workplace. When we looked at the data we had collected, we found evidence that order does indeed matter.

The notion of PSM makes explicit both the need for and nature of proper sequencing: for the achievement of competence—particularly in terms of productivity—management must first create credible conditions for collaboration, then follow up quickly on the unleashed potential for commitment by insuring conditions which allow people to act in accordance with the substantive thrust of collaborative events and, finally, guarantee access to those task and social resources needed to actualize the creative urge triggered by heightened commitment. Thus, in initiating and guiding the competence process, *the proper sequence of managerial emphasis is from collaboration to commitment to creativity.* While, ideally, conditions should probably overlap one another, we found evidence that such an ordering is a characteristic of high performing organizations while mismanagement of sequence characterizes low performers.

Violations of PSM: Short Circuiting or Aborting the Process

Before reporting fully on the relationship of sequencing to performance, we should first touch briefly on the mismanagement of sequencing, on the ways in which PSM may be violated. Mismanagement, improper sequencing, will typically take the form of either *short-circuiting* or *aborting* the competence process. The first instance involves jumping ahead in the process and the second entails failure to complete the process, once initiated.

Short-Circuiting Competence. The most common constraint on competence found in our data has been that of short-circuiting the process; that is, the bypassing of the collaboration phase in favor of an emphasis on creativity or, to a lesser degree, on commitment. Our data show that 87% of the groups reporting improper sequential management, irrespective of organization or level of performance, describe such a short-circuiting of the competence process. Though only speculation, short-circuiting seems to reflect a managerial preoccupation with getting the job done; it is probably an earmark of more traditional values to be found in organizations less attuned to more sensitive and modern philosophies of management. Just the reverse is the case with the second violation of PSM.

Aborting Competence. Less harmful to performance, but of perhaps greater significance for low morale, are practices which abort the competence process. Aborting occurs when collaborative practices are embraced by managers, but nothing is done to insure follow-up. Neither commitment nor creativity supports are provided pursuant to task accomplishment. Again, purely speculatively, we might expect a higher incidence of aborted competence among organizations heavily committed to a "human relations" philosophy, where intentions are good but appreciation of the importance of task completion for healthy productive orientation is lacking. Unless the caveat that collaboration is preparation for *doing* something is remembered, collaborative managers risk aborting the process and sowing the seeds of frustration.

Managing the Process from Start to Finish: Sequencing Effects in Performance

As a test of the implications of improper sequential management, we reviewed the competence dimensions data of the nine high and nine low performing organizations. We reviewed each organization's profile for the conditions for collaboration, commitment and creativity and then assigned it to one of three categories, depending on the nature of its sequence profile. If an organization was characterized by relatively equal supporting conditions for all three competence dimensions, it was assigned to a PSM category, indicating that the competence process was, for all intents and purposes, being managed in the proper sequential manner. If people in an organization reported conditions more supportive of collaboration or of collaboration plus commitment than of creativity, that organization was assigned to an *Aborted* category, indicating that the process was prematurely halted or lacking in supports sufficient to sustain it. Finally, those organizations described as having less support for collaboration than for commitment and/or creativity conditions were assigned to a *Short-Circuited* category, indicating bypassed collaboration and greater emphasis on latter conditions. Our findings are presented in Figure 4.

Figure 4. Patterns of performance and sequencing effects.

When we look at the proportion of organizations in each category which were either high or low performing organizations, a fairly clear picture emerges: 55% of all low performers fall in the Short-Circuited category; Short-Circuiting emerges, as the most grievous violation of the competence process, accounting for more than half of all low performers. High performers, on the other hand, are most characterized by properly sequenced conditions; the people in seven, or 78%, of the nine high-performing organizations report conditions reflecting PSM. Such results might be expected by chance one time out of 100, and we concluded that proper sequential management is a worthy operational guideline for the manager contemplating the competence process.

Finally, we looked for morale effects associated with sequencing. We found only trends, but no significant effects. Proper sequential management, we concluded, relates essentially to performance and productivity and is of prime concern in instituting the process. Once in motion, the competence process takes on its fabric-like quality, but until that time the sequencing of events matters substantially.

Such are the principles—the operational guidelines—of competence. The pursuit of competence requires much of managers. From our data it is clear that managers must undertake to learn about a social technology of the organization—about new values and new practices—and they must reconsider and give new attention to the issues of collaboration, commitment and creativity. Moreover, they must experiment and plan for achieving a proper sequence of these, concentrate on creating positively accelerated conditions to support them while weeding out those which weigh down and create drag, and—all the while—work toward that self-reinforcing process which flows from an equality among forces.

All this constitutes change from one state of competence to a higher one. While the task of effecting change is a hard one, it is not so hard as it might appear. Its apparent difficulty lies in its newness. It helps to remember that those who are managed desire such conditions and such changes. The rest is up to the manager.

Part Three

Choice Points for Competence

X

Managerial Competence: The Essential Choice

We have nearly completed our basic premise; on one hand, it has been shown that both productivity and health in our organizations vary as a function of conditions for collaboration, commitment and creativity; on the other hand, it can now be said that conditions for collaboration, commitment and creativity vary as a function of specific managerial values, beliefs and practices. *This means that organizational competence varies as a function of managerial competence.*

It also means that managers may have work to do. Just as those skills and adaptive capacities leading to personal competence are learned, so must the values, beliefs and practices characterizing managerial competence be acquired through learning. Whatever our current approaches to management might be, they have been *learned*—by trial-and-error, by imitation and emulation, in formal settings or under the eye of a mentor. But, however acquired, the test of our managerial competence is still whether it does what needs to be done; whether it yields productivity and health in the workplace. If our management does not measure up to the test of competence, we have work to do; we must reexamine some of our beliefs and preferred practices.

We have reached a choice point, a point at which each manager must decide whether or not to be a personal force for competence. The solution to organizational problems of productivity and health may require a two-fold change: conditions for collaboration, commitment and creativity must be upgraded but, for the most part, before this can truly be accomplished more competent management must be achieved. Figure 1 portrays the implicit relationship of managerial practices to organizational conditions and, ultimately, to that widespread expression of competence which we equate with productivity. Competent managerial practices lead to the creation of conditions for competence. Productive orientation is enhanced; the prospects for competent performance are reaffirmed. As more widespread expression of competence is achieved, productivity and health are enhanced. And as such practical managerial objectives are better accomplished, competent management is verified, reinforced and—one would hope—encouraged as an organizational norm, such that the cycle repeats itself and becomes self-sustaining.

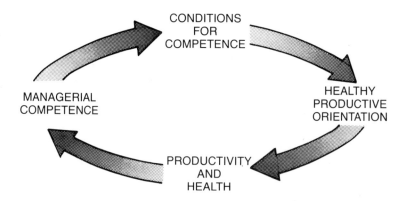

Figure 1. The self-reinforcing cycle of competence.

But first, someone must set such a chain of events in motion. Only the manager is in a position to do this. That is why competent management is so crucial for the success of the competence process and the future of our organizations.

Managerial competence is the essential choice. The individual manager must consciously decide how he or she will administer the process of management. The success of the competence process and all it entails for health and productivity boils down, in the final analysis, to the personal managerial decision to pursue more competent management. Therefore, to complete our premise that managerial competence directly affects the competence of the total organization, we must be definitive about the ingredients of competent management, about the personal values and actions which are most central to the competence process. In light of these, we can begin to appreciate the importance of the managerial and cultural tasks which lie ahead.

The Core Values of Managerial Competence

A commitment to more competent management must begin with an honest examination of one's own values, those emotionally charged beliefs and standards of conduct which underlie one's personal approach to management. Managing, at its core, is an issue of values. Our managerial practices are but reflections of our favorite assumptions about work and our notions about the best pathways to its attainment. Therefore, a change from one level of managerial competence to a greater level of competence may well involve a change in personal values as well. Values are very personal, but most of their effects are interpersonal: what we believe as individuals directly affects how we transact with others. And, while each of us must be free to choose those values which guide our actions, we would hope that our choices will be informed ones—complete with recognition of consequences and awareness of alternative courses—before, as managers, we impose them on others.

A shift in managerial values may require a good deal of work, a readjustment and radically different mindset on the part of managers. Most of the managers I know think of themselves as people who *make* things happen. Their practices are, more often than not, geared to *causing* people to do certain things, behave in particular ways. But, managing for competence entails policies and practices which *allow* something to happen: the emergence and full expression of human competence.

The goal of this chapter is to encourage an awareness of those values characterizing managerial competence so that the manager might make a more informed choice and, if the need is indicated, consider a program of personal change geared to more competent management. The stakes are high. The competence of our organizations—prevailing conditions for collaboration, commitment and creativity—and the productivity and well-being of those who do the organization's work all depend on the manager's choice.

The Essential Four

There are four core values operating in the achievement of managerial competence. Central to the competence process are positive managerial prophecies of competence which guide management practices. In addition, collaborative values of involvement, motivation and interpersonal dynamics serve to define managerial competence. Broadly defined as a set of basic beliefs which are then put into operation via specific managerial practices, each core value characterizing competent management may be thought of as a personal gyroscope which orients the manager in his or her endeavors. Values of competence constitute a guidance system which "corrects" managers when they are off course, and helps them "sense" current and future needs.

As we lay out the core values of competent management according to which collaboration, commitment and creativity vary, we will provide both a reference point for the individual manager to use in assessing personal approaches to management, as well as guideposts to more competent management. Below are presented capsule descriptions of the personal core values and related beliefs and actions necessary for creating organizational conditions for competence. While reading each capsule, the individual manager may compare his or her values and practices with those underlying the competence process by asking: To what extent do *I* subscribe to the values of competence in *my* management of *my* organization; how great is the discrepancy between what *I do* managerially and what *I must do* for competence to become a reality in my organization? In asking such questions, the manager can begin to come to grips with the personal values which underlie and govern one's approach to management. . .and how well these serve the goals of competence.

Core Value:
Positive Prophecies

The more one's management is rooted in an expectation

of competence and an abiding faith in the strength and resilience of people's drive for excellence, the more likely one's management will result in conditions for competence. Basic managerial beliefs and related practices take the following form among competent managers:

Belief

People are capable of doing what needs to be done. They have a *need* to exercise and display personal competence. And they will do so to the extent that competence is valued by management and the necessary supports are afforded. People are adaptive and resilient and, far from having an aversion to work, look to their tasks as opportunities for growth and the means to health and personal worth.

Action

Managerial practices are based on an awareness of the need for self-respect and the fact that people are entitled to pursue it as a condition of work. Practices emphasize excellence and focus on removing barriers to the expression of competence rather than on the prescription of methods or suppression of uniqueness. Collaborative problem solving, shared critique and evaluation, and an equitable distribution of authority characterize overall management.

Core Value: Involvement

The more one values and appreciates others' needs to contribute and employs practices designed to involve people in making work-related decisions, the more competently he or she will manage the conditions for work. Managerial competence reflects the following involvement beliefs and practices:

Belief

Most people put forth their best efforts when they are collaborators in the enterprise before them. When they can see that their needs and objectives are best met by achieving the goals of their organization, most people are willing to give whatever effort is required.

Action

Managerial practices are marked by a recognition that the ego-involvement of employees depends on managerial support. Practices which harness the energies, both physical and psychological, include sharing power, follow-up by management, and sharing of rewards. Such practices encourage involvement and pave the way to commitment.

Core Value:
Meaningful Work and Health

The more a manager appreciates others' needs for personal worth and self-respect, recognizes the work people do as an important means to their self-expression, growth and health, and the more he or she consciously strives to imbue tasks with features that reflect this view, the more the work context will encourage the expression of individual competence. Competent managers subscribe to the following motivational beliefs and practices:

Belief

Most people work at their highest level when they find meaning and challenge in their work. When they are able to derive a sense of personal identity and self-esteem from doing what they do and doing it well, they give more to their tasks and gain more from them. When they enjoy a sense of community, mutual respect and reliance, people will enjoy both greater health and more productive relationships.

Action

The management of employee motivation takes into consideration employee self-esteem, need for growth, and capacities for responding constructively to problem situations. Major managerial emphasis is placed on the social, esteem and growth needs of people in both design and administration of work processes.

Core Value:
Interpersonal Competence

The more conscious the manager is of the effect of social transactions on both the quality and productiveness of working relationships and the more he or she works to set a personal example of open, authentic and collaborative interpersonal practices, the more the workplace will be characterized by mutual reliance, candor, trust, and—in the best sense of the word—fun. Competent managers base their management on the following interpersonal beliefs and practices:

Belief
Most people, to perform at their best level, require opportunities for interchange and comparison with those they work with—superior, co-worker and subordinate. The clarity gained from honest discussion enables people to address their work more directly without apprehensions about failure or internal noises stemming from unexpressed feelings or opinions. Feelings of trust, respect and essentiality among people are strengthened.

Action
Managers take the initiative in establishing the norm for face-to-face relationships. Their practices promote owning up to personal ideas and feelings, sharing them openly with pertinent parties, being receptive to and encouraging others to do the same, such that a cooperative interpersonal climate free of power and bureaucratic constraints prevails.

Few of these values—the beliefs and practices described—are new. Variations on the same general themes have characterized behavioral science treatments of management and organizational theory for the past thirty-plus years. What is different is the context: these are the beliefs and practices which lead to the creation of organizational conditions for competence which, in turn, foster productivity and health in our workplaces. Our premise is that the prime significance of more competent management is that it results in more competent organizations; that is, in a better context for the expression of individual competence. The data bear us out.

Managerial Competence: The Key to Context

In a relatively small but significant study, we have found a positive relationship between managerial beliefs and practices and how much collaboration, commitment and creativity will characterize a given organization. Working with a cross-section of the engineering division of a major U.S. corporation, we asked the 224 subordinates of some 80 managers to do two things: first, we asked that each person complete the *Organizational Competence Index* to provide a measure of existing conditions within his or her organization; next, using the *Managerial Competence Review,*[1,2] we asked that each person describe the actual practices most characteristic of his or her manager. The *OCI,* the primary instrument used in the research reported up to this point, focuses on the organization. The *MCR,* on the other hand, reflects the manager's core values; it is a 60-item survey in which a manager's practices can be characterized in terms of (1) the nature of prevailing managerial beliefs regarding individual competence, (2) salient involvement practices, (3) management of motivational dynamics, and (4) the nature of overall interpersonal transactions. As such, the *MCR* provides an array of information about how a given manager approaches the task of managing and the specific practices found to be most characteristic of that person.

We used the information about the four managerial factors—the core values—to predict the levels of collaboration, commitment and creativity to be found in managers'

---

[1] Hall, J. *Managerial Competence Review.* Material from the seminar *Models II: Choice Points for Competence.* The Woodlands, Texas: Teleometrics Int'l., 1980.

[2] The reliability of the *Managerial Competence Review,* as estimated from the data of 57 individuals, is given by Cronbach's Alpha as .76 to .87 for the five styles measured.

organizations. A single approach to management—one reflecting the greatest reliance on the four core values underlying managerial competence—clearly emerged as the best predictor of organizational conditions in support of collaboration, commitment and creativity. Other practices— most notably those reflecting traditionally honored values such as procedure-bound bureaucratic and control-based autocratic practices—were found to be substantial *negative* predictors of conditions for competence. Overall, the relationship of managers' practices to the contexts for

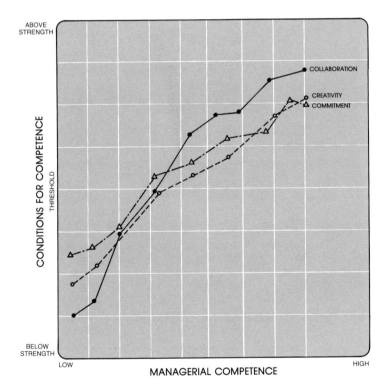

Figure 2. Growth of organizational conditions for competence as a function of individual managerial competence.

competence characterizing their workplaces is of such a magnitude as to be expected by chance fewer than one out of 10,000 times.[3] This finding confirms a major thesis sounded throughout this volume: *the burden for creating a context for the widespread expression of competence falls squarely on the shoulders of the individual manager.*

The results from this study are summarized graphically in Figure 2 so that we can see the dramatic growth which occurs in conditions for collaboration, commitment and creativity as the competence of individual managers increases. Fully operative, above threshold, supports are clearly associated with greater personal competence on the part of individual managers. On the other hand, minimal managerial competence, typically denoting a reliance on more controlling and precedent-bound autocratic-bureaucratic practices, is associated with those below threshold forces noted in Chapter IX; as managerial competence *decreases,* the organizational conditions most likely to characterize the workplace not only fail to serve competence, but actually *oppose* its expression. The message is clear: Managers—through the beliefs they hold, priorities they serve, policies they create, and procedures and practices they employ—determine whether or not their organizations will be places for sustained commitment and creative enterprise. Managerial competence is the key to collective competence.

A Crisis of Values

Taken collectively, considered as a total value system, the beliefs and practices underlying managerial competence

---

[3] See Table XI of the Statistical Appendix for a summary of the data analysis for this study.

reflect standards of empathy and concern for others rather than self-sufficiency; interdependence rather than either independence or dependence; collaboration and cooperative effort rather than competition; involvement and inclusion rather than control, conformity and elitism; candor and caring rather than deceit and indifference; and—above all else—a belief in the importance of work for reasons of health and self-regard rather than only for material comfort or economic advantage. Unfortunately, other research shows that on virtually all counts most managers are defaulting on the means to widespread competence in their organizations.

Earlier, in Chapter III, we pondered a perennial dilemma: why, given the fact of generalized competence, is workmanship sloppy and service poor; why are products shoddy and workers apathetic? Our answer was *management.* By and large, managers do not subscribe to the values, beliefs and practices necessary for competent management. Without such values and such management, it is highly unlikely that our organizations will qualify as contexts for competence. We are faced with a crisis of values.

As opposed to the values inherent in managerial competence, too many managers embrace beliefs and practices to the contrary. As an index of the current state of the art, consider the following data we have gathered about managers vis-a-vis the core values of managerial competence.

• *Positive Prophecies.* While positive prophecies are a core value of managerial competence, in a study of the managerial beliefs of 4,911 managers, we have found that only 16.7% could be characterized as subscribing to positive prophecies of the type required for competence. In another study of style practices among 4,819 managers, a like number—again only 16.7%—reported a clear preference for practices instrumental to widespread competence. *Apparently over 83% of managers today neither believe in the competence of their workers nor employ managerial practices necessary for releasing competence in their organizatons.*

• **Involvement.** While competent managers believe in and practice involvement, in a study of 12,713 subordinate critiques of their managers' involvement practices, we have found only 29.9% to report that they are involved by management in making work-related decisions. *Apparently, managers ignore the involvement needs of roughly 70% of their subordinates and fail to reap any of the salutary effects of collaboration on morale or commitment.*

• **Meaningful Work.** While managerial competence is grounded in an appreciation of meaningful work, in a study of the motivational practices of 7,573 managers, we found that only 18% place average or stronger emphasis on the social, esteem and growth needs of their employees. By contrast, we found in a study of the work motivation of 17,517 employees that social, esteem, or growth needs are of above average importance to 91%, with esteem or growth needs dominating among 78%. *Apparently, managers are mismanaging the motivation of more than 80% of the workforce.*

• **Interpersonal Competence.** While the competent manager is interpersonally competent as well, in a study of the interpersonal practices of 8,377 managers, only 7.6% could be characterized as dealing openly and candidly with their subordinates. Even fewer—3.3%—were found to transact competently with their colleagues and superiors as well. *Apparently, over 90% of managers today fail to deal* *with their co-workers in an interpersonally competent manner.*

The 40,000 managers described in the studies cited represent over 50 different types of organizations—from heavy industry to research and development, from financial institutions to health care facilities and school systems—and probably over 200 organizations in all. They reflect the whole range of organizational hierarchies, from Chief Executive Officer to first line supervisor. There is no reason to suspect that these managers are any different from managers elsewhere. If this is so, we can take these data as information about managers *in general.* And we can readily see that, as managers and workers, we are faced with a crisis of values. By rough estimate, fewer than 20% of managers today are managing in ways which encourage the expression of competence. *The individual worker's pursuit of competence, it seems, must occur in a context ill-prepared for its achievement.* The choice point inherent in a pursuit of competence becomes all the more important: to achieve competence will require, more often than not, a change in the fundamental values and practices of those who lead organizations—of managers themselves.

So it is that we maintain that the burden of competence lies with the individual manager, that conditions for competence and the productive orientation of workers—and hence, ultimate productivity—is a function of how the competence at hand is managed. It is clear that, to the extent unexpressed competence is a problem in organizations today, the responsibility lies not with those who are managed but with those who manage. This need not be the case since counterproductive values and practices can be changed—are being changed daily—because managers themselves aspire to competence. Many are willing to confront their personal values and they are open to new and better ways of managing; they embrace learning as the means to managerial competence.

If there is a commitment to competence, to creating the conditions which will support and vitalize the dimensions of competence within one's organization, then managerial competence will be learned. And, perhaps most important of all, one person—each individual manager—working from the core values of competence can become a force for competence within the organization. Competence within organizations and the solution to perennial problems of production and morale are, in the final analysis, a matter of personal commitment to more responsible and competent management. But the manager's task does not end with a personal commitment. Still more is required for competence to become the definitive feature of the manager's organization and community. Managers must look to their *own* productivity.

XI

The Productive Manager

In a 1981 speech to members of the U. S. Chamber of Commerce, Secretary of Commerce Malcolm Baldrige departed from his prepared text to express a most provocative personal opinion. "This country doesn't need more productive labor," he said. "What we need is more productive managers."[1]

Secretary Baldrige revealed a certain prescience in his ad libbed remarks. The ostensible topic of his speech—addressed to managers—was trade policy in a time of declining productivity and the erosion of the nation's historical competitive advantage. He acknowledged the traditional "solutions" to such problems—new technology, updating of plants and equipment, and capital investment—and then shocked his audience by suggesting that such aids to productivity would do little until such time as management itself became productive.

We now know that Secretary Baldrige was right on target. Many of the solutions he cited in 1981 failed, as he predicted they would, to improve either productivity, the balance of

---

[1] Baldrige, Malcolm. Speech before the Northeast Region of the Chamber of Commerce of the United States, Springfield, Mass., Sept. 30, 1981.

trade, or competitive position. What was needed then as now, it would seem, is a serious look at the extemporized notion of managerial productivity.

If, as Baldrige suggested, the real key to productivity is more productive managers, what must we do to meet the need? The answers are simple and straightforward: We must accept the fact that managers *do not* spend their time productively in "planning, directing, controlling, and coordinating," regardless of what they might have been told in Business Schools. There is more to truly productive management than playing out some armchair theory of managerial functions. Secondly, we must reacquaint ourselves with the often cited, seldom applied, psychology of the workplace. The results of forty years of psychological research have converged on a handful of managerial practices essential for both personal and organizational productivity. And, finally, we must disabuse ourselves of the notion that the task of productive management is simple and effortless. There are no one-minute shortcuts or pragmatic panaceas to excellence. Both productivity and excellence require hard work and an openness to new methods on the part of managers themselves. If we are truly interested in greater productivity and the goals of excellence in both our organizations and our nation, we can begin the quest by *redefining* the job of managers in general.

What Is A Productive Manager?

The generally accepted objective of management is the successful accomplishment of work through other people. Managers do not ordinarily do the work—make the product or provide the service—themselves. How, then, is managerial productivity gauged? What exactly does a productive manager do? These are questions that, more often than not, come up only at performance appraisal time. Historically, we have not done a very good job of answering them. The definition of productive management, however, addresses such questions head on.

The individual productivity of a manager is usually inferred from the performance of those he or she manages. Managers of low performing groups are deemed less than satisfactorily productive; managers of high performing groups are judged productive. Somehow, implicitly, there is a presumption that managers are responsible for the performance of those they manage. And this is as it should be. But, equally germane and less implicit, is the fact that productive managers *manage* differently than do unproductive managers and the performance of those who are managed differs as a result. What is the essential difference?

The key to managerial productivity can be found in the competence process. *A productive manager is one whose beliefs and practices enable and encourage those who are managed to put forth their best efforts,* or put differently, *the productive manager, through his or her own efforts, insures conditions for competence in the workplace.* Because managers represent formal authority—with all its policies and controls—and mediate organizational realities for those without formal authority, they are in significant positions of influence. Through their practices, managers literally set the tone of the workplace and "teach" others what to expect—what is tolerable, what is not; who is respected, who is not; what is rewarded, what is punished; and how much freedom and how much constraint people have in their work. In short, managers *create the conditions for work* in their organizations. Some provide conditions through their personal practices which enable and encourage people to be productive. Some do not. To be a productive manager, one must learn both what the conditions leading to productive enterprise are and which personal practices create and maintain such conditions. If managers truly desire productivity, they must learn how to facilitate and encourage the expression of human competence. But, as we have seen, the process does not begin with a focus on practices and conditions, so much as with a managerial mindset. The release of competence begins with managers who are willing to accept *personal responsibility* for the conditions of work in their organizations.

The Assumption of Responsibility

The pivotal and absolutely essential first step for productive management is a recognition by managers that *they* create—through their policies and practices—the organizational conditions governing work and that they have a choice regarding which will prevail . . . conditions for the full release of competence or conditions for something less. Productive managers choose competence and then take personal responsibility for insuring policies and practices that will facilitate its expression.

While some managers seek ways of ducking personal culpability, truly productive managers know they play a critical causal role in the chain of events leading to competent performance. While some managers fault events and people over which they have little control, productive managers accept full responsibility for the productivity and quality of life in their organizations.

Such tendencies play out in different ways. For example, managers' willingness to accept responsibility will often be revealed in a readiness to base one's practices on the assumption that people are both able and motivated to do what needs to be done. Reluctance, on the other hand, is revealed in a rejection of such notions. Differences in philosophic starting points amount to a variation on the old nature-nurture controversy in which many managers have unwittingly become embroiled over the years. When faced with unproductive, apparently incompetent, workers, some managers conclude that such malfeasance is due to the natural sloth, indolence, and ineptitude of those who work; it is the *nature* of people to avoid work and perform poorly they say, and there is little managers can do beyond insuring controls and punishments. Faced with the same dilemma, other managers conclude that people perform as they do primarily because of environmental influences, because of how they have been trained and developed; such managers fault the *nurturing* process which has fostered sloth, indolence, and ineptitude and are overwhelmed by the difficulties of undoing early influences. In either case, managers find a way to feel little real personal responsibility for performance. The truth lies somewhere in between these two positions and productive managers are blessed with a clearer perspective.

Productive managers recognize that 90 percent of the people seem able to do what needs to be done. They are mindful that this innate competence, quite simply and literally, has been necessary for the survival of the species and that our survival—particularly as punctuated by innovation and progress—is potent evidence of a natural human competence. They believe that most people, as they themselves, *want* to do what needs to be done—i.e., perform competently—because doing so enhances self-esteem and personal feelings of mastery and control. They know from personal experience that people value personal competence because it helps them feel good about themselves. *Productive managers believe that it is the nature of people to perform competently and to value competent performance as a source of important psychological rewards.*

But they also recognize that environment certainly plays a significant role. In organizations the environment consists of intangible factors such as policies, incentive systems, job descriptions, interpersonal practices, allocation of resources, and the like. The way such factors are managed defines for personnel both what is expected of them and what they, in turn, can expect. Those managers who lack a sense of personal responsibility tend to create environments that either discourage competence or prohibit it outright. In such instances, the nurturing process is at odds with the nature of the workforce. Out of frustration, poor performance and low morale result. Productive managers, on the other hand, accept their role in determining conditions and strive to create environments that support and capitalize upon peoples' natural capacity and desire for competent performance. As a result, productive managers primarily differ from their less productive colleagues in their use of managerial policies, practices, and procedures which *nurture the nature* of the workforce. They focus their energies on creating organizational conditions which encourage and enable both the individual and collective expression of competence. If all this sounds too simple, we can take comfort in the fact that it is a testable hypothesis.

A Test of Productive Practices

It is time to move from concept to action, from theory to practice. The competence process has been treated thus far as an exercise in abstractions, in terms of dimensions and conditions, polarities and sequences, and the like. But, at its core, the competence process is a matter of simple observable behaviors, verifiable practices on the part of individual managers. There are identifiable and specifiable managerial practices necessary for the creation of conditions for competence. And, in light of this fact, both productive and unproductive managers can be determined by whether or not they employ such practices.

By way of example, specific productive practices which serve the release of competence might be:

> . . . discouraging any pre-judging of anyone or looking upon people more or less favorably because of the particular work they do;

> . . . opposing factors like titles, education, or job complexity being used as a basis for special privileges or extraordinary treatment;

> . . . encouraging people to express freely their opinions and make suggestions about their work and how it might be better accomplished;

> . . . taking the actions necessary to insure that people have the information they need and access to and contact with those people with whom they must coordinate their efforts.

Such practices serve to promote the values and provide the support structure necessary for a collaborative system.

By the same token, other practices productive to the sense of impact and community necessary for widespread commitment might be:

. . . encouraging self-control and self-direction among people rather than relying on directives and prohibitions imposed by someone else;

. . . questioning people about the administrative supports—rules, policies, controls, etc.—they need to do their best work;

. . . encouraging people to learn one another's jobs so that they can help each other when the need arises;

. . . stressing the idea that people are mutually responsible to one another and that each person is best served when the common good is served as well as possible.

Such practices on the part of managers verify and translate into action many of the expectations generated by collaboration and, thereby, serve the goal of individual and collective commitment.

Or, if creativity is the objective, productive practices might be:

. . . routinely asking people what tools or equipment, freedom of layout or scheduling, they need to accomplish their work objectives in the best way possible;

. . . encouraging people to experiment with different ways of doing their work from time to time on the chance they might come up with a better way;

> . . . setting an example of candor and openness among people at work;

> . . . mingling with people in a visible and interested way to show personal involvement and that it's okay to have fun at work.

Practices like these have a productive effect on both the task environment and the social context within which people's creative urges are most likely to be aroused.

We know that managerial competence correlates significantly with conditions for competence. We know that conditions for competence correlate with organizational performance. Now, we would like to know whether managers who frequently engage in productive practices create more conditions in support of competence and its expression than unproductive managers who rarely engage in productive practices and, moreover, whether or not we can expect the productivity of organizations led by productive managers to be greater than that of organizations led by their unproductive colleagues.

We put such questions to an empirical test.

Measuring Productive Practices

As with the original research of the competence process, we began investigation of productive practices with the design of an appropriate assessment tool. Drawing from research findings and direct observation, we identified several observable behaviors like those cited earlier which we felt best served the overall dimensions of competence as well as the specific components of each. Descriptions of these behaviors were written and taken as the basis for a 72-item survey of productive practices.

The response format was straightforward; for each practice described, the question posed was essentially "do you (or does your manager) do this or not?" Respondents—managers describing themselves and subordinates describing their managers—used a nine-point frequency scale ranging from "never" to "all the time" for rating how often a given practice was employed. Thus, the survey afforded information about how often a given manager engaged in practices considered productive to the conditions for competence or, put differently, about how characteristic productive practices were of an individual in charge.

As with the conditions for competence, we were interested in not only how frequently managers were observed to use productive practices but, as well, how frequently their subordinates would ideally have them use such practices. The *actual* ratings, we reasoned, would help us determine how "productive" a given manager was and the *desired* ratings would help us verify subordinates' awareness of and desire for those practices on the part of their managers which would advance the cause of competence by encouraging and facilitating their best efforts. Moreover, the discrepancy between the two might shed light on health issues in the workplace.

Out of this approach came two surveys—one geared to managers' self-assessments and one geared to subordinate assessments of their managers—called the *Productive Practices Survey* (PPS), and the *Survey of Management Practices* (SMP), respectively. In two pilot projects, we found the

270

surveys to have good reliability[2] and proceeded to check on the construct validity of the instruments. We felt that if ratings of managers' productive practices from the SMP correlated significantly with existing conditions for competence in their organizations as revealed in OCI scores, we would be on the right track.

Working with a group of 75 subordinates of some nine managers in a manufacturing plant in the Northeast, we administered both the SMP and OCI. We found upon analysis of the data a strong system of correlation between the two sets of scores. Ratings of managers' productive practices were quite predictive—at a level to be expected by chance fewer than 1 out of 1,000 times—of the conditions for competence reported in their organizations.[3] As may be seen in Figure 1, conditions for competence within the organization vary as a direct function of the productive practices of individual managers.

Satisfied that we were measuring what we intended, we next addressed the relationship of managers' practices to the productivity of their work groups. Again, as with our original test of the competence process, we sought to evaluate the implications of productive practices or their lack among managers for productivity in organizations of varying size and mission.

---

[2] The Alpha coefficient of reliability for the Productive Practices Survey, as determined from the responses of 91 individuals, were .91, .92 and .91 for practices in support of collaboration, commitment, and creativity, respectively; from the data of 694 subordinate personnel, Alpha coefficients for the Survey of Management Practices for like practices were .94, .94 and .93, respectively.

[3] See Table XI in the Statistical Appendix for a summary of the data analysis for this test of construct validity.

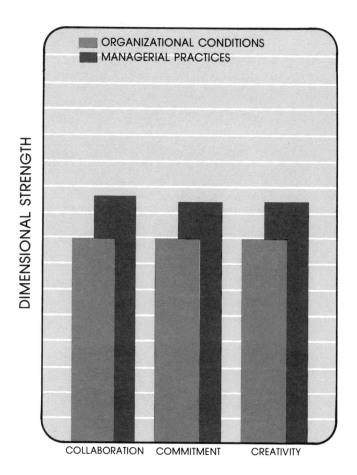

Figure 1. Conditions for competence within organizations vary as a function of managers' productive practices.

Obtaining a Representative Sample

We again sought out diverse organizations to strengthen our test and, once again, employed a matched-groups design. We wanted to compare comparable units—similar people doing the same kinds of work—within a given organization; we sought groups which could be *matched* on work, personnel, and objectives, but which *differed* in productivity. Moreover, we wanted several such pairs of high and low producers from as vastly different types of organizations as possible. If productivity across organizations of different missions and technologies was found to vary with the frequency of productive practices on the part of managers, irrespective of organization, we felt a behavioral basis for the release of competence could be pinpointed. And, to reduce the management of human competence to specific behavioral practices was our main objective.

We enlisted the aid of five different organizations, ranging from a manufacturer of hard goods to health care providers and government service. As the following descriptions will show, the nature of the work done and the criteria of productivity employed differed greatly from organization to organization. This time our point of inquiry was whether specific management practices could account for differences in productivity between otherwise comparable parts of organizations like the following:

An international container manufacturing firm. Those of us who watch television or use glass containers one way or another have very likely used the products of this well-known firm. Using an in-house rating system of productivity, the production manager of a 1,100-employee manufacturing plant in the northeast selected the highest and lowest producing shifts of a four-shift rotation in one department for study. Some 18 hourly workers in those shifts were surveyed and both union and nonunion personnel rated their managers' practices.

A neighborhood outpatient health care facility. Outpatient care is the "new look" in the health field and we wondered if the management of clinics had any bearing on the quality of services delivered. Ten departments in a major metropolitan health care clinic system were rank-ordered by an independent consultant with respect to productivity as indicated by profitability and patient interviews on quality of care. The top five were combined to form a high producing group and the remaining five formed the low producing group. A total of 23 nurses, lab technicians, and clerical personnel rated the practices of the persons in charge; often, the "managers" rated were practicing physicians.

An inpatient health care facility. Since each of us will very likely be hospitalized at some time in our lives, we felt a study of health-care quality in such institutions as a function of management practices could be of particular importance. A large metropolitan hospital system cooperated in our study and agreed to identify its highest and lowest producing hospitals as determined from physicians' comments, patient interviews, on-site standards checks for infection control and quality of patient care, and financial data. Each employee of the two hospitals—having 140 beds and 186 beds, respectively—was asked to complete the survey. A total of 333 nurses, orderlies, dieticians, physicians, and administrative personnel rated the practices of hospital administrators and department heads.

A service organization. Given the new emphasis and emerging importance of the service industry, we wanted to include a provider of intangible products in our study. The president of a privately-held West Coast accounting firm reviewed profitability records and identified, from six branches, one high producing and two low producing offices for study. Management practices were assessed by all personnel. A total of 170 people was surveyed; personnel reporting included file clerks, secretaries, computer programmers and accountants.

A government service. All of us are affected by government services and each of us has both an economic and political stake in their performance. The branch offices of a United States Government service were studied by their regional main office and two branch offices differing significantly on the basis of their weekly "Flash Reports"—a composite index of overall productivity—were selected as high and low producers. Thirty-nine carriers, clerks, drivers, and office personnel were asked to rate the practices of their management.

As can be seen, different organizations measure productivity in different ways—in terms of profits, quality of care, number of widgets, and the like—but productive outcomes are evaluated according to the same criteria *within* a particular type organization. Why does productivity vary? Does performance within organizations vary with managers' practices? Do different production objectives require different management practices or are there identifiable practices which seem to serve the cause of productivity irrespective of the type work to be done and the goals to be reached? These were the essential questions we were asking. So it was that we studied the 583 subordinate personnel of some 95 individual managers in five different organizations—doing vastly different work and pursuing vastly different production goals—regarding (1) their assessments of the day-to-day practices of their managers and (2) the practices they desired as most supportive and encouraging of their best efforts.

Results: Management Practices, Productivity, and Health

In light of our earlier findings regarding organizational performance as a function of conditions for competence and morale as a function of discrepancies between actual and existing conditions and those most desired by employees, we decided to examine our data on managerial practices in two ways. Our primary interest was in whether or not the people working in organizations identified as highly productive would assess their managers as using productive practices more frequently than did those individuals working in unproductive organizations. The core question was: Does productivity within organizations vary as a function of the frequency of productive practices of individual managers?

A related interest concerned the effects of individual managerial practices on the collective health of people on the receiving end of such individual practices. The core question was: Do the behavioral practices of individual managers impact the quality of worklife and feelings of health, fulfillment, or stress experienced by people at work?

The answers revealed to both questions offer compelling support to the notion that the nature of individual, day-to-day, managerial practices plays a significant role in determining the overall productivity of organizations and the well-being of their personnel.

Productivity as a Function of Managerial Practices

When we compared subordinates' ratings of their mana-

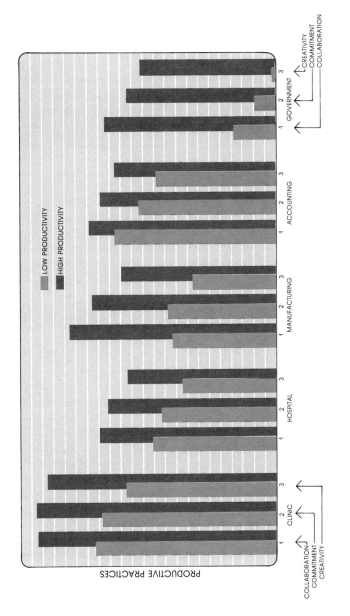

Figure 2. Productivity in five different organizations as a function of managerial practices.

gers frequency of use of productive and unproductive practices in high and low producing organizations, we found such large differences in the incidence of productive practices that they could occur by chance only one in 10,000 times.[4] Irrespective of type of organization—despite differing objectives, technologies, and criteria of productivity—the managers of productive organizations were uniformly reported to use more practices which encouraged and enabled the expression of individual and collective competence than were the managers of unproductive organizations. The consistency of these findings is revealed graphically in Figure 2, where the profiles of high and low producers for all five organizations are presented.

In each instance, the data confirm that individual managerial practices which promote and support collaboration, commitment, and creativity are associated with high productivity; and those practices which fail to serve the dimensions of competence are just as clearly associated with low productivity.

Overall, organizational differences aside, the results suggest that *organizational productivity varies as the frequency of productive practices varies among individual managers.* The overall significance of a manager's behavior for the productivity of the organization he or she managers should be clear from the data depicted in Figure 3.

It would appear that, in purely behavioral terms, what managers sow in the service of competence so do they reap in productivity. This sobering fact takes on additional meaning when we consider the practices people *desire* from their managers. The people in both productive and unproduc-

---

[4] See Table XII in the Statistical Appendix for a summary of the data analysis for this study.

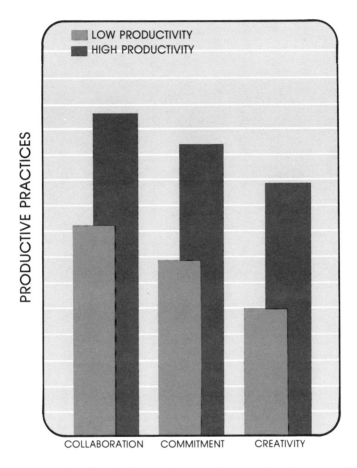

Figure 3. Productivity varies as the productive practices of managers vary.

tive organizations want to be treated the same way. Figure 4 reveals that one's current level of productivity is no indicator of the managerial practices he or she would most prefer to receive.

Figure 4. Productive managerial practices desired by people in organizations rated either productive or unproductive.

Another sobering thought: If, as we have suggested, the desire for competent performance among people is tantamount to a desire for normalcy and health, we might also expect health in the workplace to vary as managers' practices vary.

Health in the Workplace as a Function of Managerial Practices

In our earlier treatment of the results from our study of organizational conditions, we suggested that discrepancies between actual conditions and those desired by people seem to have peculiar motivational properties. Particularly when people are consciously aware of the gap between "what is" and "what might be" in the way of competence supports, discrepancies become almost palpable aspects of the work environment. People appear to experience a sense of loss and denied access to feelings of efficacy. These, in turn, show up in decreased satisfaction and heightened frustration—typical signs of "poor" morale—as discrepancies grow larger. Such findings prompted the observation that managers could do double duty—improve both productivity and morale—by taking steps to close the gap between actual and desired organizational conditions.

The same rationale applies to managerial behaviors. To the extent that people have a conscious awareness of the differences between how they are actually treated by managers on a day-to-day basis and how they would desire to be treated for maximal personal productivity, the magnitude of such behavioral discrepancies may have a bearing on signs of health in the workplace.

To test this notion, we examined subordinate assessments of managerial practices in much the same way as we did earlier with organizational conditions for competence. We computed the discrepancies between actual and desired managerial practices in support of collaboration, commitment, and creativity and assigned managers to one of four groups ranging from smallest to largest discrepancy scores.

As part of the administration of the SMP to managers' subordinates, we had asked additional questions bearing on their feelings of health, fulfillment, and stress in their work. Responses to questions like, "How often do you have a chance to feel good about yourself because of a job well done?" and "How much control do you feel you have over your own work process— how to do it, when, with whom, etc.?" and "How much fun do you have at work?" were taken as indicators of health. By the same token, answers to questions such as "To what extent are your real talents and skills utilized in doing your job?" and "At what percent of your true capacity do you feel you perform most of the time?" were taken to signify feelings of fulfillment. Stress indicators were gathered from subordinates' answers to questions like, "How often do you experience stress— headaches, upset stomach, etc.—at work?" and "In general, how frustrated do you feel with trying to work within the decision framework governing your work?"

When the subordinates' responses to such questions were analyzed relative to the Actual-Desired discrepancy scores accorded their managers, a compelling message emerged: day-to-day managerial practices—especially the gap between potentially productive and actual unproductive behaviors— have a direct and significant effect on the feelings of health, fulfillment, and stress reported by the people on the receiving end of those practices.

When we arranged the data in a predictive model for analysis, we found managers' Actual-Desired discrepancy scores for collaboration, commitment, and creativity to bear such a strong predictive relationship to subordinates' subsequent feelings of health, fulfillment, and stress that it could be expected by chance fewer than one out of 10,000 times.[5] The dramatic decline of health and fulfillment along with the equally alarming increase in stress as the Actual-Desired discrepancies of managerial practices grow is depicted graphically in Figure 5 below.

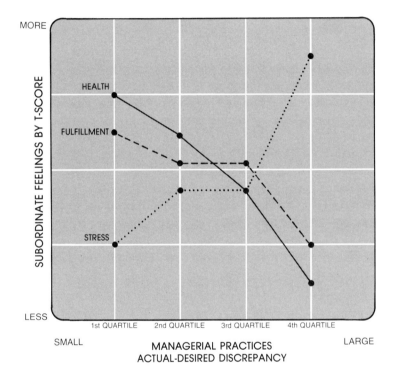

Figure 5. Health, fulfillment, and stress in the workplace as a function of the discrepancies between Actual and Desired managerial practices.

[5] See Table XIII in the Statistical Appendix for a summary of the data analysis for this study.

Clearly, how managers behave—whether or not they encourage and enable the expression of individual and collective competence—is a significant factor in determining the quality of life and a successful pursuit of efficacy and health in the workplace. This is good news, because managers have a choice in how they behave.

Choosing to Close the Gap

Managers may choose to encourage and enable the full expression of competence. In the final analysis, management boils down to behavior. The behavioral practices of managers—as well as their emotional reactions and cognitive acts of decision making and the like—are, however, based in unobservable attitudinal and philosophic considerations which organize and guide the overt acts subordinates see. This fact, coupled with the data we have just reviewed, suggests that we have some developmental work to do if managers are to serve the goals of competence effectively.

Choosing to serve the goals of both productivity and health in the workplace by closing the gap between current and desired practices, therefore, is as much an issue of managerial attitudes and philosophies as it is of behavior. In recent years, an often asked question in management development circles has been, "Does the such-and-such program have a behavioral or attitudinal focus?" The best answer for true developmental purposes is, "Both!" A focus on the acquisition of behavioral skills with little or no attention to the underlying attitudes and philosophies among managers is analogous to outfitting a sailing vessel with new sails and leaving off the rudder. Equipped with new skills in listening or creative problem solving or whatever, managers might make good speed but, without the organization and guidance of compatible values, their course will be erratic and unproductive.

By the same token, a purely philosophic focus in management development may insure a true course but, without the necessary behavioral and cognitive acts to put these in motion, the trip will be slow indeed. So, if in our management, we are to close the gap between what is and what is needed for greater productivity and health in the workplace, there is another gap we must address. We must get ourselves oriented on the basis of scientific fact rather than personal bias or armchair theorizing and, then, we must close the gap between reality and personal predilection, between what managers believe and what they do. This very likely means that many managers must be willing to rethink their approaches to managing.

It may mean, as well, that we must be willing to examine our organizations in fundamental ways. If competence is our goal, we may, literally, have to create new cultures which encourage, enable, and reward competent performance. We may have to gear our policies to the creation and support of conditions for collaboration, commitment, and creativity. We may have to fit our incentive systems to both the goals of and practices necessary for competence. Performance appraisal for managers may have to focus on the frequency of productive practices and then use the data generated to develop them further—to close the gap between their current practices and those we deem more productive— rather than the culture perpetuating approaches we've used in the past. In short, if we really choose to embrace competence—get competitive again, enhance productivity and promote health in our workplaces—we may have to ''change.'' But we are competent and adequate to the task should that be our choice.

Part Four

Adventures in Competence

XII

Competence as Change

While few organizational leaders ever intentionally choose incompetence as the path their organizations should pursue, they are apt to discover—as the data from Chapter X reveal—that a managerial decision for competence must occur against a backdrop of less than competent practices. They may find, for example, that people—managers and non-managers alike—have learned to set their sights lower than competence requires, that productive orientation has been stifled. They may discover that many of the tactics and practices employed by management and expected by workers, although part of tradition and culturally condoned, violate the basic value structure of competence. And they may find that many managers, as they try to anticipate and emulate those above them, are erratic and political in their priorities to a point that negative drift has set in, impairing adaptive fitness. In short, both the decision to become more competent organizationally and attempts to apply the principles of competence will often occur within a context ill prepared for either. A decision for competence will, more often than not, constitute a decision for change.

The pursuit of competence entails two-phased change: first, the individual manager must make a personal commitment to competence and undertake that sometimes painful examination of personal values, beliefs and practices; only by confronting one's own approach to management can the manager put his or her house in order and achieve managerial competence. But once this is done, the values, beliefs, and practices underlying the dimensions of competence must be put into action; and this involves other people—the organizational community. Therefore, personal change on the part of the manager must be followed by changes in existing conditions, prevailing norms and priorities, within the organization—all of which affect and require the support of those who do the organization's work. Many a change for the better has come to an untimely end because someone, personally commited to the cause, has failed to give those affected equal opportunity to become committed as well.

Competence, like most major organizational projects, requires both a commitment on the part of organizational leaders and a plan for its introduction and assimilation. The application of competence principles is therefore best thought of as a process of planned change. In some cases, managers take personal responsibility for introducing such change; in other instances, they employ the services of professional consultants who are skilled in the processes involved. In either event, the manager should have an understanding of the dynamics and rationale involved in effecting organizational change. Managers must monitor the change process as well as participate in it. And, because there are many different approaches—all ostensibly aimed at changing the organization—managers must be alerted to some of the issues involved if they are to make sure that a particular strategy does, in fact, serve the goals of competence.

A Competence Rationale of Planned Change

There are a number of theories of planned change, all gleaned by and large from the principles and research findings of behavioral science. But Chris Argyris has distilled the essential ingredients of these into three fundamental considerations.[1] In commenting on the functions which should be provided in a competently administered program of change, Argyris has enumerated the reigning principles which should govern any application of the competence process to organizations. In accordance with Argyris, the competence process requires: (1) the provision or stimulation of *valid and useable information* which those who comprise the organization can understand and employ in assessing both themselves and their organization pursuant to the objectives of competence; (2) the creation of conditions for realistically identifying available options and alternative courses of action, as well as the implications and full ramifications of these, so that a genuine state of *freedom of choice* is maintained throughout the competence process; and (3) ongoing attention to the need for *internal commitment,* including the creation of those conditions which most facilitate feelings of responsibility for and sense of ownership of the process.

When provided, these three functions set several important dynamics in motion. Valid and useable information aids in the creation of a cognitive map of the change process—a conscious awareness of the objectives to be served and a sense of how current practices and events must be modified, with

---

[1] Argyris, C. *Intervention Theory & Method.* Reading, Massachusetts: Addison Wesley, 1970.

their attendant costs and benefits, to move in the direction of competence objectives. Freedom of choice affords an ongoing program of evaluation and critique so that people not only have more ready access to the array of options available to them, but are free to choose among these as analysis and personal feelings dictate along the way, up to and including the choice of terminating the process. And, because conscious awareness of objectives is coupled with opportunities to shape and influence their attainment, a growing sense of ownership and personal investment in the success of the process is afforded, yielding a level of shared commitment sufficient to energize and sustain the program of change.

Valid and useable information, freedom of choice, and commitment: each is a critical facet of competently managed change, but not all programs of planned change provide for either the necessary functions or a conscious concern for their benefits. The failure of many programs of change is due in part to a neglect of such considerations and, moreover, to a gradually evolved misunderstanding of the dynamics of change: the more personally involved people have become with application, particularly with effecting change in complex organizations, the more pragmatic and technique-oriented they have become and the further they have departed from the fundamental considerations underlying the process of lasting change. The effect of this has been an aberration of the change process marked by a preoccupation with technique over objective, social processes over substance, group over individual dynamics, and pathology over health. This is why, with the thoughtful manager in mind, it is necessary and important to enunciate as clearly as possible the major considerations and priorities which comprise the competence rationale of planned change.

Competence is Geared to Objectives Rather than Technique

As irrational as it may seem, many major programs of change proceed primarily on the basis of faith alone; objectives are so ill-defined as to be literally unspeakable. No one can clearly articulate either what the goal is or what may be expected to happen. In addition to the unnecessary element of risk which this introduces, the lack of a clear focus carries with it added difficulties of evaluation. It is impossible to measure results adequately without evaluative tools appropriate to the objectives to be served; in turn, the design of appropriate tools of measurement requires a clarity of objectives before, not after, the fact. Many of the problems of organizational change—both in effecting and evaluating the process—may be subsumed by a diagnosis of unclear objectives.

The reason for this is traceable to a preoccupation with technique. In recent years more attention has been given to the *methods* of effecting change than to the *objectives* of change. In a manner of speaking, many applied social scientists have fallen into their own technological trap, becoming enamored of various consultative approaches to the point where they recommend and use them irrespective of the particular objective of concern. There was a time when sensitivity training was the solution of preference, irrespective of the problem. Team-building has often been used as a vehicle for change, even when there was not a team involved. From transactional analysis to management-by-objectives, techniques have been applied indiscriminately. Technique is seductive and may be employed independently of either theory or the realities of the situation. So it is that managers have encountered a proliferation of programs and strategies with little measurable impact.

In the competence rationale, objectives come first: *The top priority in a competence program of organizational change is the establishment of those conditions which have been verified as critical supports to collaboration, commitment, and creativity.* In the competence process we can be clear about what is required for credibility, for example, or relevance, or a creative social context. Since the conditions for both competence and its alternatives can be specified, measurement can occur and specific objectives can be enunciated, allowing for informative and practical performance-based evaluation of the process. Moreover, focusing on the objectives of competence affords a certain eclecticism and flexibility where technique is concerned; the competence rationale recognizes that just as objectives differ—community as compared to task environment goals, for example—so do the means for achieving them. If there is a problem of community or social ambience, then some form of team-building might be appropriate. But if the problem lies with management values, value training might be the appropriate intervention. The method deemed most appropriate to a given objective becomes the technique which should be selected. No longer are results subordinated to technique when competence is the aim.

Competence Values both Process and Substance

It has been my experience that most programs of change flowing from a social science rationale are marked by a decided preoccupation with process issues to the virtual neglect of substantive issues. Perhaps in an attempt to counteract the average manager's concern for *what* is to be done—the substantive, intellective, cognitive aspects of work—many change agents focus almost exclusively on process, *how* things are done—the nature of those social dynamics and interpersonal transactions which primarily affect the emotional tone of the workplace.

In competence we are concerned with both process and substance. At virtually every juncture of the competence premise we have expressed concern for the manner in which social dynamics affect one's performance and feelings of efficacy and personal worth. But we are equally concerned with the substance of work: we are every bit as interested in what the millwright *knows* about the capabilities and limitations of his milling machine as we are in how he feels about his supervisor; we are equally as concerned with the facilitating and inhibiting effects of rules and regulations on the government worker's performance as we are with his reasons for working where he does; and we are just as concerned with the pedagogical principles of a new educational project as we are with how the decisions leading up to it were made.

Process cannot realistically be separated from substance because *process is an outgrowth, a direct by-product, of efforts to deal with substantive issues having interpersonal consequences.* Problems of process virtually always occur within a context of substance; it is while we are trying to accomplish something substantive—solve a problem, reach agreement, give direction, effect a change—that *how* we behave becomes important. If the substantive content of our decisions affected no one other than ourselves, the social dynamics of process would be of little concern to us. But this is seldom the case. The beliefs we hold and the conclusions we draw individually are, like our fates, intertwined with the beliefs and conclusions of others. This is why it is artificial and of limited value to treat process as if it occurs in a vacuum, to subordinate substance to procedural concerns. Managers have been ill at ease with such treatments for years, and rightfully so.

In the competence process, a concern for substance is built in at every stage. The nature of that policy which sets the stage for collaboration—the fundamental *management values*—is a substantive issue. The planning of a collaborative *support structure* proceeds from substantive considerations. And the assurance of commitment based on *relevance* and a creative *task environment* requires a substantive awareness and understanding of the work itself. Under the competence rationale, therefore, substance is equally as important to change as process issues are in collaboration, commitment, and creativity.

Competence Focuses on the Individual Rather than the Group

Years ago Kurt Lewin observed that it was easier to effect a change in individual attitudes and behavior within a group context than in an individualized one-to-one setting.[2] Citing the powerful influence of group norms and social comparison processes in shaping personal beliefs and practices, Lewin discovered that such forces could be harnessed in the service of change when the appropriate group was involved in the process. This insight has had a profound effect on the evolution of change strategies. And it has produced one of the more noteworthy aberrations of the change process.

[2] Lewin, K. "Group Decisions and Social Change." In E. Macoby, T. Newcomb & E. Hartley (Eds.), *Readings in Social Psychology*. New York: Henry Holt and Company, 1958.

Over time many people responsible for the planning of programs of change have come to take Lewin too literally. They have discounted the importance of the individual while insisting that the group—the work team, the board, or the crew—is the only appropriate target of change efforts. Change strategies have become almost exclusively geared to group dynamics. Indeed, many people have come to act as if it is the group which *thinks,* the group which *learns,* the group which *feels,* and the group which *acts.*

Such a rationale dredges up a number of hoary notions, long since discounted, like that of "group mind" or "aggregate effect." And it prompts resentment among those who sense a loss of their individualism. It is important to bear in mind that groups are comprised of *individuals* and, if to digress a moment, to remind ourselves that unless we have a shared purpose, mutual attraction, commitment to common norms, and some agreement on power structure, we do not really have a group at all. The point is that, as Lewin said, the group is a *context* for *individual* change; it is a vehicle for change, not the target.

Under the competence rationale we recognize that individuals make organizations function as they do; we recognize that, while groups may exert tremendous influence on their members, it is still individuals who find a particular message persuasive or who make the decision to commit themselves in a particular direction. It is the individual who ultimately embraces change or opts for the status quo.

That is why the pursuit of competence proceeds according to an individually oriented rationale. Maintenance of individual integrity and the assurance of freedom of choice require an individual focus. And while this focus may well be brought to bear within a group context, using the group structure as a unifying vehicle, the strategy for change is geared to individual dynamics. It is only by insuring that the goals of learning, performance feedback, incentives for change, and the like are *personally* germane that we can achieve that sense of personal responsibility which will result in separate individuals voluntarily joining together in collective action. Competence demands the best that *each* of us can offer. And it is important to remember that our best is very, very good.

Competence Assumes Health Rather than Pathology

We began our discussion of competence with a reminder that we are good at what we do. Many programs of change ignore this vital sign. The trend in planning change has become one of assuming *pathology*. For some reason an implicit acceptance of the idea that our organizations are sick—that someone is hurting or that there is a critical problem—has come to dominate thinking about change. Most resulting strategies of change are geared to curing organizational ills. But well intended curative measures used with people who are already healthy sometimes have toxic effects. A more responsible approach is called for.

Under the competence rationale, we assume health until it is undeniably contra-indicated. The major focus of the competence process is simply on that healthy human desire to do better. The fact that one is concerned about not performing or feeling as well as he or she might, in no way indicates that a person is necessarily ill; it may simply signify a desire to perform and feel better still. As we all know, you don't have to be sick to get better. Such considerations are at the core of the competence motive and we should remind ourselves once again that people in low performing organizations aspire to the same competence ideal as those in high performing systems. Competence and adaptive fitness, by definition, pertain to health. The competence process proceeds according to a basic premise of health and it succeeds because the premise is valid and has credibility among those who do the work of our organizations.

The Competence Strategy: Change via Credibility

A strength of the competence rationale is that it can proceed on the basis of validated objectives. The basic research undertaken to validate the competence process not only verified the working assumptions of competence but yielded operational principles germane to its application, all of which serve to give a direction and structure to the change process often found lacking in unvalidated approaches. The importance of a validated premise cannot be emphasized too greatly in a program of lasting change: data help overcome many of the personal biases and apprehensions that the prospect of change evokes under less structured rationales. By the same token, the provision of valid and useable information, freedom of choice, and conditions for commitment ease the way for personal acceptance of the fundamental premise of competence. When the competence rationale is operationalized as a change strategy, the validity of its objectives and its sensitivities to the personal meanings of change combine to produce a foundation for credibility, the cornerstone of lasting change.

A valid and personally credible premise is critical to lasting change. Psychologist Herbert Kelman of Harvard University has demonstrated that, while short term change may be effected in a number of ways, lasting change may only be achieved when its essence is internalized, when the values and implications for action are adopted as one's own and become a source of personal guidance.[3]

To be internalized, change must enjoy personal credibility: It must be relevant to one's goals, it must have meaning in terms of one's aspirations, it must be amenable to personal influence, it must be based in reality, it must be both feasible and verifiable, and it must incorporate and reflect one's own priorities and capabilities. When the value structure of change can meet these requirements, it is literally taken over by a person as a viable guideline for daily living. Competence lends itself to change based on credibility.

The issues in effecting change competently are much the same as those in achieving competent performance. Conditions must be created by the manager which insure and encourage those affected by change to *collaborate* in planning for its implementation; conditions for *commitment*—the power, relevance, and shared reliance necessary for putting the plan into effect—must be accorded those who implement; and the resources, feedback mechanisms, and problem-solving supports needed for *creativity* in fashioning and implementing change must be assured by management. The competence process per se becomes the major vehicle for introducing and achieving those changes deemed necessary for the more widespread expression of competence to occur. The involvement, sharing of power, assurance of relevance, access to resources, and solving of problems for common acceptance which mark the competence process may also be brought to bear on the plan-

---

[3] Kelman, H. "Compliance, Identification, and Internalization." *Journal of Conflict Resolution,* 1958, Vol. 2, pp. 51-60.

ning and implementing of change. This is a major strength of the competence process, for as people come to grips with the issues governing competence in their workplace they will, in fact, be working on change and performance simultaneously. The outcome of such a process will enjoy personal credibility among those who fashioned it. And it will be embraced and acted upon by those most important to the success of the competence process: those who do the work that needs to be done. In the following chapters we will describe how the competence process may be set in motion and share some of the reports we have received about what happens when such a program of change is undertaken.

XIII

Organizational Reconstruction: Applying the Process

It is time to move from theoretical to practical concerns, from issues of development and validation to those of application. The objective of the competence process is, after all, to create organizations which enable and encourage the release of commitment and creativity. More often than not, this means the organization must be changed. In this chapter we will explain how this can be accomplished.

Applying the competence process begins on a positive note because of the fact that organizations *can* and *do* change. This is an important point to bear in mind because, when we opt for a more competent organization, we are not setting ourselves up for an impossible task. The job of changing an entire culture is not easy, but it is doable. It may be facilitated and accelerated if we keep a few points in mind.

Management is the Key

Management is the key to organizational competence. Proper management can unlock the structure, ease access, and release the commitment and creativity of people so that these may be channeled toward organizational objectives. Improper management, as we have seen, can jam the mechanism and maintain barriers to any sense of personal efficacy or reasonable expectation of productive outcome. If we are interested in moving our organizations from a state of lesser to greater competence—if we are ready to embrace change—we must first be willing to examine our management and determine whether or not it impedes or facilitates the expression of competence. Such an examination entails facing up to some critical facts.

Personalizing the Process

One of the first steps in such a process is that of explicitly *personalizing* management. Competence cannot tolerate, much less flourish under, anonymous authority. Management is practiced by *people*—as individuals—and, as such, is a direct product of the personal beliefs and practices of our fellow human beings. Situations do not dictate, objectives do not demand, circumstances do not require that certain policies or practices be employed; *people*—managers —*decide* what policies and practices will characterize their management. This means that any serious program of organizational change must involve those who run the organization—each individual person in a position of formal authority—and center the locus of control where it belongs, in people rather than in some inaccessible or ill-defined notion of "they" or "the system." If we are willing to personalize our management, we can then begin to ask why we have chosen to manage as we do.

A Testing of Premises

If, as Argyris claims, we have constructed organizations that ignore competence, alienate and frustrate workers, and lead them to fight the organization, now is a good time to ask why. Why have managers ignored, perhaps rejected outright, the potential for competence around them? Why have they pursued policies and practices that alienate, frustrate and antagonize those who do the organization's work? Is it because they are evil people? Is it because they are themselves exceptions to the rule of widespread competence? Of course not!

The problem, I submit, is that managers have simply based their management in *faulty premises.* Any action based in a faulty starting premise, however good one's intentions, will hardly ever achieve the results desired. Therefore, a second step for those contemplating organizational change, assuming they have accepted personal responsibility, is a willingness to test the premises upon which their management is founded. For those premises which fail to stand up to the test, more valid alternatives must be found. And this will entail a learning process, a reconstruction of managers' formulations of the practice of management.

Reconstructing the Managerial Mindset

Most managers manage as they do because they have *learned* to do so. Whether in a Business School, with a mentor, or in an in-house management development program, managers pick up concepts and principles which they look to for guidance in their work. In the process they may be exposed to a variety of "explanatory" notions, not all of which will necessarily be compatible or mutually reinforcing. At the local B School, for example, they may hear about the functions of management—planning, directing, controlling—and take these as role-defining reference points. Macro-economics and micro systems, strategic planning, and the seven steps in decision making tend to be big ticket items in such settings. Or, they may hear about how to motivate workers or how best to fit their particular predilections to the situation most favorable to them. Buzzwords like flexibility, worker maturity, direction and support creep into the managerial lexicon as items on the checklist for success.

If management theory were a musical score, such notes would be sharp or flat . . . just off-target enough to promote discord rather than harmony. Rather than providing a coherent and testable set of assumptions, such premises divert attention from the fundamental objectives of management . . . to enable and encourage competence.

Indeed, seldom do managers hear about concepts of competence; nor are they asked to evaluate what they hear in terms of its utility for releasing competence in their organizations. But they do learn a mindset and it is this mindset that must be examined—and perhaps reconstructed —if competence is to be served.

George A. Kelly,[1] an eminent psychologist and theorist, has offered a unique and practical explanation of human behavior. He proposes that people think, feel and behave as they do because of the particular way in which they interpret, deduce and explain for themselves, current and future events. They observe, look for relationships, reflect, and eventually build for themselves an explanatory construct or *model* of their experience to give meaning and guidance in any similar setting in the future. Moreover, Kelly says, experience is not the best teacher as we've always heard.

---

[1] Kelly, George A. *The psychology of personal constructs.* New York: Norton, 1955, Vol. 1.

People do not learn from their experiences so much as from the models of those experiences which they construct. This is why six people may have the same identical experience and come away with six different learnings. Models form the core of learning in Kelly's view and he is quick to note that there is nothing inherent in the nature of things to make a person prefer one model over another; anything which dispels doubt and allows movement will suffice. Personal comfort and relief from uncertainty seem to be their own rewards.

This means that the *validity* of the model may be of less importance to a person than its power to reassure or provide direction, even misdirection. But sooner or later, thoughts, feelings and actions based in invalid models will prove counterproductive, perhaps destructive—both for the individual and those affected by his or her thoughts, feelings and actions. Required then is a search for more viable models.

So it is with managers, I feel, and if we are to help them change their practices we must help them find more viable and productive models to guide their management. Therefore, the objective of change in the service of competence is a *reconstruction* of mindset, of the manager's formulation of productive management, based on viable models for management.

A Search for Viable Models

Just because we choose to believe something, doesn't mean it is valid and true. The only true test of validity is replication, a dependable time-after-time occurrence which is consistent with the premise and what it leads us to expect.

We can have confidence in a model of nature that says the sun will rise or water will run downhill, because they always do. We might be less confident of the notion that love conquers all, because it doesn't always turn out that way. The point, of course, is that in selecting their models for management, managers should choose those that can be tested and, then, actually put them to a test of repeatability to see if they warrant confidence.

Such a rule of evaluation can move managers away from the *ex cathedra* pronouncements and simplistic shortcuts they have been subjected to and toward a management based in more scientific and verifiable premises. A major objective in any change effort, therefore, should be to provide both scientifically verified models of management and practical opportunities for managers to verify such models themselves. Through self-convincing experiences, managers can achieve a reconstruction of their personal approaches as well as guidelines for testing and evaluating the viability of other premises they might encounter. If we are lucky, managers might someday ask of any idea or practice prescribed for them, *How does it serve the release of competence?*

* * *

A change effort based in considerations like the foregoing must be carefully thought through and implemented. Over a twenty-five-year period, such a design has evolved.

To prepare managers for the competence process, we reasoned, we must address in a personally relevant way the issues of management centrality, personal culpability, the validity of basic managerial premises, and how and what managers learn. A design which accomplishes this must be both instructive and heuristic, provide information and allow for personal discovery. In the best sense of the word, it must be educational. So it is that the competence process begins as an educational vehicle for accomplishing cultural change. It focuses on both the organizational system and those individual managers who make it run as it does. But it does this in a somewhat different manner—drawing on unique and more dynamic processes—than most programs of management education and, always, against the backdrop of widespread human competence waiting to be released.

There are five basic phases in applying the process. Each takes into account not only the reconstructive objectives necessary for achieving personal learning—the *substantive* material for change—but Argyris' requirements of valid and useable information, freedom of choice, and attention to commitment, issues critical to the *motivation* for change. With this brief background, we may now consider how the organization itself may be reconstructed for competence.

Organizational Reconstruction

The long-term objective of the competence process is one of creating an organizational culture—a system of norms, policies, practices, incentives, and expectancies—within which individual and collective competence may flourish. In practical terms this means that the conditions of work, more often than not, must be changed and that the mindsets and assumptions of those responsible for those conditions must be changed as well. Under the competence process, therefore, we do not seek to *develop* the organization as our colleagues in organization development (OD) would propose, so much as we try to *reconstruct* the organization, provide more viable models for managing and organizing the competence at hand.

Prime Objectives

While the specific conditions characterizing a given organization at the time of intervention may differ from one organization to another, the basic conditions of concern and their effects on competence are the same in any case. This is because the competence process addresses the *social* technology of the organization rather than the specific *work* technology characterizing its efforts. Organizations differ from one another primarily in terms of the commodities or services they produce and, consequently, in terms of the technologies required to accomplish their work objectives. They are alike, however, in the processes of importance in harnessing human potential and this calls for a common set of social skills and principles which may be applied uniformly from organization to organization, irrespective of product, size, personnel or task complexity. Table I below summarizes the points of emphasis, desired characteristics and end objectives of the competence process. Movement toward these objectives is initiated by assessing the organization's *need* for change through *Competence Analysis,* a survey of current and desired conditions and estimates of the resulting level of organizational competence. If a need is verified, three educational interventions—in the form of the *Models for Management Series*—may be used in reconstructing both managers' and workers' conceptions of productive effort and the conditions needed for this to be achieved. Finally, *Competence Analysis* is repeated as a measure of the degree, direction and significance of movement toward the objectives of competence. Following are brief capsule descriptions of each of the major intervention steps—their objectives and methodologies—for achieving organizational competence.

Table 1
An Overview of the Components of Competence

Management Values

Major
Characteristics:
- Reflects basic organizational culture
- Affirms organization's concern for excellence (i.e., doing the best possible work)
- Gives evidence that management values the resources of its personnel and acknowledges the humanity of employees

When Properly
Managed:
- Enhances feelings of self-esteem
- Diminishes the power-based class system
- Instills self-confidence

Support Structure

Major
Characteristics:
- Addresses both the physical and psychological structuring of relationships
- Maintains both the technical and social system
- Facilitates information flow
- Insures access to both information and other people

When Properly
Managed:
- Translates "philosophy" into action
- Opens communication channels
- Initiates and nurtures collaboration

Managerial Credibility

Major
Characteristics:
- Emphasizes the need for basic trust in management
- Stresses the importance of feedback as evidence that management will do what it says it will do
- Promotes a norm of reciprocity

When Properly
Managed:
- Clarifies what may be expected to happen
- Promotes flexibility
- Stimulates employee input
- Reaffirms management intent

Impact

Major
Characteristics:
- People *can* cause things to happen
- Verifies that one's involvement or collaboration does lead to personal impact
- Those who need authority get it without regard to rank or position

When Properly Managed:	• Formalizes the sharing of power
	• Improves morale *and* productivity
	• Encourages people to invest themselves and give their "best"

Relevance

Major Characteristics:	• People spend their time in *core* activities
	• There is a logic involved in the work which allows people to find challenge and maintain a sense of purpose
	• People can *do* rather than just getting ready to do or analyzing what to do

When Properly Managed:	• Sustains a sense of purpose
	• Integrates personal goals and organizational objectives
	• Lends coherence to job activities

Community

Major Characteristics:	• Encourages and rewards interdependence and mutual reliance and respect
	• Promotes the need for shared responsibility and a concern for the common good
	• Minimizes issues of "territoriality"
	• Avoids win-lose dynamics or individualistic posturing
	• Makes commitment a widespread commodity
	• Promotes greater identification with work group and organization

Task Environment

Major Characteristics:	• Acknowledges that work must be structured and priorities set, but minimizes emphasis on conformity to procedures
	• People have access to needed resources
	• Allows personal control over work activities

When Properly Managed:	• Stimulates creative problem solving
	• Rewards accomplishment through personal initiative
	• Eliminates inefficient methods and procedures

Social Context

Major Characteristics:	• Promotes and legitimizes the sharing of ideas and opinions
	• Capitalizes on the positive aspects of social facilitation, i.e., fun and stimulation
	• Encourages innovation and promotes a norm of candor and openness

When Properly Managed:	• Creates excitement, not boredom, in workplace • Avoids the depersonalization of individuals • Makes work fun rather than a chore • Establishes honesty and critique as norms of day-to-day behavior

Problem Solving

Major Characteristics:	• Emphasizes that problem solving is basically a process issue and not a task issue • All resources are utilized—not just those of a single individual or privileged few • Conflict is not avoided but is utilized as a source of potential creativity
When Properly Managed:	• Encourages abstract thinking • Ignites collective creativity • Reinforces personal impact • Insures review and evaluation of multiple alternatives

Competence Analysis ™

No organization should undertake change just for the sake of change. Only when people are doing less well than they might, when current policies and practices have proved counterproductive or inadequate to the task, or when the organization is faced with changing demands from its marketplace or for its function should wholesale change be contemplated. The fundamental concern is to keep—or make—the organization adaptively fit. Therefore, the competence process begins with a *Competence Analysis,* a computer-based assessment of the organization's strengths and weaknesses, to determine whether or not change is both necessary and desirable. Originally designed for top decision makers in the organization, practical use of the analysis has often been extended down to first level supervision as a powerful management tool. Properly managed, the data afforded can become a reliable and valid foundation for planned change; moreover, it can begin the personalization process.

As Brian Warner, Director of International Training for Wang Laboratories, views the analysis, "Managers don't take their own influence on the workforce seriously. Until *Competence Analysis* was developed, an analysis of how behavior impacts productivity never existed. *Competence Analysis* has provided a research-based model that gives managers the information they need to increase productivity. It has impacted a lot of people here . . . it enables managers to see how their behavior affects the workforce much more deeply than they imagined."

Competence Analysis is a means of determining what life is really like in the organization. It is a survey of whether or not people think the conditions for competence exist in their work and, if they do not, what conditions they feel oppose competence and what they need instead to do their best. The analysis is employed in a cross-section of the organization—from the top down to the very bottom—and is designed to provide organizational decision makers with information about the state of the organization they have created.

Competence Analysis measures both the *actual* and *desired* conditions characterizing an organization and its people. Using the same *Organizational Competence Index* instrument as used in the original research on the process, current policies and practices are assessed for their contribution to competence and specific measurements are made for each of the conditions of concern. *Actual* measurements reveal "what is" and establish the causes of current performance and productivity. *Desired* data reveal the competence motivation of the organization's human resources and their *readiness* for more competent performance.

From *Competence Analysis* data, managers can immediately determine what areas require attention. Moreover, they can gain insight into those practices and options that have the greatest potential for enhancing the competence of the organization. When shared with the workforce, *Competence Analysis* can be the first important step in a serious program for creating a truly competent organization.

Competence Analysis presents a statistically accurate profile of current working conditions and can be done for an entire organization or any part thereof. It provides a focus for change efforts and a normative context so managers might compare their organization with others. It results in a 20-page report containing specific organizational data. A major utility of *Competence Analysis* is that, in addition to providing analyses of balance, polarity and sequence effects, it examines the components of competence in detail. Statistical tests of significance are provided for all observed differences so that managers may concern themselves with those discrepancies that are "real" with confidence. Finally, detailed capsule descriptions of both actual and desired conditions are provided so that people have an understanding of not only what they are currently doing but what they need to do differently to release competence.

The message implicit in the analysis is that if managers want high performance, quality and productivity over the long term they must constantly emphasize to all their people their belief in collaboration, commitment and creativity. If managers are actually going to solve productivity problems, they have to somehow break out of the confines of conventional wisdom and involve those who do the work. They have to come to know the difference between old myths and current realities and begin to use practices which create competence. It is in this sorting out and starting out phase that *Competence Analysis* is most useful. Because the analysis specifies and quantifies as it measures, problems are not only identified but solution priorities become obvious.

As Ray Jensen, Supervisor of Advanced Concepts, Ford Motor Company, reports, "*Competence Analysis* showed where the company is now and where the employees want it to be. We learned that we had a great deal of unused potential. That was a problem we'd never really considered before. We learned that most of us were managing people, when we should have been managing the environment."

On the basis of valid and useable information about their organization, managers can gain new insights and give serious consideration to the need and desirability for change. If they opt to proceed, they will next embark on some 80 hours of seminar-based learning.

The Models for Management Series

The Models for Management series is comprised of three different educational experiences. The first, which participants have titled Models I, is designed to personalize management. The focus is on the individual manager, with heavy emphasis on the nature and effects of his or her current practices.

The second in the series, Closing the Loop, is designed to extend to the workforce the awareness gained by managers in the Models I seminar. As a means of sharing new ideas and values and enlisting the help of those who are managed, this one-day seminar also makes public a commitment to new ways of working.

The third seminar in the series, Choice Points for Competence, shifts the focus away from the individual manager onto the organizational system and how much it enables and encourages competence. It is here that serious action planning is begun.

The Models I Seminar

"You feel pretty beat up after *Competence Analysis*," says Don Kopka, Vice President of Ford's Design Staff. "But it's nothing compared to the seminar. The Models I seminar is awful! Here's where you learn that everything you thought you were doing right is wrong. I guess self-analysis is supposed to be painful. But this is like standing out in a snowstorm and beating yourself with a stick. Believe me, it's uphill from there . . . but, what it taught us is how to use the resources we have effectively. We now have to work with fewer people and smaller budgets, so we have to work smarter. The seminar is the ultimate in employee involvement. And it works!"

The Models I Seminar is a 40-hour program for executives, managers and supervisors. It is designed to teach them the behavioral practices necessary to succeed as managers of other people. Participants in this seminar are exposed to those same behavioral philosophies and practices which formed the basis for a major research effort involving over 16,000 managers.[2] The research project identified, and the seminar presents, those beliefs and behaviors which characterize high achieving managers and which significantly distinguish them from their less achieving colleagues. As it turns out, these are the

---

[2] Hall, Jay and Donnell, Susan M. "Managerial achievement: The personal side of behavioral theory." *Human Relations,* Vol. 32, No. 1, January, 1979.

managerial beliefs and practices necessary for releasing competence in the organization.

The Models I Seminar is penetrating and engrossing. While people who attend may enjoy the experience, entertainment is not its purpose. It is based on a well-validated theory of human learning and represents a serious effort to provide insights which will enable a manager to become more effective in those human interactions which are essential to personal achievement. Many participants have referred to this program as a "turning point" in their careers.

The objectives of the Models I Seminar are:

- To stress the role of the manager's personal choice, and therefore, responsibility in managing.

- To help managers identify their personal ideas about managerial effectiveness—the "best way" to make decisions, how to motivate, etc.

- To introduce and allow managers to experiment with validated behavioral science models of personal and organizational effectiveness.

- To compare managers' personal ideas with behavioral science models so that they may achieve data-based insights into their current and potential effectiveness.

- To provide feedback opportunities for managers, both as self-appraisals and co-worker critiques, of their practices from a behavioral science perspective.

- To link the seminar experience to real people in the real world via subordinate appraisals of managers' practices.

- To achieve a broad base of behavioral science thought so that managers may come to understand and make enlightened choices about their personal interactions.

The numerous behavioral models employed in the seminar, when taken together, reveal the concepts and practices necessary for implementing the competence process. Each of the models presented during the seminar is then used as the basis for personal assessment so that managers may receive critiques of their practices within the framework of those models most critical to the dynamics of competence. In this way, they gain awareness of the personal significance of their practices for achieving the goals of widespread competence.

Beginning the Process. The learning from the Models I Seminar is not confined to the program itself. It may be more accurate to think of it as a process initiated by the individual and terminated only when that person decides to go no further. The process actually begins when participants receive learning instruments to be completed before the seminar along with materials for several subordinates or colleagues. The subordinate materials will provide feedback to the participant when they are examined and placed in an appropriate context during the seminar. These data from the workplace make the learning have real meaning and, of course, it is to the workplace that participants will return to apply the process and test its utility. It is this "linkage" between the seminar and the real world that enables participants to actually use what they learn.

Awareness precedes choice. The central role of managers' assumptions in guiding their practices is stressed. The way managers think about and plan for the future, the actions they see as desirable and feasible, and the feelings they experience in the world of work all stem from personal "theories" of management. The seminar creates conditions under which participants may become aware of these personal theories and of their impact on others, as well as of alternative theories or models. Such awareness becomes the basis for making enlightened choices among identified options, and the resulting decisions may lead to change in the service of personal excellence.

Group problem solving. As in many other behavioral science seminars, the group is the basic vehicle for learning in the Models I experience. But, whereas many learning designs focus primarily on the group, the Models I design recognizes a more basic truth: groups—and organizations—are composed of individuals, each of whom has different needs, resources and preferences. Personal identity is never lost in the Models I Seminar; nor should it ever be, for the key to group and organizational effectiveness is the creative use of individual resources. Group problem solving has therefore become a major part of the Models I experience.

Structured process. Activities in the seminar never occur randomly or in a vacuum. Using unique, specially designed work booklets, each group session is presented within an appropriate structure. Participants are often unaware of certain aspects of learning at the time they occur, and the structured process allows them to recall, capture and learn from these otherwise elusive dynamics. This learning is enhanced because the seminar design allows participants to conduct this recall process for themselves. They do not rely on group facilitators for their insights.

Organizational dynamics. Many of the dynamics which characterize small group work in the program simply mirror the dynamics of organizational life. In the seminar, therefore, participants may study at close range, under more systematic and less anxiety-producing conditions, the cause-and-effect relationships underlying both the effectiveness and the ineffectiveness of organizational systems. For example, how often do people seem committed to decisions and then fail to follow that commitment with affirmative action? More importantly, why? Or, why do some people seem to distrust any kind of group action while others revel in committee meetings? Understanding one's group in the seminar setting provides the framework for understanding the real life systems to which one belongs.

Linkage: the real world revealed. Under the best of conditions, a management seminar suffers two limitations: artificiality and difficulty of transfer to the real world. Linkage materials overcome such shortcomings. The co-worker materials sent to participants prior to the seminar provide much needed, but difficult to obtain, feedback data from associates. These linkage materials inject a *realism* into the seminar that is unmatched in other programs. At the same time, they provide the mechanism for *transferring* seminar learning to the real world of work. When the results and the learning instruments which generate them are used as a basis for back-home discussion and critique—as called for as part of a learning contract—they substantially assist managers in applying what they have learned in the seminar to the people within the organization back home.

Synthesis. Many seminars concern themselves with a single behavioral theory or model, as if it covered the whole spectrum of managerial and organizational issues. A more comprehensive approach, however, is designed into the

Models I experience. There are several models that apply to the process of managing and to the effectiveness of organizations. All of these models address the nature of people in the workplace. Because they do, it is possible to explain them in terms of one another and greatly expand a participant's grasp of each of the individual models and their interrelationship. It is this process of synthesizing which is unique to the seminar that enables the manager to understand his or her own behavior and the behavior of others in the organization.

Reconstruction and reaction: putting it all together. It is not uncommon for a learning experience to be followed by an "incubation effect" in which the real learnings only become apparent and usable at some later time, as one reflects upon and attempts to formulate what has really been learned, after all. For this reason, numerous aids to reconstruction are designed into the Models I experience . . . data summaries, personal feedback materials, structured processes, and conceptual frameworks are provided as reference points for interpreting events and to enhance one's back-home reconstruction. The reasons so many other seminar experiences fail to transfer the learning to the workplace may be traced to their lack of reconstructive aids.

Back-home linkage sessions. The real payoff from the seminar is realized in the manager's back-home linkage session. Managers are encouraged to set up a meeting, upon their return to work, with those co-workers who supplied feedback materials for their seminar experience. The purpose of these sessions is two-fold: first, to share the concepts and data from the seminar with those who did not attend and, secondly, to begin discussions of the manager's feedback material . . . reasons and implications of the scores received. These meetings are often spread over several days and may take in excess of nine hours. Not only are new ideas and awarenesses disseminated more widely in the back-home organization, but linkage sessions establish a new norm of critique and planning for improvement where manager-subordinate relationships are concerned. These sessions can be profound experiences for those involved and sow the seeds for commitment and a more serious pursuit of competence.

Mike Adler, President of Moto-Photo Labs, had this reaction to the seminar: "I'm sure I'd been exposed before to 90% of what I learned, but somehow it never sunk in. When I went to this seminar, I had a real-life Aha! experience. It really excited me. We started out intending to send only our managers through the program. We ended up sending every one of our 800 employees."

As the first in the Models series, the seminar focuses on the efficacy of one's managerial beliefs and practices and triggers a search for more viable alternatives where needed. Because the seminar deals with generic issues of importance in any authority relationship—manager and subordinate, teacher and student, parent and child—it can be used with all levels of an organization. The same learning experience may be afforded people from top to bottom in the hierarchy, irrespective of title or responsibility, and it is not uncommon that Presidents and CEO's speak in the same terms as first line supervisors in discussing their management. Such a shared perspective prepares people for the next step in the process.

Closing the Loop

"As a result of the Models I seminar, as managers we had all changed," said Ray Jensen, "and our people were suspicious. It was hard to convince them that we meant what we said. We wanted their ideas. We wanted them to participate. They thought it was just management trying some crazy new scheme. We felt Closing the Loop was essential to making the new management work."

A major goal of the competence process is one of working for a more collaborative organization. The idea that managers should work to involve their subordinates is over forty years old, but only recently have managers begun to give the concept more than lip service. Today, many managers are seriously looking for the keys to a more collaborative approach because they feel the times demand it. In applying the competence process we are mindful of an important fact in this regard: a truly collaborative organization requires a workforce that is both involved and willing to collaborate.

Involving non-management employees. As we noted earlier, a pursuit of competence will seldom occur against a blank slate. For collaborative management to work, managers will need the help and cooperation of those who are managed. And the pursuit of more competent management must take into account the past history and culture of the organization. Doubt and opposition must be anticipated in direct proportion to the lack of managerial competence in the past. For these reasons—the possibility of an unfriendly past history, managers' need for help and cooperation from their subordinates, and because collaboration is a two-way street among equally informed parties—Closing the Loop sessions have been designed for non-management employees.

Developed and tested with over 4,000 employees within one of the top five corporations in the Fortune 500, Closing the Loop sessions are designed to inform and set the norm for involvement among those who are managed. The program is a six-hour overview of the concepts and experiences offered to managers and supervisors in their Models for Management seminars. Closing the Loop sessions, however, are specifically designed for those people upon whom the manager depends daily.

Natural work groups. Closing the Loop sessions occur in natural work groups with the manager sitting in. Specially designed materials are provided for each employee and, as they hear summary presentations of the same concepts their managers have recently heard, individual workers are encouraged to assess their own philosophies, practices, motives and styles. Through the use of learning instruments designed for these sessions, self-assessment is harnessed as a learning tool and extended to those directly responsible for production. Work group discussion and problem solving follow each theory presentation and period of self-assessment. Managers and their subordinates discuss the ways in which, together, they can practice concepts in the workplace. Critiques of current practices, identification of areas in need of change, specific efforts required, and the roles to be played by all members of the work group are the typical immediate outcomes of Closing the Loop.

A six-month plan for change. In order to continue the development process after the session, resource material and guidelines for follow-up activities are provided for each participant. A six-month program is outlined for achieving 1) clear communications, 2) productive job conditions, 3) managerial competence and 4) team effectiveness.

Several themes dominate these sessions. Among them, the most important are:

- It is just as important for employees to be informed and committed regarding new ways of thinking about manager-subordinate relationships as it is for managers.

- Shared knowledge and information are the foundations for productive collaboration between managers and workers.

- Managers need and want the opinions and suggestions of those they manage.

- Joint problem solving where appropriate is a profitable and satisfying way of working.

- Learning about, discussing, and planning for new ways to manage and work is everybody's business.

- Managers are willing to work for a more competent organization, but they need the help and cooperation of the workforce.

Closing the Loop sessions are dynamic and powerful opportunities for management to prove its commitment to organizational competence, especially in those instances where *Competence Analysis* data have been presented to the workforce. Closing the Loop sessions can verify the fact that management is serious and willing to work for a more competent organization. More importantly, these sessions are the first step toward gaining the commitment of the employees themselves and preparing the entire group for a serious examination of its own competence. In one organization, over 12,000 hourly workers have participated in Closing the Loop sessions "on the clock." Assembly lines were literally shut down to allow attendance. Workers uniformly produced more in the resulting four-day week than they had in the full five-day weeks leading up to the session. Through such experiences the fabric of competence begins to take shape. Readiness is affirmed and the next step is to tackle the process explicitly and head-on.

Choice Points for Competence

By the time they have been through information-gathering and decision-making activities, training and self-assessment, the sharing of agenda with subordinates and the solicitation of their support, managers should find both the climate and the practices of their organization beginning to change. This, then, is the appropriate time to insure that change—on the organizational level—has an underlying structure. The third in the Models for Management series, Choice Points for Competence, is a vehicle for introducing managers to those issues under their control which affect organizational competence. This seminar directly confronts the requirements of organizational competence and the role played by managers in its achievement. As one manager said, "This is where you stop preaching and start meddling."

Choice Points for Competence is conducted for *actual* work groups and is "organization specific." That is, the issues that arise and the learning that occurs during the seminar are directed specifically to those people who will be responsible for causing competence to become a reality in that organization. It is the intent of the seminar to provide participants with a clear understanding of what they must do to remedy counterforces to competence and to create conditions which support competence in their stead.

Process and objectives. This seminar builds on the first in the series and shifts the focus from individual behaviors to the organization itself—the policies and working conditions created by managers. Using the same involvement-feedback-awareness learning formula as in the Productive Manager Seminar, Choice Points for Competence begins with an "update" of managerial practices impacted by the initial Models for Management experience and then moves on to more organization-bound issues. The objectives of the seminar are:

- To refine the level of personal awareness obtained in the Models for Management seminar, i.e., to review managers' understanding and interpretation of behavioral theories and values as a beginning point for assessing current practices.

- To provide both personal assessments and feedback from co-workers with respect to the nature of those choices pursued by managers since the first seminar and their implications for managerial competence; i.e., to answer the question, "How am I doing?"

- To introduce new considerations bearing on managerial competence and to provide an opportunity for personal appraisal in light of such considerations.

- To relate managers' personal choices—their basic values and related practices—to the competence of the organization; i.e., to determine the impact of managerial influence on the organization's ability to respond in a committed and creative manner to the demands it encounters.

- To provide feedback and "linkage" materials to ease the transfer of learning to managers' back-home situations.

- To provide the tools for creating a self-reinforcing cycle of competence.

This 30-hour learning experience moves participants from a plateau of self-analysis to a penetrating diagnosis of organizational dynamics. Not only do participants receive heretofore unobtainable information about the organization they have created but, because of specially designed sessions, they have the opportunity to formulate realistic action plans for renewed growth and vigor.

Review. Competent management is still the key to organizational competence. For this reason—and even though managerial competence was the objective of the first seminar—managers need an opportunity to assess their understanding of the issues underlying managerial competence. Review exercises are conducted to provide such assessments and to provide opportunities for clarifying concepts.

Core values. By the same token, managers need an opportunity to evaluate their own progress. They need to know how they are doing in their attempts to change the way they manage. Using the Four Core Values necessary for competence as criteria, both managers and their subordinates have an opportunity to appraise managerial performance since the Productive Manager seminar. The relationship of Core Values to organizational competence is stressed and managers have an opportunity to seek help in areas still in need of improvement.

Power dynamics. The issue of power—a most critical and volatile issue in formal organizations—is addressed from the standpoint of both style and motivation. Managers have an opportunity to examine power dynamics in depth, determining those practices and personal motives most instrumental to organizational competence. In this instance they prepare self-assessments and receive subordinate appraisals regarding their customary management of power dynamics. Such considerations lay the foundation for many of the actions which will be required in their pursuit of organizational competence.

Sense of competence. Participants are confronted with the competence of their part of the organization. Using instrumented feedback, the organization is portrayed according to the dimensions and conditions necessary for organizational competence. Managers and their co-workers have an opportunity to take a close look at the organization they have created. They receive an estimate of actual competence and, from subordinate personnel, an estimate of those conditions which would most allow people to do their best work. This latter information amounts to both a statement of potential competence for the organization and an index of peoples' readiness for necessary changes. In addition, if a *Competence Analysis* was conducted as a beginning step to organizational change, managers have an opportunity to judge the impact of activities undertaken since that time on organizational conditions. During this session, nearly all groups discover that they have made substantial improvements in organizational conditions just as a result of the Productive Manager and Closing the Loop sessions. In any event, participants will learn how to accomplish the work that still needs to be done if they are seriously committed to a more competent organization.

Diagnosis. For the first time, participants have an opportunity to examine in detail the current practices, policies
and procedures characterizing the organization and the
implications these have for greater competence. Prevailing
policies, common practices, and standard procedures are each
evaluated in terms of their effect on conditions for
competence within the organization. Participants are able
to see their management in a new light, and sacred cows
and cultural myths are called into question. This intensive
diagnostic activity is the foundation for action planning.

Linkage. As with the Models I seminar, provisions are
made and materials are furnished for linking the learning
and data from Choice Points for Competence with those co-
workers not in attendance. While linkage sessions in the first
seminar concerned the manager and his or her relationships
and practices with others, linkage sessions from this seminar
address both managerial practices and conditions for competence. Actual action planning may be begun during
Choice Point linkage sessions but the manager has the
option of widening these sessions to include all who are
affected.

Outcome. Participants leave the Choice Points for Competence experience with knowledge and linkage tools
which are at the cutting edge of organizational excellence.
The reasons for past and current problems of productivity
and quality of worklife are made patently clear. Invaluable
insights into the specific steps necessary for problem solution are guaranteed and, of major importance, a reliable
index of readiness for change is implicit in the data
generated. Armed with scientifically tested and verified
concepts, managers are ready for the hard work of achieving a more competent organization for everyone involved.

Competence Analysis:
Evaluating Results

After several months of investing both time and money, managers should pause to take stock of their efforts, *Is the change effort working? Are we moving toward greater organizational competence? Have conditions changed and, if so, in which direction?* Such questions can best be answered through a second *Competence Analysis*, as widespread and in-depth as the one conducted initially. By surveying all levels of the organization, managers can get answers to their questions, identify areas still in need of work, and plan those additional follow-up activities which may be needed. It is at this time that the entire effort can be objectively evaluated because a cycle of competence is now in place and both productivity and the quality of worklife should show it!

While a post-series *Competence Analysis* can provide statistically reliable evidence of the movement achieved— and most organizations can expect to double their starting conditions in a few months time—the real value of a periodic evaluation is less apparent. First of all, as managers begin to trust their data and take their scores from an analysis as evaluative guidelines, they move more and more toward internalizing the norms of competence in both their policies and practices. This is the essence of cultural change. Secondly, a post-series analysis can often alert managers to potentially unwanted trends. For example, in their zeal to overcome autocratic and unilateral past practices, managers may become so preoccupied with collaboration that they neglect conditions for commitment and creativity, thereby risking aborting the process. Or, perhaps fascinated by the creativity unleashed, they may risk short-circuiting by concentrating too much on output. A periodic *Competence Analysis* can prevent such slip-ups and keep the process on track, until a self-reinforcing cycle of competence becomes the dominant theme of the organization.

Thus, applying the competence process rests on a reeducation of both managers and workers such that a new culture begins to take shape, a culture in which collaboration, commitment, creativity and respect for human competence are the accepted order of things. While some individuals will find the shift in values and practices more difficult than others, virtually all can learn and commit themselves to the new system, given the time and freedom of choice. One of the interesting features of the five-phase approach employed is the short time it takes. Conventional wisdom in organizational development circles is that change of such a magnitude—reconstructing the basic culture of an organization—of necessity takes years to accomplish. The Competence Process has been fully set in place in as little as eight months and the expected time-frame is less than 18 months on the average. But, although accomplished in but a brief fragment of an organization's life span, its effects are both profound and long-lived. In the next chapter we will see what happens once the competence process is in place.

XIV

War Stories:
First Hand Accounts of the
Liberation of Competence

"A culture can't be changed overnight," said Don Kopka, Head of Ford Motor's Design Staff. "But our objective is clear to us. We have to create an environment where our people have an opportunity to contribute more. It's better for them, sure, but it's better for management too.

"Creative output is an essential part of what we do in design. We have to create an environment where people have the opportunity to contribute the most. Competence Analysis™ showed that our original efforts weren't working . . .we identified a real need for change in our organization."

And change they did. In this chapter we will share some eyewitness accounts, from several different organizations, of what can happen when the competence process is seriously applied. These are decidedly unscientific reports. They do not represent well-designed empirical studies; there were no control groups or statistical tests of significance. We cannot claim cause-and-effect connections between what was done and what happened. Unlike previous chapters, all we can offer are the observations and personal conclusions of those who actually lived out the competence process experience. But, lack of scientific rigor notwithstanding, these true life dramas can add to our understanding of the practical implications of the adventure of competence.

Probe V

Due largely to the efforts of Gale Cook, an in-house consultant with Ford's Management and Technical Training Center, in 1981 the Body and Electrical Engineering Division undertook a Competence Analysis™ as part of its developmental efforts. The scores were extremely low. Subdued but resolute, department executives committed themselves to doing something about the situation. They set a goal of applying the competence process, reeducating all supervisors and managers over a two-year period. The program's success caught the attention of top level executives, which at that time included Ford's current president, Red Poling. Poling and his colleagues on the Executive Committee were so intrigued, they voted to conduct a Competence Analysis™ for themselves. When the results were presented, they too recognized the need for some changes and embarked on both the Models I and Choice Points for Competence seminars. With the results of these experiences in hand, they next approached then-President and now Chairman of the Board, Don Peterson, to talk about going forward. As a result, he too decided to familiarize himself with the personal feedback materials and concepts from the Models I program in a one-on-one session with the same consultant used by the Executive Committee. Peterson, too, said "Move ahead."

During the four years since Ford first elected to try the competence process, it has conducted 20 Competence

Analyses™ and sent some 30,000 employees (both managers and rank-and-file workers) to the Models Series seminars. It has been sanctioned not only by the president and his executives but by union leaders as well. And, although no single department has been required to take advantage of the program, many have requested it. Enthusiasm is widespread.

One of the most enthusiastic groups of graduates is the Design Department. They are one of the few departments who, at the time of writing, have completed the entire program from Competence Analysis™ to Closing the Loop to Choice Points; their follow-up analysis is pending. Although they were aware of problems when they began, they had no idea of the depth of those problems.

"I thought—we all thought, 'How bad can it be?'" said Vice President, Don Kopka. "But the Competence Analysis™ was a real eye-opener. In fact, it was devastating. We thought we were good managers, but that's not exactly how our employees perceived us. But once we looked beyond our own feelings, we were able to identify a real need for change."

The analysis proved a valuable starting point for executives in the design area. "It showed where the company is now and where the employees want to be," explained Ray Jensen, of the Advanced Concepts Section. "We learned that we had a great deal of unused potential, of people actually capable and wanting to do a better job. That was a new idea for us."

The need for change was undeniable. Consequently, the Design management team was asked to participate in the first Models seminar. Dave Rees, Director of International

Design, had his doubts. "In the beginning, I had mixed emotions. Whenever you try anything new, there are bound to be failures. We're in an environment where you don't get second chances. But we have learned to accept the fact that there may be failures. And we've learned that management has to support failure. Out of failure comes a better solution. The program has influenced how I operate. I guess the delegation of responsibility is the biggest change that affects people here and at Ghia. One of the messages in the competence process is that the more power you share the more powerful you are. I'm finding that to be very true."

Others shared Dave's reaction and experimentation with new methods began to spread. About six months after the first seminar, management had a chance to see how they were doing. As part of their Choice Points for Competence experience, which they had elected to try, managers received a mini-version of the Competence Analysis,™ reflecting current conditions in Design. Using their first analysis, conducted some eight months previously, as a baseline they discovered that following their participation in the first seminar, people reported that conditions for competence had increased a whopping 271%, an amount to be expected by chance fewer than five times out of 1,000.

Kopka picks up the narrative, "After management had been through both the Models I and Choice Points seminars, we felt we had to complete the process by having the employees go through Closing the Loop. We had all changed and people were wondering what we were up to. So we had to convince them of the mutual benefit of complete collaboration. As a result, our employees are happier and more productive. They are working better by communicating more effectively. Many of them are like born-again evangelists. They're out preaching to everybody else.''

So, the retraining effort did not end with management. Rank-and-file workers were sent to the Closing the Loop session as well.

The program's worth was tested late in 1984 by a group of designers and modelers who volunteered for assignment to the Probe V team. The task was to develop a model for showing at the 1985 Auto Show to be held in Japan. The annual event is an important opportunity for car makers to show their stuff and Ford executives do not take it lightly. Dave Rees was taking a chance by testing the program's value on this project.

''We tested what we learned about the competence process on the Probe V project,'' said Rees. ''The clay modelers, all of whom had been through Closing the Loop, really took it seriously. The results—new approaches—were fantastic. For example, they developed a new way of looking at a vehicle's environmental armature. In the past, engineers spent weeks doing drawings which were then sent to woodshop where a model was constructed. It took weeks to build. By the time it came back, the design had changed. It cost thousands of dollars. The modelers came up with the idea of building the armature out of tubing, which was much less expensive and much easier to change. And from the beginning of the project, they worked with the engineers, something they'd never done before. The benefit of that was that the engineers could identify potential problems early, before they became expensive. I'm very sensitive to seeing the same kind of success in other projects.''

The team that assembled to work on the Probe V was instructed to use all the team skills they'd learned from the Models Series. For the first time, the team, not management, was responsible for creating the best product possible and for deciding how to do it.

"It was hard at first," said Chuck Thomas, one of the clay modelers. "We were used to getting a sheet of paper listing things we were supposed to do and here we were in brainstorming sessions. It was a tremendous learning process. We learned that sometimes *we* know the answers. We learned to get more people involved in the beginning so that problems are taken care of early on. The Probe V became ours. It was more than just a job."

The Probe V model was completed in a record time of two months, despite limited manpower and financial resources. And, in the eyes of management—as well as the automotive world—their creation was a winner.

The Probe V has a coefficient of drag lower than that of the F-15 jet fighter aircraft. It also features flush glass, wrapover sliding doors, a vertical stabilizer, enclosed underbody, and covered wheel openings. The interior is highlighted by a projected holographic display of the electronic instrumentation and a unique tilt/telescoping steering wheel.

Rees said, "The results of our test were more than convincing. Some of our people really blossomed under the new system. They were able to complete the project by the deadline and save tens of thousands of dollars in the process with the approaches they came up with. They even came up with an inexpensive and fast method of examining the environmental armature which they call the ergonomic buck—an environmental bucket. This will be invaluable to us in years to come!

"The culture we're creating is opposed to the culture we've had. Before, you never made suggestions. Natural change that might have occurred by itself never did because new people copied the behavior of the people they perceived as successful. The authoritarian mode has never been challenged. We've always told people what to do and how to do it. Collaboration, though, is a faster problem solver. You can cut through the smoke and get right to the point. Communications is the key. We have learned how to foster an environment that invites communication. To get employees to collaborate you have to do more than pay it lip service. You've got to carry it through and support employees when things go wrong. You've got to earn their trust. It hasn't all been a bed of roses. Employees resisted at first. They thought they were being set up or asked to do the boss' job. You see, many of us made significant changes in our management styles. It will be awhile before all the wrinkles are worked out, but the benefits outweigh all the other issues. It's a real pleasure to see how our people behave, their attitudes. They're motivated. There's no way we can go back to the way we were. The momentum is just incredible!"

"Management support made a big difference," said John Jackson, a Master Modeler. "If we made a mistake, they said, 'Go try again.' It became an issue of where do we stop and how far do we go? I think the result has been that all of us have increased feelings of self-confidence and mutual respect. We're not afraid to get involved. We used to hide projects we wanted to do so that management wouldn't stop us. I don't think anybody here does that anymore."

According to John Hutchison, International and Advanced Concepts Modeling Coordinator, there are other benefits to the new team system. "We used to have to borrow people from other areas to work overtime to complete a project. We don't do that anymore. Team members are so involved with their projects that they are willing to work whenever necessary to see it through. They even call the office when they're on vacation to check on their projects."

One index of the new commitment was an extracurricular project initiated by the clay modelers themselves. So enriched were their worklives by the new approach to management, their personal involvement in Closing the Loop sessions, and the heady success of Probe V that they decided to do what they could to make sure that the process continued. On weekends they put together a presentation for management—drawing on the models and principles from their six-hour seminar sessions—and related the effects of the competence process to their own performance and morale. Top management, in turn, was so impressed by this spontaneous show of support and encouragement that they asked the modelers to repeat the presentation—this time for all management and, moreover, before video cameras. The resulting tape is now widely shown throughout the company.

The Probe V experience was, in many respects, tangible proof for the Design Staff that competence abounds and needs only the support of an enlightened management to be released. Don Kopka sums up the lesson learned: "There was a period when we were worried about our future. But now we are all prepared to compete regardless of what happens in the marketplace. The secret is our people. But it's much more than that. You can have the best and brightest on your side, but if you're standing in their way they won't do you much good. The real advantage we have is that we now know how to let our people work for us.''

* * *

Turn Around in Dayton

For an example of how the competence process works on a smaller scale than in one of the world's largest companies, we can turn to Progressive Industries of Dayton, Ohio. Progressive was, at the time of embarking on the competence process, a small film processing company with a growing network of Foto Fair outlets. After a good start in the early '70s, by 1978 Progressive was in trouble. The words that follow are, for the most part, those of Mike Adler, President, and Paul Pieschel, Progressive's Vice President of Human Resource Development.

Mike Adler set the stage. ''Back in 1978, Progressive Industries started losing money, for the usual reasons: competition, inconsistent quality, etc. Morale was mercurial. There was a very high turnover. We brought in a consulting company, which recommended we replace the president (me). I did not consider that a viable option! My first thought was that we paid lots of money to these guys and they didn't know anything about our business. They called me a benevolent dictator. Anyway, the consultant told us that people felt left out of decision making and did not understand decisions, and therefore would not commit to them. There was no consistency in decisions. Although in general, our employees liked the company, this thread of dissatisfaction kept reappearing. We decided to change the way we managed.

"We asked ourselves: Why are we in trouble as a company? We have good people working for us, our gross sales are at an all-time high, we are at the forefront of our technology. We have the newest and best equipment available. Yet, with all of this going for us, we are not only losing money, but we face the real possibility of extinction. Why can't intelligent people who know their field survive in this business? Why are some of our competitors doing so well when there appears to be little difference between them and us?"

These questions and others being asked by Adler had far-reaching significance. Progressive Industries, not unlike many organizations, had a history of attempting to solve its problems and cope with changes in its market by trying to become more technically competent, by purchasing more and better equipment, by increasing sales, by reducing budgets, by hiring smarter people, and the like.

The questions were being asked because in that year a sales volume of $24.5 million produced a pre-tax *loss* of $1.7 million. It was apparent that if Progressive Industries were to survive, let alone move forward, creative solutions to its problems had to be found.

While Adler didn't care for all the implications of the consultant's report, its findings were sobering. Adler and Pieschel decided to take a closer look at what was going on in-house. To gain a better understanding of the situation, each manager was interviewed in order to determine problem areas. In addition, a questionnaire soliciting similar information was sent to all personnel who had left the company within the last three years. A summary of the primary findings indicated that goals were vague and there was little organizational integration among the various departments; the functional structure was obsolete, resulting in dual accountability and poor horizontal communication; decision making was not sufficiently delegated, frequently resulting in a loss of valuable information and a perception that decisions were predetermined. Consequently, there was a low level of commitment among the workforce.

In meeting the challenge to resolve these problems, management focused on two primary areas: organizational structure and management style. The first was easiest to address and a solution quickly came off the drawing board—a new divisional organizational structure. Recognizing, however, that the best structure would fail without a consistent management style capable of gaining the commitment of the entire workforce, top management also began to study what amounted to the social technology of the work setting, and looked for ways of achieving a more participative style of management.

Adler continues, "Through the grapevine, we heard about the Competence Process. My first inclination was to send Paul Pieschel down to Houston to check it out. But since I was the problem, I was nominated to test the program. Paul went with me to make sure I didn't cut any classes."

Based on their Models I seminar experience, Adler and Pieschel decided to move ahead at top speed. In six months, all of Progressive's managers, as well as the representative from the union local and the chief steward, participated in the first of the Models series. In the months that followed, management began to put into practice the social science principles they had been taught about employee involvement, motivation, communication and management style. Top executives—who once went six months without meeting—established a regular schedule of meetings to exchange ideas and critique operations. General managers began to meet with their staffs once a week; the corporate executive committee started meeting every two weeks; and everyone got together at least once a month. This was part of an effort to decentralize and improve decision making. A norm of 'decision-by-consensus' was introduced with interesting results. Managers who were previously silent began to speak up, and managers with known combative instincts began to try to solve problems instead of pick fights. Pieschel reflects, "Progressive began making better decisions at all levels of management, and commitment to decisions improved. We saw the difference between logical commitment and *psychological* commitment."

Buoyed by its success at the management level, Progressive began to bring its hourly employees into the decision-making process, with the same creative results. By the end of the year, Progressive was managing in a different fashion than ever before. During the next year, it would know in no uncertain terms if this new way of managing made any difference in its struggle for survival and success.

Adler continues. "We brought the business agents and chief stewards through the program. It was a built-in challenge. They knew what we knew.

"As a result, we saw a dramatic improvement in quality and consistency of quality in our product. In addition, morale began to improve; there was less tension. Of course, the profit looked better, too.

"Nine months after we'd all been through the program, we realized we needed wage reviews. Unfortunately, because the industry was so fiercely competitive, we could not afford to pay salary increases. But we knew that our people needed more money. We (management) didn't know what to do. But we'd learned from the Competence Process that a good manager commits to both profits and people. If you're compromising, something is wrong. So we said, 'Hey, let the people make the decision.' They came up with two programs, a food co-op to save employees money on food; and a vegetable garden for employees on our property."

Early in the new year, Progressive asked its employees to reflect on the changes it saw compared to previous years: "Was there more involvement?" "Were there stronger feelings of commitment to the organization?" And, if so, "Were managers able to translate positive feelings into productive enterprise?" A post hoc Competence Analysis™ was conducted and, in a truly unscientific procedure, current conditions were compared with those "recalled" from a year prior. Even so, there was an estimated 200% increase in conditions for competence within Progressive, enough to be expected by chance fewer than two times out of 1,000. Survey data indicated substantial increases—in everyone's minds' eye things were much better at Progressive; but a collective impression, albeit positive, is not enough to make a payroll. Harder data, the kind budget officers are fond of, were used in the final analyses.

The profit/loss statement, productivity, quality of services, costs and performance results, using year-end data for Years I-III, provided a before and after view of Progressive's change effort. For Year I, on sales of $24,627,000, Progressive experienced a pre-tax loss of $1,713,000. The "before" picture was clearly dismal. In Year II, on sales of $14,821,000, the pre-tax loss was cut to $268,000. Improved, but still less than healthy. But by the end of fiscal

Year III, on sales of $15,000,000, Progressive turned a *profit* of $1,013,000. Moreover, service schedule rose to the 95% level compared with 85% in Year II, and 80% in Year I. Quality standards, seriously below forecast before, were consistently above forecast in Year III. Budgeted results were exceeded for the first time and productivity increased an average of 15%.

Progressive achieved a dramatic turnaround of its economic picture, not because of traditional economic measures but because, apparently, it began to focus on the social technology of the firm, at least in part because management worked to increase the conditions for competence within the organization. All this in not quite three years. Despite its small size and greater ease of coordination, the Progressive experience was not unlike that of Ford. But the story doesn't end there.

Adler describes the big turnaround. "Our first two or three years after the Models seminars helped us change our management were dramatic (internally). Then our business began to change rapidly. Our management decided we no longer had the resources to compete. We had to change in order to grow. It was a painful decision. We called everyone together and explained the situation to them, and they understood. We bought the franchise then.

"When we decided to become a franchise business, we were at a crossroad. We had tested a new method of photofinishing that we thought would revolutionize the business, but it would cost millions of dollars more than we had to invest. Franchising was the natural solution. We noticed, though, that some other franchises were not very successful, primarily because the franchisor tends to 'boss' the franchisee. Normally, the former doesn't give the latter much involvement, if any. Corporate executives usually make the decisions and tell everybody else to follow them. But thanks to the Competence Process, we knew how we could make a franchise system work. We had learned that commitment comes from collaboration, and if you treat others as if they are capable, they will reward you. We consider our franchisees our partners. They are always involved in decision making that affects them. And we get a better decision because of their involvement.

"Franchising embodies the concepts we learned from the Competence Process better than any other structure. It is a real partnership, where the partners are mutually dependent, legally, economically and psychologically. Our franchisee training program includes this management philosophy. We know that our competitors are as technically astute as we are. But we teach our 'partners' that our management tone will help us be better."

Today, Progressive is known as Moto-Photo Labs. It is currently one of the top 200 franchises in the country and the number one photo-finishing franchise. There is no way to pinpoint causality for all this. The best explanation is that management enabled and encouraged the expression of competence among its people. But Mike Adler has his own opinion. "I attribute our success as a franchise to the Competence Process. Before we got involved in franchising we heard a lot of horror stories about franchises that didn't work. We could see that the reason they didn't work was that the franchisor felt he was more capable than the franchisee. We approached it differently. We consider each franchisee as our partner, our equal. Partnerships have more potential than dictatorships."

* * *

When East Meets West

For Brian Warner, the major strength of the Competence Process is its applicability across cultures. "As Director of International Training for Wang Laboratories," said Warner, "I had the opportunity to observe the effects of the Competence Process in several different countries. Regardless of language, no matter what the prevailing norms governing management and workers, the process struck the same human chord and yielded the same results."

The setting against which Warner worked was not always as receptive or conducive to change as he wished. Indeed, Warner likened management of Wang International in the early 1980's to some hybrid sport that people made up as they went along. He describes the history of Wang International and his experience with the Competence Process as follows.

"Working at Wang is a little like trying to play baseball when everybody is an individual and people just do as they please. The rules change so quickly it's hard to keep your feet on the ground. The ball is pitched; you hit it and run toward first base, only to find that the first baseman has taken the base to center field. You say, 'Hey, this is different . . .' and take off after the guy who ends up running around the whole ball park with first base under his arm.

"That's like Wang in the early 80's. Trying to add some measure of stability to the way people think about managing others and the way that managers can influence others to improve productivity appeared to be an impossible task. But that's where it started five years ago. The average manager stayed in his job about five to nine months and then was promoted. The company was growing at a staggering rate—35 to 45 percent a year—and it was impossible not to get caught up in the frantic pace which characterized Wang at this time.

"The company grew by 20,000 people in a four-year period. But fast growth and profits are not the whole story. Salesmen in the field were 'turning over' at an average of 35 percent a year and their bosses were leaving slightly faster at 38 percent. Nobody was willing to take a close look at the cost of this turnover, but if you take your calculator out, you quickly realize that many millions of dollars were lost every year. We're not just talking about a couple of million dollars. In 1984, turnover of sales-related functions in the U.S. cost the company over 30 million dollars.

"This was the stage that was set for the introduction of a different value set in managing people. Carl Masi, at that time newly-appointed Vice President of European Operations, characterized the need to move his management and executive group from '. . . high tech to high touch.'

"In January of 1982, Masi spent four days with all of his European management team, country managers and his direct staff, going through the Models I program. 'The most unique thing about that meeting,' Masi recalls, 'was the fact that for the first time, key management people were getting a chance to examine the impact of their assumptions and behavior on their direct reports. It was an eye-opening experience for all of us.'

"In the meeting that followed Models 1, the significant decision was made to formalize management—each local manager would be held accountable for productivity in their own subsidiaries. One manager realized that his own development was critical to his success. He made significant attempts to change and improve his management style based on what he learned in Models I. He implemented a more collaborative approach. That subsidiary has really taken off.

"Since that time, every European subsidiary has implemented the Models I program with all of their management staff. A new language of management was created in Europe that year. The conversation was no longer solely concerning bookings and revenues. Now managers were talking about 'styles of management and tracking toward competence.'

"The level of commitment is different when the program involves people who work together. The collaborative element reinforces learning. We developed a human resources planning system for managers to implement, following guidelines set by the company, so managers are rewarded for implementing human resource activities that support the competence process. Productivity is measured by the manager.

"Ian Diery is the best example I can think of when I try to describe the effects of the Competence Process on managers. Ian is a success story in Wang, par excellence. He is a native Australian that 'hitchhiked' cross continent to England in 1980. He was driving a mini-cab in London when he answered an advert in the London Times for word-processing salesmen at Wang U.K. He was tremendously successful and one year later became branch manager; 12 months later district manager; 14 months later national sales manager; and then country manager of Wang U.K.

"Ian Diery, as Managing Director of Wang U.K., describes

his experience with the Competence Process this way: 'For me, this was the first time I ever really had a measure and direction to my management tactics, and the effects of this were profound. When I came to the realization that my people needed to be involved in the decision-making process, it was like a light was turned on. We formed an executive committee that, in effect, began to run the operation and take responsibility. It was no longer just me. We had fantastic results from that change. Each manager then did the same thing within their own functions. Our success and phenomenal growth in the UK market is directly related to how we work together and the Competence Process has played a big part in this.'

"Diery continues, 'When we implemented the Models II, Choice Points for Competence, program in July of 1983, the entire upper management staff participated, some fifty managers. Instead of talking about managing people, we were now discussing how to create conditions for competence and building an organization that could maintain a 30 to 40 percent growth pattern without killing everybody in the process.

'We were able to identify weaknesses and develop plans for improvement that were committed to by the entire group. It was interesting to see how closely the OCI scores from the Models II program compared to our own productivity measures for all of our sales, service and support functions. We even took the time to analyze our own Employee Opinion Survey results, by question, as they related to the OCI scores. Some people needed proof and they got it.'

"That year," Brian Warner resumes the story, "Wang UK broke the 100 million mark in revenues—the first of any international subsidiary to do so. Ian Diery is holding true to his record and after 13 months in the job was promoted to Vice President of European Operations.

''But that's not the only success story from Wang in the use of the Competence Process. We put it to its ultimate cross-cultural test. From the West we went to the Far East and we found yet another example of management growth springing out of Hong Kong, Taiwan, Singapore and mainland China. Ed Yang, Vice President of the Asia area for Wang talks about building his management team: 'It's difficult to change some management concepts that people hold. The Chinese culture is very much based on respect for authority and management. This comes from the fact that all Chinese cultures have deep respect and commitment for the family and the authority of parents. It is easy to see how managers can get 'carried away' with their authority.

'When we completed the Models I and II programs as a group, we found that we had broken down some of the barriers that prevented us from communicating effectively. Some of us thought that the Competence Process concepts would not apply to the Asian cultures, but when we looked at the feedback instruments that our people filled out as part of the programs, they were saying that these principles are universal for managers and if we wanted them to be more productive, then we had better start using them.'''

Warner concludes, ''Wang is currently expanding its operations into China in cooperation with the Chinese government. Ed Yang has spearheaded this new venture for Wang.

''We knew that many companies had failed to be effective in China because of their attitudes and style in doing business in the mainland. We thought about this carefully. Other companies would take their most successful managers in Hong Kong or other parts of Asia and put them into China, often times with disastrous results. We considered carefully the style and skill of each manager that accepted an assignment in China. This market has tremendous potential and we wanted managers that could create a productive environment—conditions for competence—with their employees and staff. We achieved what we set out to do. Our understanding and ability to do this was directly related to the concepts and management principles that were learned in Models I and II, in the Competence Process.''

Warner concludes with some impressions about the computer industry and customer service. ''Our industry was, and is, a high-tech industry. Profitability and marketshare center around technology. New-fangled gizmos drive the marketplace. We are entering a stage where that has to change. The market is glutted with high-tech whiz-bangs. The customer is saying, 'That doesn't meet our needs. Until you allow me to participate in the decisions you make on my behalf, you don't have my business.' Slow down in business is the result. Competence Process concepts, then, need to be used in customer, as well as employee, relations. Interaction with customers impacts image, how you do marketing and strategic planning. Our industry has historically been short-term. Products and people would come and go. It has been very short-sighted. At Wang, that's starting to change.

''The Competence Process provides a research-based model that gives managers the information they need to increase productivity. Until the OCI was developed, an analysis of how behavior impacts productivity never existed. Using it has enabled us to make progress. It has impacted a lot of key people here. In a lot of places, the quick-fix is the popular thing. I call one-minute solutions and simplistic 'pragmatics' laetrile management. It's comfortable. It doesn't require anything of the manager. Unfortunately, it doesn't work either. It's difficult to change that mentality. It's hard sometimes to get managers to change or to commit to process. It takes thought and effort. But it works. People don't take seriously their own influence on the workforce. The Competence Process enables managers to see how their behavior affects the workforce much more deeply than they imagined. It teaches them to take their own behavior seriously. That's not a bad place to start.''

* * *

From research and development, manufacturing, service, and high technology organizations, reports are the same. When the Competence Process is seriously applied, potential is released and both people and productivity prosper.

In each of the cases presented, the Competence Process was used to solve existing problems of poor morale and lagging productivity. It was tried as an experimental curative. But this need not be, nor is it always, the case. The Competence Process is perhaps best used as a preventive measure, as an approach to managing and organizing that avoids the problems of worker malaise and declining production by working for competence and health in the first place.

* * *

Creating a Culture from Scratch

An interesting opportunity to use the competence process as a preventive mechanism was provided by the management of Mazda Motor Manufacturing (USA) Corporation. They decided to manage for competence and health from the outset. In preparing to open their new — and first—U.S. plant in Detroit, management worked from a preventive posture and used the Competence Process to set the norms and standards necessary for organizational competence *in advance.* People were hired and the plant was constructed; and then, before either working relationships were established or a single piece of work was accomplished, management addressed both its workers and itself to the conscious creation of a culture in support of competence.

Much of the work required for this novel approach to organizing the technical and social resources for productive outcomes fell to the Training and Development staff. Ken Kumiega, Director of Training and Development for Mazda USA, describes the process thusly:

"Our approach was one of pro-active norm setting and organizational influence. From the outset, we wanted both our goals and the pathways to their attainment to be clear and shared on everyone's part.

"As it turns out, the basic concepts and values of the competence process are ingrained in our organizational and training philosophies and guiding principles. In fact, the readiness to operationalize these was merely waiting to be realized; the Detroit plant provided the opportunity. At Mazda our philosophies depict mutual respect among people, positive relations with the community, business concerns for quality and cost, human concerns for interpersonal skills and the involvement of people, and working together to achieve the common goals of the company and all of its members. In addition, we share concerns for working effectively in a structured way to create ideas, for the improvement of methods and quality, for effective communications, and providing support for each other and between functional areas. We have a concern that the individual person be able to grow and, in turn, help the company grow. Finally, we are committed to managing our business in a rational and humanistic way. A common phrase at Mazda has been "Rationality and Humanity," to be used as our check and balance when we make decisions or implement our work plans. The values and supporting conditions for collaboration, commitment, and creativity are very consistent with the objectives we are preparing to serve.

"Our development strategy in building a new culture was to provide organizational targets to all of our new hires and then to determine ways to grow together to achieve these. We understood that, very likely, people would have to change their behavior, attitudes and techniques in some way to function within the Mazda philosophy. So we trained both ends of the organization — top to bottom — with common training so everyone could speak the same language — that is, use a common terminology and employ shared concepts — and have the same expectations. We also provided applications and techniques, not just words, of motivation or direction. Again, this training was provided to every person hired, not just the select few.

"With our supervisory levels we went a step further and provided training on behavioral science concepts and, most importantly, how these concepts are applied by managers considered to be successful. This, of course, is described in Models I of the competence process. Because we are a very young organization without a history of working relationships or work situations, we chose a different strategy for introducing the competence process.

"We decided to conduct our sessions in two parts. The first part, we decided, would set the stage by clearly defining the targets of the organization and the use of behavioral science concepts. Part two would measure and provide personal feedback to participants regarding their achievement of these targets. This was done by first conducting the Models I program and withholding subordinate evaluations; because supervisory relationships didn't exist or were too young for accurate assessment, we reasoned that subordinate feedback should be used later as a developmental tool. Therefore, we scheduled the second step to be conducted 6-9 months later with subordinate feedback to provide measurement for leaders of their use of Models I concepts.

"Also, currently, we are creating the next level of learning and growth by introducing the personal and behavioral effects of a leader's power style, as opposed to just the structural organizational power significance of a leadership position. We are just entering this stage and, hopefully, we will see the results of our efforts in the coming year.

"Results seen so far from part one of our approach are: an understanding among people of social science concepts to the point of now knowing how to apply them; a sense of confidence among leaders that they are able to work with their subordinates in a participative way; an eagerness on everyone's part to reach the targets identified; and a focused sense of how to apply social science concepts towards chosen outcomes, rather than managing by trial and error. Again, as Jay Hall pointed out at the beginning of this chapter, these are not scientific results but observations and personal conclusions based on our own experiences at Mazda. We are making good progress with this approach toward our five-year objectives.

"For Mazda, the competence process has been a working concept that reinforces our existing corporate feeling that teams require three types of skills to be successful; namely, Technical skills — that is, skills necessary to perform a technical task regardless of the functional area or responsibility to include both Manufacturing and Administration; Interpersonal skills — those skills necessary for people to interact in a constructive way vertically and horizontally to create and maintain a positive environment, and Group skills — those practices necessary for people in groups to contribute and be involved in effective and efficient ways.

"The competence process at Mazda has proved to be a relevant and practical approach to effective organizational operation; it has helped us begin an organization to "do what makes sense" and utilize all the talents it contains. The key word here, in my opinion, is "process" not "product." This may sound strange, but if leaders focus on the product, they may never find the best process; and, as a result, never obtain the best product. The point is, if leaders focus on the process, they will find the best process; and their product will naturally follow as the best product. The concepts of the competence structure, I believe, have helped our organization find the best process."

Just as we don't have to be sick to get better, we don't have to bottom out before we become willing to rethink our assumptions and our priorities. We can—at any time, if we choose—base our management and structure our organizations according to a prophecy of competence.

XV

When Prophecies are Fulfilled

We can fulfill our prophecies of competence if we are willing to change, if we can honestly review both our organizational priorities and our managerial practices. Contrary to conventional wisdom, most people welcome change when they have reason to believe it is for the better. As their values shift and they gain new insights into more preferred practices, they will often set to with uncommon zeal. They will undertake new tasks and pursue new directions with enthusiasm. This can be a mixed blessing in the case of competence.

On one hand, while the typical organization is not initially structured in support of competence dynamics, with proper commitment from management it may fairly easily become so because of the widespread desire among its people for the conditions of competence. A major strength of the competence process is that it strikes a responsive chord; people are receptive to its promise. But, on the other hand, there is always a tendency to expect too much when we embrace new ways. Many of us often anticipate that we can solve more problems—make more things right—than we actually can. And, more often than not, think we can do it all overnight. Unbridled enthusiasm sets us up for disappointment. One of the major pitfalls encountered by social scientists in the past has been the tendency among those people who were persuaded at all to view their findings and solutions as virtual cure-alls. There are no cure-alls, least of all the competence process. But there can be more affirmative action; there can be the excitement of discovery and progress; there can be feelings of efficacy and worth from engaging and solving the problems of competence.

Problems of Competence

The Competence process is not a panacea. It will solve some problems and not others; it will cause some erstwhile unapparent problems to surface and others, apparently solved, only to go undercover. We should be clear that a commitment to competence will not free us of organizational, managerial, or interpersonal problems. What such a commitment can do, however, is change the *nature* of the problems we must deal with as managers.

Problems of Growth Rather than Stagnation

As competence becomes a reality, managers will find that they have exchanged many of the problems of stagnation for problems associated with personal and organizational growth. As Chris Argyris pointed out, most of the problems confronting organizations are of their own making.[1] By ignoring or attempting to reverse the natural human tendency for growth—the needs for maturity and autonomy—organizations have traditionally created stagnation. By

[1] Argyris, C. *Personality and Organization*. New York: Harper, 1957.

creating places where work is to be endured, not enjoyed, where people mark time rather than make progress, we have encouraged decay of the very spirit which underlies health and productivity. And the problems of apathy, hostility, slavish conformity, and apparent incompetence are simply the signs of this stagnation.

The competence process can renew the growth process. And, doing so, it will release a multitude of new considerations, a host of new "problems," which will vie for managerial attention. Managers will find, for example, that people are less tolerant of boredom. When competence becomes the priority, people will not only find that their work is enriched but they will come to *expect* that work will be meaningful most of the time. They will chafe more publicly when little is required of them or the tasks to be done fall too far below their levels of competence.

By the same token, managers may anticipate that once involvement is valued and collaborative dynamics are set in motion and verified, people will often seek to broaden their collaboration to other areas. Their sense of ownership and desire to contribute will be so great that they will have opinions—and a need to express them—about issues and practices well beyond the scope of their particular tasks.

Frequently managers will be confronted with problems of too much extended effort: they will find some people intent on doing more than is either required or desired. It will sometimes prove hard to keep a simple task simple or, once a goal has been reached, to lay it aside for another.

Self-esteem will emerge as a double-edged sword which the manager must handle deftly. In one respect, an emphasis on competence will unleash nearly all the constructive energies associated with ego dynamics. The will to produce will intensify; opportunities to express—indeed, display— one's special competencies will be more highly valued; and the bonds of personal identification with one's work will be strengthened. But, at the same time, less mature personal needs associated with ego may be expressed more freely and openly as well. Some people will experience episodic bouts of personal aggrandizement and become unduly preoccupied with recognition and personal status. Having been rewarded for essentiality, some people will come to feel indispensable. They will, from time to time, become hypersensitive to signs of managerial neglect and uncomfortable with the rule of equity implicit in the competence process. They will worry about whether they are as fully appreciated as they should be.

Managers may well find that they must contend with the counterproductive forces of what some organizational consultants have called the "love puddle" syndrome. One of the boomerang effects associated with the new competence values of openness, mutuality, cooperation, and respect is the unspoken—and unintended—notion that everyone must *love* one another. As Freud has said, to love and be loved is one of the two fundamentals of life; but quite frankly, there are better places for its accomplishment than in the workplace. Organizations exist so that objectives may be reached, goods produced, and services rendered. Performance and quality are inherent in organizational purpose. Some people believe that mature love must be unconditional. Not only does that lack of conditionality make the use of candor and equity more difficult, but it is devoid of performance considerations. This is another growth problem.

Competence is not concerned with love so much as with mutual *respect*. Love and respect are different qualities, but the manager may find that people will attempt to confuse the two. Respect is tied directly to accomplishment. Both self-respect and that of others flow from behaving competently, from doing what needs to be done. And task accomplishment is a fundamental requirement of the competent organization. Managers, therefore, must learn to promote values of respect based on doing while guarding against the immobilization of interpersonal competence and diminished sense of accountability which unconstrained affection can foster.

And there will be those who are uncomfortable with the demands of renewed growth. We discussed in Chapter II the manner in which traditional organizational values often lead to an extinction of the competent response; seldom rewarded and sometimes punished, competent behavior is simply dropped from one's on-the-job repertoire. This is the major effect of stagnation in an organization and it exacts a tremendous emotional toll. The desire for competence is so frustrated and the trauma is so great that competence is subverted and displaced by cynicism and diminished productive outlook for many people. Not only do these people no longer look to the organization as a place where their needs for competence can be acted upon, but they have learned to accommodate themselves to less-than conditions for competence for the eight or so hours a day they must spend in the organization. This is such a fundamental compromise of basic human aspirations that it requires an enormous investment on the part of those individuals who are able to pull it off. They will often be reluctant to give up the familiar pain of stagnation to risk once again attaining the unknown, almost forgotten, rewards of growth. These are the casualties of organizational life, but they must be reclaimed. Like the other problems which will characterize a commitment to competence, they too are amenable to proper management.

Problems of growth can be addressed by competent management. Managers will find that they must become more creative themselves. In dealing with the growth problems of competence, they must be able to help people perceive reality more accurately; they must be able to convey the fact that an organization can neither be all things to all people nor a realistic substitute for life outside the organization. It cannot be these things, nor *should* it be. Managers may have to rethink traditional approaches to incentives, the proper role of seniority, and the many ways in which respect may or may not be conveyed across the board in an organization. In short, managers must become more competent. And this may be the ultimate problem of growth: Managers themselves must grow; creating a new system of values pursuant to more appropriate managerial practices will be the key to creating a management that is consistent with the competence of its people.

The important thing to bear in mind when contemplating the problems of growth which competence may set in motion is that, all the while, *people are doing what needs to be done.* They are busy producing and pursuing health in their workplaces. If we can solve the problems of managerial competence, performance will be uniformly high and the problems of growth which arise will simply be a sign of life itself.

Problems of Managerial Competence

Organizational leaders will find that a commitment to competence requires more of managers than has been the case in the past. Competence will require different values, practices, and skills than those traditionally emphasized among managers. It may well require a rethinking of priorities in the selection and development of managerial talent. Competence will require professionalism. No longer will technical expertise automatically qualify one to manage the collective efforts of other people. The importance of work technology notwithstanding, the competent manager will be the one who has mastered the *social technology* of the job: those values, principles and practices necessary for providing the conditions under which *people,* not machines, work together to do what needs to be done.

In what I have long considered to be an aberration of the traditional organizational emphasis on "selection procedures," candidates for management are frequently identified because they have performed well *in some other profession.* The outstanding engineer, for example, is often rewarded by a "promotion" to management. Good teachers frequently end up as Principals or Deans, their days filled with administrative issues not even philosophically related to their classroom specialities. For many years we were convinced that it took a qualified physician—a person with medical knowledge—to head up a hospital; only recently have we begun to recognize that the management of a health facility is itself a profession. My point is that we have filled the ranks of management in our organizations in ways which reflect priorities other than the competent management of those organizations. Expertise in one narrow area does not imply competence in another broader one.

These are manifestations of our confused priorities—of our preoccupation with technology and related expertise rather than with issues of how and why people work. We have produced several generations of *inanimate* management, people who are more at home with figuring budgets, developing plans, and designing machines than they are with dealing competently with other people. Some have even come to define management in such terms. But technological expertise is not—has never been—a valid index of one's ability to listen to, support, free, or encourage other human beings to perform at their highest level of competence. The skills required for competent management involve people, not "things," and the sooner we face this fact the sooner we will be able to make widespread competence a reality in our organizations.

A commitment to competence will, if it is to be realized, require a different kind of management. It will require managers who can deal in a productive way with the multitude of human forces—some constructive, some problematic—which are unleashed in the organizational community. All that is required to insure such management is to recognize the dependency of organizational competence on managerial competence and develop managers accordingly. This will entail a review of current selection procedures and, certainly, a rethinking of training and development priorities. But the social technology of management development is well documented and available for application when organizational leaders are sincere in their commitment to competence.[2,3,4]

Just as the conditions for competence must be

2 Shtogren, J. A. (Ed.), *Models for Management: The Structure of Competence*. The Woodlands, Texas: Teleometrics Int'l., 1980.

3 Hornstein, H., B. Bunker, W. Burke, M. Gindes, & R. Lewicki. *Social Intervention*. New York: The Free Press, 1971.

4 Argyris, C. *Intervention Theory and Method*. Reading, Massachusetts: Addison Wesley, 1970.

systematically planned for and created within an organization for it to become competent as a totality, the value structure and skills associated with competence must be examined and learned by the person who would manage for competence. Thirty years of social science research and practical application are at our disposal for such purposes. And when enough people equip themselves to manage the competence process within their organizations, we may well discover that not only the organization and its people will prosper but that we foster more competent communities as well, for organizations set the tone of the communities in which they function.

Organizations and Managers as Social Forces

Of the people who work, probably 95% or more do so in a formal organization. This means that the formal organization—its values and procedures—is second only to the family as a formative influence on the individual. Think about that for a moment. One's feelings of efficacy and worth, self-respect, sense of normalcy, health, and fundamental humanness are as much affected, perhaps even determined, by the way we run our organizations as by what transpires in the basic family unit.

If we wish to delude ourselves about the enormity of this organizational potential for influence, we might embrace the notion that most people divorce themselves from their work upon leaving it for the day or the weekend. Many, executives and blue-collar workers alike, would disagree; and so would I. Not only do we fail to shut out our world of work upon crossing the family threshold, but many people find that their experiences at work have a direct bearing on both the type and quality of interactions they have with other family members. Kicking the family cat in reaction to the day's frustrations at work is an old managerial chestnut. But, be that as it may, it is not my purpose to delve into the sociological impact of organizational life on family dynamics. My point is simply that where we work affects how we live elsewhere and organizations committed to competence will have different impacts on the lives of their people than organizations committed to alternative values.

It is not too farfetched to anticipate that people who enjoy a sense of efficacy and worth at work are better equipped motivationally to function as competent members of the community. They are more likely than others to believe that there is more than merely symbolic value in civic involvements, that the individual can have an impact, that a sense of community is to be preferred over self-serving competitiveness, and that we are creative enough to solve most of the problems confronting us. These are, after all, reflections of the core values of competence.

But what of the influence of organizations which embrace less than competence? Having employed practices and promoted values which impair the adaptive fitness of people at work, can we then expect that they send these same people out into their communities unimpaired? I suspect not. But the implications of such organizations for our communities is, I think, more profound and insidious than just the effect on the individual and his or her family. There are too many Love Canals, Three Mile Islands, and Bhopals in our history. But, beyond such flagrant betrayals of trust, there are more subtle and potentially unhealthy influences. *I believe that entire communities mirror their dominant organizations, both in philosophy and practice.* This, to the extent it is a valid premise, adds a new dimension to the issue of competence within organizations.

My experience has been that virtually all the organizations which go to make up a community—school boards, PTA's, vestries and boards of deacons, trustees for hospitals and service organizations, regents, volunteer agencies, and even groups of appointed officials—seek to emulate the structure and practices of their local businesses and industries. It is commonplace enough that it may be taken as axiomatic that, in filling vacancies and identifying leadership for such groups, the rule is to look to "successful" businesspeople or "prominent" citizens. The desire is explicit: "Help us run this board the way you run your organization!"

The people who serve in such capacities in their communities take the charge seriously. They will bring all the acumen and experience at their command to bear on the problems of the community. My point is a simple one: if they represent organizations committed to competence, they will exert influence for competence in the community. If they come from more traditional settings, they will, with all good intentions, try to steer their community boards and committees in other less viable directions toward priorities of budget, control, and compromise. In this way, I believe, the practices and commitments of our organizations and those who lead them tend to be spread throughout the community. And we will encounter their influence well beyond the factory door or executive suite.

If competence, doing well what needs to be done, is the priority, the community will know it from the actions and programs which pour forth. But if competence is subverted to more traditional priorities, we have to look more closely.

Often the logic and values of formal organizations, when imposed on communities, do not reveal their effects until it is too late. For example, I have seen small towns stagnate and decay because raising the funds to refurbish buildings was seen by the city fathers as potentially unpopular and politically risky. I know of a school board—composed of prominent citizens and business leaders from the community—which committed its school system to build several new elementary and intermediate school buildings according to the Open System concept. This decision was not reached on the basis of pedagogical considerations; teachers were not even provided the specialized training called for under the Open concept. Rather, the school board chose such buildings because their round configurations, with few interior walls, allowed more *cost-effective* construction. The trustees risked and misappropriated the funds of a hospital endowment because it was the financially savvy thing to do. What was the cost to property owners, to teachers and students? To patients? Did anyone bother to ask? We don't know; but we do know that school experiences, for example, affect esteem and health—sow the seeds of productive orientation—just as surely as work experiences do. This point is, of course, that in committing to competence within their organizations, managers must adopt a larger view; they must, in addition, consider how they can be the messengers of competence in their communities.

For years now, social philosophers have commented freely on the social responsibility of business and industry, the economic organs of society. I believe that *all* organizations have a very important social responsibility; but it is not one of supporting local charities or granting scholarships or sponsoring research as is often considered the case. These are all worthwhile pursuits; but far and away the most important and far-reaching contribution any organization and its management might make to its community is to become a force for competence. To so organize and manage itself that the people who comprise the organization reflect its competence in their daily lives and thus spread its effects throughout the community. The uneducated, ex-longshoreman, and prizewinning philosopher, Eric Hoffer said, "To be human is to be competent." We need to reflect such thinking in both our organizations and communities so that we can deal more competently with both our internal and external realities.

Once, not too long ago, after I had completed a presentation of the competence process to a group of leaders from several different organizations, one of them—a top-level executive—said, "Do you want me to do this stuff or do you want me to do my job?" I had heard variations on the question before, so I replied with a question of my own. "What is your job?" And without hesitation, the man answered, "My job is to help my organization *compete!*"

The need to compete effectively is a part of that external reality with which organizations must contend, particularly in the private sector and internationally. But it is best served by tending to the internal realities of our organizations.

"It seems to me," I said to the executive, "that your problem holds the seeds of the solution you want. I believe the organization that is truly productive and enjoys good health in the workplace will be the one most able to compete effectively. Maybe you've been putting all the emphasis on the wrong syllables. To me, the word *com-pete* is only the first part of the word competence. In my opinion, the organization which acknowledges and encourages and enables the fullest expression of its human competence is an organization best equipped to compete. And that's a matter of leadership.

"You see," I said to the man, "*you* are the competence connection. Because you are a leader, it is up to you whether or not the competence of the people you lead will ever be brought to bear on, meshed with, connected to the work that needs to be done."

Each of us is a competence connection in one way or another. We can, if we choose, work to join the competence around us to the jobs that need doing. We can encourage and enable productivity and health in our places of work. And maybe, in the process, we can even help tone up the whole society.

That's really what it is all about, isn't it?

Epilogue

Like the children of Israel, we have wandered too long in the wilderness. Our self-deceptions have kept us there, blinding us to both the competence around us and our responsibilities for seeing to its release. The following excerpt from Frederick Winslow Taylor's *The Principles of Scientific Management* is offered as a counterpoint to the themes of competence developed in this book. As a major influence on management thinking since its publication in 1911, it exemplifies how a competence so apparent, that of the pig-iron worker Schmidt, may be ignored and mismanaged when management control and executive judgment are deemed more valuable than feelings of efficacy and worth among those who do the work.

He was a little Pennsylvania Dutchman who had been observed to trot back home for a mile or so after his work in the evening about as fresh as he was when he came trotting down to work in the morning. We found that upon wages of $1.15 a day he had succeeded in buying a small plot of ground, and that he was engaged in putting up the walls of a little house for himself in the morning before starting to work and at night after leaving. He also had the reputation of being exceedingly "close," that is, of placing a very high value on a dollar. As one man whom we talked *to about him said, "A penny looks about the size of a cart-wheel to him." This man we will call Schmidt.*

The task before us, then, narrowed itself down to getting Schmidt to handle 47 tons of pig iron per day and making him glad to do it. This was done as follows. Schmidt was called out from among the gang of pig-iron handlers and talked to somewhat in this way:

"Schmidt, are you a high-priced man?"

"Vell, I don't know vat you mean."

"Oh yes, you do. What I want to know is whether you are a high-priced man or not."

"Vell, I don't know vat you mean."

"Oh, come now, you answer my questions. What I want to find out is whether you are a high-priced man or one of these cheap fellows here. What I want to find out is whether you want to earn $1.85 a day or whether you are satisfied with $1.15, just the same as all those cheap fellows are getting."

"Did I vant $1.85 a day? Vas dot a high-priced man? Vell, yes, I vas a high-priced man."

"Oh, you're aggravating me. Of course you want $1.85 a day—everyone wants it! You know perfectly well that that has very little to do with your being a high-priced man. For goodness' sake answer my questions, and don't waste any more of my time. Now come over here. You see that pile of pig iron?

"Yes."

"You see that car?"

"Yes."

"Well, if you are a high-priced man, you will load that pig iron on that car to-morrow for $1.85. Now do wake up and answer my question. Tell me whether you are a high-priced man or not."

"Vell—did I got $1.85 for loading dot pig iron on dot car to-morrow?"

"Yes, of course you do, and you get $1.85 for loading a pile like that every day right through the year. That is what a high-priced man does, and you know it just as well as I do."

"Vell, dot's all right. I could load dot pig iron on the car to-morrow for $1.85, and I get it every day, don't I?"

"Certainly you do—certainly you do."

"Vell, den, I vas a high-priced man."

"Now, hold on, hold on. You know just as well as I do that a high-priced man has to do exactly as he's told from morning till night. You have seen this man here before haven't you?"

"No, I never saw him."

"Well, if you are a high-priced man, you will do exactly as this man tells you to-morrow, from morning till night. When he tells you to pick up a pig and walk, you pick it

up and you walk, and when he tells you to sit down and rest, you sit down. You do that right straight through the day. And what's more, no back talk. Now a high priced man does just what he's told to do, and no back talk. Do you understand that? When this man tells you to walk, you walk; when he tells you to sit down, you sit down, and you don't talk back at him. Now you come on to work here to-morrow morning and I'll know before night whether you are really a high-priced man or not."

This seems to be rather rough talk. And indeed it would be if applied to an educated mechanic, or even an intelligent laborer. With a man of the mentally sluggish type of Schmidt it is appropriate and not unkind, since it is effective in fixing his attention on the high wages which he wants and away from what, if it were called to his attention, he probably would consider impossibly hard work.

What would Schmidt's answer be if he were talked to in a manner which is usual under the management of "initiative and incentive?" say, as follows:

"Now, Schmidt, you are a first-class pig-iron handler and know your business well. You have been handling at the rate of 12½ tons per day. I have given considerable study to handling pig iron, and feel sure that you could do a much larger day's work than you have been doing. Now don't you think that if you really tried you could handle 47 tons of pig iron per day, instead of 12½ tons?"

What do you think Schmidt's answer would be to this?

From: The Principles of Scientific Management
Frederick Winslow Taylor, 1911

Statistical Appendix

Tests of Statistical Significance

In the following pages may be found summaries of the various statistical analyses made of competence data. These pages reflect a personal bias. They are not included with any anticipation that their content will be widely read or studied. They are included for only two reasons, really: for those who are interested in the statistical processes which led to the various conclusions characterizing the competence process and, of a more personal nature, because I believe statistics tell us when we are on firm scientific ground and when we are not.

Statistics keep us honest and help us avoid self-deception. Perhaps of greater importance, they prevent us from deceiving others. In my view, those of us who offer suggestions about how organizations might function or what managers might do differently are obligated—scientifically and morally—to first insure that we are not merely mouthing some "common sense" solutions to complex problems or "new" insights based on single chance occurrences. The stakes are too large; too many people are affected. For those who would advise or prescribe there is no substitute for the hard work of research. It is only through the systematic and, one would hope, scientific collections and analysis of data, accomplished more than once, that we can claim to speak with any confidence that what we describe and *recommend* is based in fact rather than personal fantasy. Statistical analysis is the handmaiden of this process. And, for this reason more than any other, the following tables and summaries are presented. Nothing preceeding these entries should be taken seriously if these analyses are found wanting.

— Table I —

Relationship of Opportunities for Collaboration to Productive Orientation

Summary of multiple discriminant function analysis of feelings characterizing productive orientation.

$\Lambda = .634$
$F_{5,9594} = 1109.553$
$p = .0000$

	CENTROID SCORES		χ^2	df	p
	LOW PARTICIPATION	HIGH PARTICIPATION			
ROOT I	6.4792	9.3480	4379.065	5	.0000

Summary of univariate ANOVA of feelings characterizing productive orientation.

VARIABLE	$F_{1,9598}$	p
Satisfaction	5021.4330	.0000
Responsibility	1162.8697	.0000
Commitment	2243.1385	.0000
Frustration	907.7608	.0000
Pride	1072.9574	.0000

— Table II —

Conditions for Competence and Organizational Performance

Summary of a multivatiate ANOVA of the effects of conditions for collaboration, commitment, and creativity on performance in nine organizations.

SOURCE	df	MS	F	p
COLLABORATION				
A. High vs. Low	1	19703.86	30.66	.000
B. Organizations	8	1386.37	2.16	.029
Interaction A x B	8	1322.43	2.06	.038
Residual (Error)	558	642.60		
COMMITMENT				
A. High vs. Low	1	15321.68	28.29	.000
B. Organizations	8	2989.43	5.52	.000
Interaction A x B	8	1554.15	2.87	.004
Residual (Error)	558	541.61		
CREATIVITY				
A. High vs. Low	1	8097.46	18.21	.000
B. Organizations	8	3852.28	8.67	.000
Interaction A x B	8	790.24	1.78	.079
Residual (Error)	558	444.57		

— Table III —
Comparison of Actual and Desired Conditions for Competence among Low and High Performing Organizations

Summary of ANOVA of actual vs. desired scores by performance level.

CONDITIONS	MEAN T-SCORES		SOURCE	MEAN SQUARE	df	F	p
	ACTUAL	DESIRED					
COLLABORATION			Between				
LOW	47	62	Group	15701.36	1	27.62	.000
			Error (B)	568.52	574		
HIGH	52	62	Within				
			Trials[a]	317964.81	1	775.03	.000
			Group x Trial[b]	12788.72	1	31.17	.000
			Error (W)	410.26	574		
COMMITMENT			Between				
LOW	47	62	Group	10114.84	1	17.89	.000
			Error (B)	565.33	574		
HIGH	52	63	Within				
			Trials[a]	262584.02	1	799.42	.000
			Group x Trial[b]	6741.13	1	20.52	.000
			Error (W)	328.47	574		
CREATIVITY			Between				
LOW	48	60	Group	8987.58	1	13.39	.000
			Error (B)	671.04	574		
HIGH	52	62	Within				
			Trials[a]	121486.59	1	302.12	.000
			Group x Trial[b]	1070.19	1	2.66	.103
			Error (W)	402.26	574		

[a]Comparison of Actual and Desired conditions across groups.
[b]Comparison of Actual and Desired conditions for Low and High performers.

— Table IV —

Differences in Morale Factors between Organizations

Summary of multiple discriminant function analysis of organizational types and morale factors.

$\Lambda = .759$ $F_{36.1364} = 2.455$ $p < .0000$	ORGANIZATION							χ^2	df	p
	Super Market	Fast Food	Petro-chemical	Manufacturing	Engineering	Banking	R & D			
ROOT I (Commitment/Satisfaction)	-.231	-.304	.149	.328	.410	-.091	.965	32.01	11	.001
ROOT II (Accountability)	8.074	8.122	7.842	8.698	8.188	7.338	8.384	28.698	9	.001
ROOT III (Involvement)	.239	.948	.904	.509	.691	.439	.625	17.302	7	.02

— Table V —

Predicting Morale as a Function of Conditions for Competence

Summary of CANONA of conditions for competence and morale data.

ROOT NO.	ROOT VALUE	CORRESPONDING CANONICAL R	χ^2	df	p
1	.2002	.45	55.5038	5	.0000
2	.0141	.12	3.5383	3	ns
3	.0005	.02	.1133	1	ns

Canonical vector for predictor (conditions for competence) and criterion (morale factors) scores.

VECTOR I			
PREDICTOR		CRITERION	
Collaboration	.4912	Involvement	.4165
Commitment	.5280	Commitment	.6132
Creativity	.6928	Pride	.6712

Summary of bivariate correlations among conditions for competence and morale factors.*

CONDITIONS VARIABLE	MORALE FACTOR		
	INVOLVEMENT	COMMITMENT	PRIDE
Collaboration	.2624	.2799	.3588
Commitment	.2714	.3228	.3408
Creativity	.2862	.3347	.3138

*p < .001 for all correlations

— Table VI —

Productive Orientation as a Function of Competence Dimensions

Summary of ANOVA of productive orientation factors by competence level.

MEAN T-SCORES BY COMPETENCE LEVEL		SOURCE	MEAN SQUARE	df	F	p
FEELINGS OF INVOLVEMENT						
LOW	40.0	Total	4.0404	95		
MODERATE	44.6	Groups	33.9764	2	10.003	.0003
HIGH	52.4	Error	3.3966	93		
FEELINGS OF COMMITMENT						
LOW	40.5	Total	3.1719	95		
MODERATE	42.5	Groups	30.8369	2	11.966	.0001
HIGH	54.4	Error	2.577	93		
FEELINGS OF PRIDE						
LOW	39.0	Total	2.0982	95		
MODERATE	48.0	Groups	31.2972	2	21.286	.0000
HIGH	55.0	Error	1.4703	93		

— Table VII —

The Effect of Discrepancies between Actual and Desired Competence on Morale Factors

Summary of CANONA of desired-actual discrepancy and satisfaction-frustration data.

ROOT NO.	ROOT VALUE	CORRESPONDING CANONICAL R	χ^2	df	p
1	.1954	.44	54.1298	4	.0000
2	.0077	.09	1.9156	2	ns

Canonical vector for predictor (desired-actual discrepancy) and criterion (satisfaction-frustration) scores.

VECTOR I			
PREDICTOR		CRITERION	
Collaboration$_{dis}$	.8165	Satisfaction	−.6915
Commitment$_{dis}$	.9772	Frustration	.8831
Creativity$_{dis}$	.7314		

Summary of bivariate correlations among discrepancy and satisfaction-frustration scores.

DISCREPANCY VARIABLE	MORALE FACTOR			
	SATISFACTION	p	FRUSTRATION	p
Collaboration$_{dis}$	−.2277	.001	.3329	.001
Commitment$_{dis}$	−.2991	.001	.3812	.001
Creativity$_{dis}$	−.2584	.001	.2629	.001

— Table VIII —

Predicting Unhealthy Productive Orientation from Discrepancies in Actual vs. Desired Conditions for Competence

Summary of multiple discriminant function analysis of morale factors and actual-desired competence discrepancies.

$\Lambda = .541$ $F_{15.216} = 3.583$ $p < .0001$	DISCREPANCY QUARTILE				χ^2	df	p
	Smallest	Next	Next	Largest			
ROOT I (Pride vs. Frustration)	2.332	2.851	1.462	.684	34.936	7	.0001
ROOT II (Commitment)	13.270	11.903	13.725	12.391	12.146	5	.03

Summary of ANOVA of morale factors by amount of actual-desired discrepancy.

MORALE FACTORS	STANDARD SCORES				$F_{3.82}$	p
	1st Quartile	2nd Quartile	3rd Quartile	4th Quartile		
Satisfaction	52	45	46	41	4.209	.008
Responsibility	51	49	53	44	3.144	.029
Commitment	53	45	52	40	4.973	.004
Frustration	51	49	55	56	10.186	.0001
Pride	53	49	47	39	8.063	.0002

— Table IX —
A Test of the Isodynamic Principle of Competence

Summary of multiple discriminant function analysis of competence structure and productive orientation.

$\Lambda = .634$ $F_{42,1129} = 2.747$ $p < .0000$	TYPE ORGANIZATION								df	x^2	p
	000	100	020	003	023	103	120	123			
ROOT I (Productive Orientation)	39.5	43.6	50.9	46.8	58.2	57.6	56.1	65.4	12	81.37	.0000
ROOT II (Accountability vs. Complacency)	70.6	70.7	72.6	77.0	77.2	72.2	61.9	71.5	10	20.29	.03

Summary of univariate ANOVA of productive orientation indices.

VARIABLE	$F_{7,245}$	p
Involvement	3.261	.003
Satisfaction	6.667	.0000
Responsibility	2.451	.02
Commitment	4.599	.0002
Frustration	7.075	.0000
Pride	7.199	.0000

— Table X —

Personal Managerial Competence as a Predictor of Organizational Conditions for Competence

Summary of CANONA of managerial styles and conditions for competence as described by subordinate personnel.

ROOT NO.	ROOT VALUE	CORRESPONDING CANONICAL R	χ^2	df	p
1	.2184	.4673	53.836	7	.0000
2	.0232	.1523	5.139	5	ns
3	.0093	.0964	2.037	3	ns

Canonical vectors for predictor (managerial style) and criterion (conditions for competence) ratings.

VECTOR I			
Predictors (styles)		Criteria (conditions)	
Collaborative	.94	Collaboration	.92
Beneficent	.55	Commitment	.85
Bureaucratic	−.63	Creativity	.79
Autocratic	−.48		

Summary of bivariate correlations among managerial style ratings and organizational conditions for competence.

MANAGERIAL STYLE	DIMENSIONS OF COMPETENCE		
	COLLABORATION	COMMITMENT	CREATIVITY
Collaborative	.412***	.377***	.341***
Manipulative	.077	.005	−.272***
Autocratic	−.201**	−.186**	−.202**
Beneficent	.272***	.225**	.140*
Bureaucratic	−.281***	−.218**	−.256***

*** $p < .001$
** $p < .01$
* $p < .05$

— Table XI —

Managers' Productive Practices as a Predictor of Organizational Conditions for Competence

Summary of CANONA of managerial practices and conditions for competence as described by subordinate personnel.

ROOT NO.	ROOT VALUE	CORRESPONDING CANONICAL R	χ^2	df	p
1	.248	.498	24.792	9	.003
2	.065	.255	4.738	4	ns

Canonical vectors for predictor (productive practices) and criterion (conditions for competence) ratings.

VECTOR I			
Predictors (practices)		Criteria (conditions)	
Collaboration	.935	Collaboration	.583
Commitment	.783	Commitment	.878
Creativity	.638	Creativity	.839

Summary of bivariate correlations among productive practices ratings and organizational conditions for competence.

PRODUCTIVE PRACTICES	DIMENSIONS OF COMPETENCE		
	COLLABORATION	COMMITMENT	CREATIVITY
Collaboration	.289**	.386***	.432***
Commitment	.254*	.307**	.391***
Creativity	.229*	.221*	.371***

*** $p < .001$
** $p < .01$
* $p < .05$

— Table XII —

Productive Practices and Organizational Performance

Summary of a multivariate ANOVA of the effects of practices for collaboration, commitment, and creativity on performance in five organizations.

SOURCE	df	MS	F	p
COLLABORATION				
A. High vs. Low	1	48680.41	26.62	.000
B. Organizations	4	10381.40	5.68	.000
Interaction A x B	4	4566.96	2.50	.042
Residual (Error)	573	1828.55		
COMMITMENT				
A. High vs. Low	1	46069.31	24.54	.000
B. Organizations	4	12091.58	6.44	.000
Interaction A x B	4	3076.80	1.75	.163
Residual (Error)	573	541.61		
CREATIVITY				
A. High vs. Low	1	51947.67	16.62	.000
B. Organizations	4	12288.16	6.21	.000
Interaction A x B	4	3108.11	1.57	.180
Residual (Error)	573	1978.24		

— Table XIII —

Predicting Health in the Workplace from Discrepancies in Actual vs. Desired Productive Practices for the Release of Competence

Summary of multiple discriminant function analysis of health factors and actual-desired competence discrepancies.

Λ = .599 $F_{9,668}$ = 15.873 p < .0001	CENTROID SCORES BY DISCREPANCY QUARTILE				χ^2	df	p
	Smallest	Next	Next	Largest			
ROOT I (Health vs. Stress)	14.91	12.89	11.31	7.32	120.061	9	.000

Summary of ANOVA of health factors by amount of actual-desired discrepancy.

HEALTH FACTORS	STANDARD SCORES				$F_{3,252}$	p
	1st Quartile	2nd Quartile	3rd Quartile	4th Quartile		
Health	55	52	48	42	40.817	.000
Stress	45	48	48	58	35.307	.000
Fulfillment	53	50	50	44	16.086	.000

Index

Index